OUTNUMBERED

This edition published in 2013 by
CRESTLINE
a division of BOOK SALES, Inc.
276 Fifth Avenue Suite 206
New York, New York 10001
USA

This edition published by arrangement with Fair Winds Press.

First published in the USA in 2010 by
Fair Winds Press, a member of
Quayside Publishing Group
100 Cummings Center
Suite 406-L
Beverly, MA 01915-6101
www.fairwindspress.com

10 9 8 7 6 5 4 3 2 1

ISBN-13: 978-0-7858-3059-7

Library of Congress Cataloging-in-Publication Data

Cover and book design: Peter Long
Book layout: Megan Jones Design
Cover: Alesia Besieged by Julius Caesar, 52 BCE, by Melchior Feselen (d. 1538).
During the actual battle, Julius Caesar used eleven miles of Roman-engineered field-
works to trap his Gallic enemies and defeat a force around four times the size of his
own. Feselen's dramatic painting, filled with uniforms and weaponry from his own
time, is a look at the ancient world through a sixteenth-century lens.
Alte Pinakothek, Munich, Germany / Lauros / Giraudon / The Bridgeman Art Library International

Printed and bound in China

OUTNUMBERED

INCREDIBLE STORIES OF HISTORY'S MOST SURPRISING BATTLEFIELD UPSETS

CORMAC O'BRIEN

CONTENTS

INTRODUCTION

"It often happens, that fortune in war and love turns out more
favorable and wonderful than could have been hoped for or expected."
—Jean Froissart, *Chronicles*

IN SUMMER 480 BCE, A GREEK ARMY PLANNED TO THWART a Persian invasion by occupying the pass of Thermopylae, the "Hot Gates" as it is known to the Greeks, where the mountains came down to the Strait of Euboea to create a choke point for anyone hoping to invade Greece.

The Persians owned a vast empire, the greatest humanity had ever seen. Filled with troops from across Asia, the army of the Persian king was an unprecedented host, numbered in the hundreds of thousands, all bearing down on the glorified mule track of Thermopylae. There the Greeks waited for them.

The men of Greece were Thebans, Athenians, Corinthians, and Spartans. They hailed from myriad city states, at once divided and united by the sea, jealous of each other's power and yet proud to identify themselves as brothers in a Hellenic heritage. They traded as often as they battled, fixed in their parochial view of the world. Above all things, they valued civic independence.

Fiercely agonistic, they nevertheless understood the scale of the Persian threat and organized, in their way, a concerted response. And Thermopylae was to be its greatest effort.

After two days of fierce battle in the narrow pass, the Persians, foiled by the heavily armored Greeks, discovered a path through the mountains that allowed them to deliver a force around the Greek rear. Learning of the flanking maneuver, the commander of the Greeks, King Leonidas of Sparta, elected to stay in the pass with a token force to give the rest of the army an opportunity to withdraw before the trap closed.

The brave gambit allowed the majority of the Greeks to fight another day. For Leonidas and his fellows, however, the end was near. On the third day, 300 Spartans, accompanied by contingents of Thespians and Thebans, received the Persian onslaught from both ends of the pass. Wildly outnumbered, they all died, fighting to the last.

History remembers the 300 Spartans (though it is considerably less kind to the Thespians and Thebans who died with them) in film, literature, and legend. The popular imagination is enthralled by their sacrifice. Moreover, Leonidas and his little command actually achieved what they set out to do: delay the Persian onslaught. In combination with the battles waged at sea, Thermopylae set the tight Persian timetable back just long enough to limit the enemy's options. By the time summer gave way to fall, the Persian king had yet to crush the Greek alliance, whose bold and clever resistance ultimately forced the invaders to decamp before the onset of winter.

This book takes a look at armies that faced similarly daunting odds but that went one step further—not only did they achieve their missions, they survived to tell the tale. From ancient times to the Second World War, *Outnumbered* explores one of the most compelling phenomena in war: the upset victory against dreadful odds.

The causes for victory or defeat, it will be seen, are as diverse as the reasons for going to war in the first place. In many instances, genius makes an appearance, whether through assiduous preparation, an uncanny appreciation of events, or some prescient judgment call. But just as often, the numerically superior force lays the groundwork for its own defeat: Overconfidence, disastrous decision-making, ineffectual staff work, and good old stupidity rear their ugly heads again and again. Sometimes technology proves decisive, and terrain plays a role in nearly every clash.

Perhaps nothing, however, is as common in the following pages as a difference in doctrine—the gulf that yawns between two armies in the *way* they make war, often because of cultural differences. From divergent ethics to variations in weaponry, this is as much a saga of human diversity as it is a history of beating the odds.

Finally, there is luck. As Prussian military thinker Carl von Clausewitz asserted, "War is the province of uncertainty." Truer words were never written. Battle is the (often futile) act of finding order in chaos, an unavoidable fact that underpins everything in the hellish, murderous confusion of mass killing. Though it is often difficult to remember from our removed perspective, it is vital to understand that Lady Luck plays a role in every military clash—a sobering reminder that humankind's quest for a foolproof weapon or stratagem is a futile one.

—CORMAC O'BRIEN

CHAPTER 1

SALAMIS
480 BCE

GREEK AUDACITY AND COURAGE DEFY
THE WORLD'S GREATEST EMPIRE

375 GREEK SHIPS VERSUS
1,000 PERSIAN SHIPS

I N 498 BCE, THE GREAT ANATOLIAN CITY OF SARDIS FELL
prey to one of the most notorious acts of arson in history. Seat of the local
satrap, or Persian governor, Sardis was besieged by rebels—most of them
Greeks—who hoped to throw off Persian rule in Ionia. They forced their way into
the city, only to see the garrison retreat safely into the citadel.

A standoff ensued. The streets may have belonged to the attackers, but the
Persian soldiers made a mockery of the Greek occupation by their very presence
in the fortress, whose walls defied any hope of breaching. During this period of
inertia a fire broke out, probably started by Greeks. Raging out of control, the
flames claimed scores of homes and the temple of Cybele, the city's patron goddess. The Greeks ultimately retreated from Sardis, only to be thrashed by Persian
relief forces and scattered. Within four years, the Ionian revolt was suppressed.

The burning of Sardis, however, left an ugly scar on the consciousness of the
Persian king, Darius. Most abominable of all was the defilement of Cybele's sacred
temple, which was reduced to a smoldering ruin. To those who worshipped this
ancient Asian goddess, patroness of fertility and strength, blasphemy had occurred
within the very walls of a Persian city. Vengeance was compulsory.

But against whom? For Darius, the answer was obvious. Athens had openly aided the Ionian rebels and led the attack on Sardis. Ionia, comprising the Mediterranean coast of modern Turkey, was a land of Greek city states founded centuries earlier by voyagers from the Greek mainland—thriving communities that looked to the free cities of Athens and Sparta as cultural progenitors while living under the domination of Persian masters. To secure their own independence, the Ionian rebels turned to Sparta, greatest military power of the Greek world, for help. They were rebuffed. Athens was more supportive: The warriors who had marched on Sardis and watched its buildings burn were mostly Athenian.

Darius now had a slave stand at his side at every meal to whisper a mantra into his ear: "Remember the Athenians." In fact, the king hardly needed a reminder. To the Persian ruler, the distant Greek heartland had become an instigator of treason for the Greeks living within his empire. And Athens was the principal offender. Ruling the Ionians was impossible as long as their independent countrymen across the Aegean remained free to foment insurrection—and condemn Persian property to the flames. Athens, in short, had become the apotheosis of Persia's unfinished business. Conquering her would mean more than avenging the wrong of Sardis; it would also represent Persia's domination over European Greece itself, with its bustling cities and bountiful resources. The Persian "King of Kings" already reigned over the greatest empire the world had ever seen. How difficult could it be to add a handful of fractious Greek city states to his realm?

DARIUS NOW HAD A SLAVE STAND AT HIS SIDE AT EVERY MEAL TO WHISPER A MANTRA INTO HIS EAR: "REMEMBER THE ATHENIANS."

Actually, it would be very difficult indeed. The Persians were about to embark on one of the toughest campaigns of their imperial history, an endeavor made all the more difficult by the illusion of its ease. A hard, warrior people who had conquered a titanic empire from their remote highland homeland, the Persians were taking on a population of philosophizing agriculturalists whose obsession with independence and competition virtually guaranteed the failure of concerted action.

But the Greeks were also a warrior people. And the heroic effort they mounted in response to invasion did more than shock their "barbarian" foes—it helped shape the course of Western civilization.

THE FIST IS CLENCHED

The Achaemenid Persians ruled an empire that stretched from the shores of the Mediterranean to the banks of the Indus River in India. The ruler of this colossal expanse of territory was referred to as *shahanshah*, "King of Kings," and for good reason—subject monarchs literally paid homage to him at his magnificent palace in Persepolis. As heir to a Near Eastern imperial tradition that went back centuries, Darius could be forgiven for looking with disdain on his Greek adversaries.

In 491 BCE, he dispatched ambassadors to Greece with a very simple, very important mission: secure gifts of earth and water from the city states as symbols

of submission. A standard practice in Iranian tradition, the process amounted to a first wave to prepare the way for absorption into the Persian Empire.

The king's representatives met with success in all but two cities. After putting their Persian visitors on public trial, the Athenians elected to execute them. The Spartans simply threw theirs down a well.

An incredulous Darius now prepared to send more than emissaries. The following year, a Persian expeditionary force of around 25,000 landed in Attica, north of Athens, and destroyed Eritrea, the only city besides Athens to have actively supported the Ionian revolt. Athens, however, proved more resilient.

Mustering an army of Greek hoplites, the Athenians marched north to meet the invaders and crushed them in the Battle of Marathon. Though outnumbered, the heavily armored Greek warriors—protected by bronze helmet, *greaves*, or shin guards, and a massive round shield—proved more than a match for the Persians, whose cavalry, usually decisive, were either poorly used or absent from the fight entirely. Though the numbers of Persians arrayed against them remain a matter of conjecture, the Athenians had saved their city and bloodied the mightiest empire on Earth.

DARIUS I, ACHAEMENID KING OF PERSIA FROM 521 TO 486 BCE, FAILED IN HIS INVASION OF GREECE IN 490 BCE, LEAVING THE TASK OF PUNISHING ATHENS TO HIS SON, XERXES.

© Image Asset Management Ltd. / SuperStock 1746-501-A-P30R

Darius could only dream of vengeance, as a revolt in Egypt compelled him to put his Greek plans on hold. He would never see them through, dying in 486 BCE.

The throne now passed to his son Xerxes, along with a hatred of Greeks that bordered on the obsessive. A man of outsized ambition and implacable determination, King Xerxes meant to descend on Greece like a force of nature. No one had ever harnessed the full potential of an empire so vast, and he intended to remedy that. His invasion of the West would be an awe-inspiring affair—a triumph of inexorable grandiosity over parochial petulance.

No effort was spared. Originally hailing from the high Iranian plateau, the Persians felt at home in the saddle, producing excellent cavalry. But conquering and maintaining an empire had made them deliberate and technically skilled, as well, with a fascination for the possibilities of engineering. Xerxes insisted on marching across the Hellespont, the narrow channel dividing Europe and Asia known today as the Dardanelles; his laborers produced two massive pontoon bridges, each over a mile (1.6 km) long, complete with earthen floors and high wicker walls to keep the horses from spooking. While his army would walk on water, his navy would sail through land: In northern Greece, Persian engineers dug a canal across the Athos Peninsula, allowing ships to avoid a much longer, more treacherous route.

These two staggering engineering achievements, along with an elaborate logistical system established by the court, were meant to ease the passage of an invasion of unprecedented scope that finally got underway in 480 BCE. Debate surrounds the size of Xerxes's army, but it was almost certainly larger than 100,000 and conceivably three times that size. It included slingers and archers, infantrymen and cavalry, from places as diverse as Bactria, Arabia, Lebanon, and Mesopotamia. Its columns stretched for miles, throwing up cloudbanks of dust and denuding the countryside of food and fodder. It was a living, moving wonder of the ancient world.

Shadowing it along the coast was a navy of more than 1,000 fighting vessels, accompanied by innumerable cargo ships and support craft. This huge armada, however, disguised a fundamental weakness. Dedicated landsmen, the Persians in their stables looked to the sea with a blend of wonder and disdain. Once in the empire business, they were forced to wrestle with its challenges—a task made simpler by such subject peoples as the Egyptians, Phoenicians, Cypriots, Cilicians, and Ionian Greeks, all of whom were venerated mariners. These peoples now rowed for Persia under widely varying degrees of duress. Though Persian rule afforded a liberal degree of local cultural autonomy, it came with the requirement of military service that forced men into obeying a master they would not otherwise have fought for willingly. To offset this, the Achaemenids predictably included a complement of Persian soldiers on their ships, guarding as much against the crew's perfidy as the threat of enemy boarders.

Despite these complications, however, Xerxes floated more than three times the number of warships that all the Greek city states could produce combined. And nothing in Greek history suggested that cooperation among the city states, even against a threat as grave as the Persian Empire, was in the cards. How, with a navy like this and probably the largest army to invade Europe until the twentieth century CE, could the King of Kings fail?

The answer lay, ironically enough, in the ground—and in the capacity of Athens to produce leaders who, despite lacking the pedigree of Xerxes, possessed abilities that proved more than a match for his seemingly invincible power.

FLIGHT OF THE OWLS

The Persian juggernaut swept westward through Thrace and Macedonia, its very approach compelling numerous Greek communities to *Medize*—to submit utterly to the Great King before his enormous army even came into sight. Not everyone in Greece, however, was so conciliatory.

That many of Greece's infamously divisive city states could arrange themselves into a coalition for mutual defense speaks volumes about the enormity of the threat bearing down on them. Led (unsurprisingly) by Athens and Sparta, the Greek alliance—some of whose members were still technically at war with each other—meant to achieve the impossible by fighting a war against a superior enemy by popular vote. This was Greek culture at its best and worst all at once, representing a stalwart distaste for tyranny that, however attractive, undermined the effort to ensure survival. Xerxes called councils of war only to inform his own judgment; the ultimate decision was his, and was carried out with ruthlessly efficient dispatch. Those opposing him in his Greek venture could rely on no such alacrity.

But they could rely on sound leadership. In the effort to defend Greece from the Persians, one figure stood out. Themistocles, an Athenian who had risen to power and influence through a generous inheritance and a lot of hard-headed maneuvering, was the mirror image of his opponent. While Xerxes was constrained to act within courtly parameters, Themistocles was an opportunist who battled in the scrum of politics. Both came to positions of influence by birth; but Xerxes exercised his right as an autocrat, while Themistocles wagered his fortune and future on his ability to manipulate the votes of his fellow democrats. Both, however, were vulnerable: A vote by his fellow citizens could deprive Themistocles of his citizenship, condemning him to exile. Xerxes, on the other hand, had to impress the families that influenced his court—an aristocracy capable of overthrowing him should his star fall too far, too quickly.

Themistocles lacked breeding but possessed vision in abundance. Luck was also with him. In 483 BCE, as rumors of Xerxes's preparations for invasion raced across Greece, Athens struck a new vein of silver at Laurium. A cratered wasteland southeast of Athens, where slaves were worked savagely to scratch precious metal out of the ground, Laurium was the cash cow of Athens—a warren of mines that allowed the city to literally bankroll its own success. Athenian coins, commonly known as *owls* for the owl of Athena stamped on one side, were a familiar sight in marketplaces throughout the Greek world.

Voices in the assembly clamored for a distribution of the newfound wealth to the Athenian people. But Themistocles had another idea, pushing for the creation of a fleet—200 triremes that would make Athens the mightiest naval power in the Greek world. With eloquence and deft politicking, he eventually got his way.

It is difficult to exaggerate the significance of this decision. Themistocles, through sheer willpower and personality, had set his city on a new course. He had also saved the future of a free Greece. In the ensuing months, Athens made itself into a base for building a state-of-the-art navy. And it was around the Athenian fleet that the desperate Greek defense would achieve its greatest triumph.

SEASON OF FIRE AND DOUBT

The summer of 480 BCE proved a mostly successful campaigning season for Xerxes and his two-headed leviathan. The military might of the Persian Empire traced a path around the northern arch of the Aegean, the army shadowed by its naval companion off the coast. The terrain, however, favored the locals.

Outnumbered in every way, the Greek allies that converged on the Isthmus of Corinth knew their mountainous homeland offered certain opportunities—choke points through which the enormous Persian force must pass to reach Athens and the rest of Greece. Such terrain features could dramatically offset the numerical disparity between the two armies. After an initial attempt to guard the Vale of Tempe in far northern Greece proved untenable, the allies settled upon a surer bottleneck farther south. Known as Thermopylae, or the "Hot Gates," this narrow pass, bordered by mountains on one side and seaside cliffs on the other, offered little more than a glorified mule track for passage by an army. Despite its narrowness, any large force headed south needed to use it. Moreover, it stood fewer than fifty miles (80.5 km) from Artemesium, a town guarding the approaches to the narrow channel separating the island of Euboea from the Greek mainland, through which the Persian navy was sure to pass. In other words, the Greek high command could block both prongs of the Persian advance at almost the same point on the coast— while hoplites fended off an attack at Thermopylae, Greek triremes could grapple with their opposites at Artemesium, holding up the Persian offense completely until more reinforcements could be brought to bear.

It was a solid plan, and it worked—sort of. In what quickly became one of the most celebrated acts of sacrifice in Western history, King Leonidas of Sparta and 300 of his elite hoplites—in addition, it must be remembered, to a host of fighters from Thespiae, a city of Boeotia near Thebes—gave their lives at Thermopylae to allow the rest of the army an escape and the opportunity to galvanize further Greek resistance. At sea, the Greeks fared better, fighting the Persian crews to a strategic draw at the Battle of Artemesium. Once the land complement had been defeated, however, the triremes at Artemesium—led by Themistocles—retreated south to aid in the evacuation of Athens. Xerxes had hit a speed bump, but he would not be thwarted.

Soon, much of Boeotia and Attica were ablaze, the horribly outnumbered allies incapable of doing anything but pulling back in frustration. Xerxes entered a deathly quiet Athens and set its acropolis to the torch before turning it into a huge Persian camp. Victory, it seemed, was in his grasp.

Or was it? Athens may have been his, but the cities of the Peloponnese, including Sparta, still remained, and the summer had been full of hard lessons for the Persians. To begin with, the Greek force at Thermopylae had been able to hold back an army many times its size for several days before being overwhelmed. Dealing with Greek hoplites, with their heavy panoply of armor, shield, and thrusting spear, proved difficult for even the finest Persian infantry, most of which—even the celebrated Immortals, the Great King's personal shock troops—went into battle with little more than tunics and wicker shields. To complete his conquest of Greece, Xerxes needed to get his army south to the Peloponnese. But the only land route into it, the Isthmus of Corinth, was blocked by an army of allied hoplites waiting behind carefully prepared defenses—yet another place in which his splendid cavalry would be a nuisance to the enemy at best. If Thermopylae had been a bloody affair, an attack across the Isthmus could prove disastrous.

Amphibious operations were the only option open now for Xerxes. But the sea battle at Artemesium, along with attrition from storms, had whittled down his navy considerably from its top strength of around 1,200 fighting vessels. And the allied fleet still cruised to the south, its crews guarding the refugees from Athens. Until this formidable force was decisively defeated, Greece's fate remained an open question. Xerxes could not land his army in safety on the shores of the

Peloponnese, nor could he be sure that the allied triremes might not attempt a landing in his rear to harass his tenuous communications. This was the hard reality of the campaign that Xerxes and his generals had always feared: Greece, a mountainous land of harbors, islands, and coastlines, could just as easily trap a mighty army as fall to it, should the seas remain in enemy hands.

Worst of all, time was against Xerxes. Indeed, it is easy to imagine the Great King brooding as the temples of Athens smoldered before him under a September sun. He had his vengeance, but not Greece. Not yet. And winter was fast approaching, during which all campaigning would need to cease—and he would have failed to subdue this fractured land of bumptious farmers in one season, a dire prospect

THEMISTOCLES, THE VISIONARY ATHENIAN STATESMAN WHO LED THE BATTLE, SUCCESSFULLY LURED THE PERSIANS TO FIGHT IN WATERS OF HIS OWN CHOOSING-AND TO DO SO ON THE VERGE OF EXHAUSTION.

for his reputation at court. Besides, it was dangerous for a king to be away from his throne for this long, especially this far from the heart of the empire. Plotters might have an opportunity to strike, their cause fortified by a Greek debacle. His father Darius had come to power under the very same mysterious circumstances—Xerxes himself was heir to a usurper.

All the facts pointed to a need for decisive action. However, Xerxes got something just as good—a lucky break. On a late September evening, word reached him that Themistocles had sent a servant to deliver a message: the Athenian had Medized. Moreover, he was offering to serve up the allied fleet in a trap.

Perhaps the gods were with Xerxes after all.

DO OR DIE

Herodotus, still our principal source on the Battle of Salamis, was once dismissed as a spinner of fantasies. But archaeology has vindicated so many of his writings in the past few decades that a complete reappraisal of the "Father of History" has restored his lost respect. It is ironic that the story he relates about the events that precipitated this most significant of naval clashes is worthy of the finest fiction—a moment in history as pregnant with contingency as it was instrumental in altering the course of civilizations.

If Xerxes was vexed by the strategic situation as it stood in September 480, his opponents were hardly better off. With cities such as Thebes Medizing throughout the land, manpower for the Greek resistance had been hard to come by. The allies were an argumentative rabble taking on an empire that spanned the known world—an empire that ruled countless other Greeks, many of whose hands now pulled the oars on ships answering to Persian admirals. It was a war of awkward and uncomfortable alliances, in which some Greeks fought for independence against a regime that others accepted as inevitable, almost divinely ordained. How could the allies hope to succeed, let alone defeat the greatest army ever assembled?

Now Athens groaned under Persian occupation, its acropolis a charred ruin. Thermopylae had been a defeat, no matter its contribution to Greek pride, and Xerxes's throngs now controlled everything north of the Peloponnese.

The leaders of the fleet, the last best hope of Greek resistance, debated what to do. The ships controlled the strait between the Greek mainland near Athens and the large island of Salamis. But to what end? Some argued for a blockade of the Saronic Gulf south of Salamis, protecting the marine flank of the allied army assembled on the Isthmus of Corinth. But this idea smacked of the sort of passivity that Themistocles, for one, believed the fleet could ill afford. Options were running out, to be sure. But to his thinking, using the fleet in a gamble that could prove decisive was better than waiting for the barbarians to decide events.

This line of thinking ran into resistance, and for good reason. The Greek allies had right around 375 triremes, a figure extrapolated by modern historians from conflicting figures given by ancient sources. As for the Persians, figures vary. It is safe to put their numbers at 700, but 800 to 900 would not be off the charts. Faced with this chilling disparity, some of the allied commanders balked at the notion of taking the fight to the Persians.

So Themistocles, as Herodotus tells us, improvised.

Convinced that allied crews were better led and firmer in purpose than their subject enemies, Themistocles needed to bring the two fleets together, to arrange the climactic clash that, he hoped, would lead to a Greek victory and render the Persian presence in Greece untenable. Consequently, he sent his servant Sicinnus, a teacher schooled in languages, to deliver a daring bit of misinformation. Once his small vessel was in shouting range of Persian forces, the messenger barked his scandalous news: Themistocles, like so many Greeks before him, had seen the change in the wind and gone over to Xerxes. He also informed the King of Kings that the allied fleet hoped to evacuate soon, and that blocking both ends of the straits would secure its doom.

Xerxes, calling a council of war, chose to act on the information. His reasoning was sound. To begin with, his cause was flooded with Greeks who believed the future was with Persia. Could Themistocles be so different? Granted, Athens was a mortal enemy whose sacred space Xerxes had recently violated. But could not many Athenians have seen the light, so to speak, in the fires of their city's destruction? Themistocles, greatest of Athenians, was a typical agonistic player—a man whose canny instincts were born of an opportunism that Persians disdained and came to expect in their Hellene neighbors. Greeks, independent to a fault, were notorious for putting a price on defiance. Little wonder so many of them bowed to the Great King.

Besides, Xerxes needed to move. Hope in the news from Themistocles may well have clouded his objective judgment of the situation and of his adversary. Whatever the Great King's reasoning, the results were fateful. Confident in his superior numbers, his cause, and his intelligence, Xerxes prepared a perch for himself on the heights overlooking Salamis to view the morning's *coup de grâce*. Meanwhile, his navy labored to deploy in the darkness, rowing in silence to avoid detection by Greeks at sea and on land.

They did not go unnoticed. Upon receiving news of the Persian movements, the Greek command, fearing a trap in the straits within which they were stationed, debated heatedly. Themistocles, right on cue, presented the news as a fait accompli. They now had no choice but to fight. Running was impossible, and the narrow straits offered ideal geography for fighting a superior opponent. Fate was upon them. The light of dawn would bring a grim choice: do or die.

Themistocles had gotten his fight.

DAY OF THE RAM

Mediterranean naval battles in 480 BCE were about speed. Without catapults or other large missile engines, necessity dictated turning the ship itself into a weapon—to mount a massive, bronze-plated ram on the prow and train the crew behind it to row hard into enemy ships like a giant torpedo.

The trireme was designed for just such a purpose. Probably originated by the Phoenicians, the trireme quickly became the state-of-the-art war vessel, requiring its adoption by any polity interested in projecting power beyond its harbor. It was a sleek design, around 120 feet (36.5 m) long, as short on seaworthiness as it was long on speed. It was therefore incapable of remaining at sea for a long time, and so habitually hugged the coastline. Trireme crews hauled their craft onto beaches for overnight stays rather than leaving them exposed to a capricious sea. Nor was there enough room on such a ship for supplies, the majority of its design being given over to the swift delivery of a lethal thrust. Blockades, with their long tours at sea, were impractical for trireme fleets, whose crews expected either to exert themselves in the kill or rest on land with proper victuals.

For all these reasons, naval warfare in the ancient Mediterranean favored the tactical over the strategic—the decisive battle over the drawn-out chess match. No ship on either side at Salamis employed anything but paid freemen; in a world supported by slaves, virtually none were to be  found at the slaughter in the Straits. Though exorbitant, this made perfect sense: getting a crew of 170 rowers on three decks to pull their oars in unison and endure the punishment of combat was no small feat, and required willing, paid citizens who could pride themselves on their ability and endurance.

Synchronicity was life on the trireme, where the unit depended on teamwork to an extent that ancient land forces did not. Listening at once to the bark of officers' orders and the rhythmic tune of the piper keeping time, three decks of rowers— from top to bottom, the *thranites*, *zygites*, and *thalamites*—concentrated on heaving in unison often in relative ignorance of the events in which their vessel was

participating. Twenty to thirty marines filled out the ship's complement, including archers and infantry, whose duty it was to fight enemy crewmen after a collision, as well as defend the virtually naked crew from enemy boarders.

Everything, however, depended on the ram and the crew's ability to steer it at speed into an enemy's hull. Though the ship's pilot controlled the tiller, velocity was provided by the crewmen, exerting themselves in unison in foul, sweat-soaked conditions toward a looming target most of them couldn't see. The victims of such collisions would have fallen abruptly into a nightmare—a concussive tangle of flesh, wood, and bronze. Missiles and screams would have filled the air,

THIS FANCIFUL IMAGE OF A TRIREME WAS MADE CENTURIES AFTER SALAMIS. IN THE FIFTH CENTURY BCE, SUCH WARSHIPS WERE MUCH LONGER AND LEANER.

Getty Images

hapless rowers swept under by a thrashing sea. Under such circumstances, the several decks of crewmen that had only moments earlier performed in seamless unison would now fall apart into a myriad of private hells.

Once an enemy ship had been rammed, the attacker's first priority was to reverse momentum to avoid becoming lodged in the hull of the impaled victim, a reversal of effort that alone must have challenged the finest crews. Should the two ships remain locked in a mortal embrace, their joined decks would have erupted into something very like a miniature land battle, with infantry and archers swarming over the groaning hulks in furious, close-quarters fighting.

At Salamis, those plunging into the water would find no sanctuary. This was one reason why archers prowled the decks of ancient triremes: to loose a final judgment on enemy swimmers. But the straits offered an additional opportunity for murder, depending on which side of the watery expanse one's vessel went down. For soldiers and guerillas lined the coast to slaughter enemies coming ashore.

Under these circumstances, coordination and physical vitality mattered as much as numbers and experience. The Greek allies had the advantage of rest, their crews having waited in the sheltering confines of the island of Salamis while Xerxes's ships spent the night scrambling into position for a trap they hoped in vain to close. When the sun rose, painting the heights of Salamis and the mainland with orange, the Greek crews were ready for action. Contrary to Xerxes's intelligence, the allies were not trying to flee the straits—they were, in fact, waiting like predators for the moment to strike.

Though many details of the battle remain sketchy, it appears certain that the Persian fleet—originally based along the beaches of Phaleron Bay, south of Athens—entered the strait in three large groups on the night of September 24–25. Persian soldiers had occupied the island of Psyttaleia, which guards the entrance to the strait, in anticipation of its importance as a place of refuge for drowning sailors. Moving in columns, the Persian fleet entered the strait north of Psyttaleia, its 700-plus vessels making an enormous bridge over the water in the darkness. Once in the channel, they hugged the coast opposite Salamis, their ships forming up in great lines beneath the black mass of Mt. Aegaleos, where their Great King would watch the action come morning.

The king's most trusted ships anchored the western end of the line. These were the Phoenicians, whose ancient maritime traditions were respected throughout the Mediterranean and Near East. At the other end of the line, nearest to the

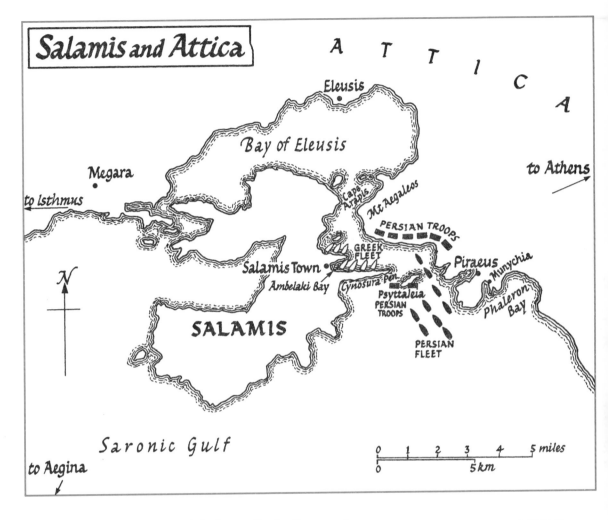

Salamis and Attica

ATTICA

Eleusis

Bay of Eleusis

Megara

to Isthmus

Cape Arapis

Mt Aegaleos

PERSIAN TROOPS

GREEK FLEET

to Athens

Piraeus

Munychia

Salamis Town

Ambelaki Bay

Cynosura Pt.

Psyttaleia
PERSIAN
TROOPS

Phaleron Bay

N

SALAMIS

PERSIAN
FLEET

Saronic Gulf

to Aegina

0   1   2   3   4   5 miles
0   5 km

eastern mouth of the strait, stood the Ionian Greeks. Between these two groups were vessels from all over the eastern Mediterranean, offering colorful testament to the vast breadth of Persia's dominance—Carians, Cypriots, Cilicians, and others. The Egyptians were there as well, though probably waiting outside the strait to catch fleeing enemies.

By the time dawn broke, the Persians had spent an entire night at the oars, first to get into the strait and then to right themselves and remain in a semblance of order—all in darkness, a tremendous and exhausting feat. It wasn't long into the morning before the Greeks began to appreciate this, by which time they began to issue forth from the confines of Ambelaki Bay on the northern shore of the island of Salamis to pounce on their disorganized foes across the channel.

WHILE THE GREEKS HUDDLED AGAINST THE COAST OF SALAMIS, THE BULK OF THE PERSIAN FLEET ENTERED THE STRAITS FROM THE SOUTH, WHERE THEY TOOK UP POSITIONS BENEATH MT. AEGALEOS, SHOWN HERE.

Desperate to sort themselves out in what must have been a press of ships, the Persians, feeling the eyes of Xerxes upon them, looked south to see the Greek triremes emerge from Salamis. As they grew closer, an eerie sound came over the water—the Greek paean, or battle hymn to Apollo.

Heavily built triremes, with armored hoplites crowding their decks, must have made a chilling sight. Most of them were Athenian. The rest hailed from a host of proud city states—Aegina and Corinth, Naxos and Styra, Ambracia and Melos, each contributing what they could. Though nominally led by Eurybiades, a Spartan, the fleet rallied to the Athenian Themistocles, who led his countrymen on the line opposite the Phoenicians.

The Greeks found their rhythm, only to founder inexplicably. Whether because of the huge Persian numbers, or because of some loss of alignment in the dawn light, a stutter in the tempo of the oars swept through the allied fleet. Doubt raced from crew to crew, communicating a primeval fear, and the Greeks began to slow and reverse course.

This is one of the strangest moments in the record, for which little explanation is provided. But it seems the Greek fleet—a composite force of mutually antagonistic cities—found the need to right itself properly after a poorly coordinated beginning. Or perhaps too many of the crews had second thoughts about heading into a battle of such unprecedented scale. In any event, an Attic captain named Aminias broke the spell by commanding his vessel forward, ramming an enemy for all to see. His countrymen, horrified at the prospect of being shamed, dipped their oars and picked up speed.

Pulling hard now, the adrenaline of imminent violence coursing through them, the Greek crews came to ramming speed and seized the initiative. It appears they never lost it. Better rested than their foes, the allies took grisly advantage of the narrow strait to cancel the Persian numbers. Xerxes looked on with horror as his ships, stacked in rows against the shore, jostled in vain for space to maneuver. "For as the Greeks fought in order and kept their line," wrote Herodotus, "while the barbarians were in confusion and had no plan in anything that they did, the issue of the battle could scarce be other than it was." The strait became a watery slaughter pen to the nations of the Persian Empire.

THE TIDE RECEDES

Salamis proved disastrous for Xerxes, who lost as many as 200 ships that long, bloody day. The Greek allies lost perhaps forty. Though it seemed a miracle, Themistocles and his fellows had managed, through cunning and boldness, to get the enemy to fight in waters of their own choosing—and to do so on the verge of exhaustion. At Salamis, Xerxes's numbers counted for little.

Other factors favored the Greeks, as well. Unlike their opposites, they were of a single culture. Perpetually divided and fiercely independent, the allied city states nevertheless spoke a single language, prayed to the same gods, and followed the same customs. Coordination of such a force must have been much easier in battle. Just as important, they were fighting to defend their homelands—a strong motivator in any age.

With no conceivable way of conquering the Peloponnese before the onset of winter, King Xerxes departed for home, taking much of his army with him. A reduced Persian force would remain in Greece, only to suffer defeat at the Battle of Plataea the following year. Greek independence had been saved. Though Greek culture would have survived under Persian rule, the course of Western history would undoubtedly have been very different. The so-called Golden Age of Athens, after all, was just about to begin—a flexing of military and cultural muscle that was made possible by Salamis. Little wonder we remain fascinated by this epic battle.

CHAPTER 2

ISSUS
333 BCE

ALEXANDER THE GREAT LEADS A
MARTIAL STORM INTO MIGHTY PERSIA

**40,000 MACEDONIANS AND GREEKS
VERSUS 100,000 PERSIANS**

I T WAS A MOMENT LATER CAUGHT FAMOUSLY IN MOSAIC ART— a young warrior king, his helmet having been knocked from his blond head by an enemy blade, riding his horse into a throng of enemies and piercing one of them through the stomach with his spear. The king's eyes flash, however, not at his victim but at his nemesis across the melee: Darius III, king of Persia, whose face clearly shows worry at the furious approach of his young would-be assassin.

The helmetless fighter, of course, is none other than Alexander the Great, and on a pleasant November day in 333 BCE, near the coast of the Gulf of Issus in what is now Turkey, he may have looked as he appears in the panorama depicting his charge toward Darius that now resides in the Archaeological Museum in Naples, Italy. Then again, maybe not.

Though a general and ruler of a kingdom, Alexander led from the front. The famous mosaic shows a moment frozen in time, but the reality must have been far more gruesome: a blur of frantic action, with spears thrusting and breaking, the ground littered with wounded men and animals screaming in the crush of bodies. Alexander himself would have been all but sheathed in viscera—a ghastly remembrance of those who had tried to oppose his manic assault against the Persian line.

But there is no doubt that the eyes of the two rulers met, however briefly, as the melee swarmed toward Darius's chariot. This was the meeting of two disparate cultures with divergent ways of making war—a gulf whose distinguishing characteristics were on display not seventy years earlier on another famous battlefield.

THE TEN THOUSAND

In 401 BCE, two armies clashed at Cunaxa, a day's ride north of Babylon, over the throne of the world's greatest empire. Since 404, Artaxerxes II had ruled as Great King of Persia more in name than fact, his legitimacy challenged openly by his younger brother Cyrus. Now, on the left bank of the fabled Euphrates River, these two sons of Darius II came to settle the issue and write the future of their colossal realm in blood.

The two mighty hosts that faced each other that day looked more alike than not; after all, this was a civil war. Both had large contingents of archers and lightly armored Persian-style infantry, as well as throngs of swift cavalry and chariots with scythed wheels. But in Cyrus's ranks stood a mass of notorious outsiders—mercenaries from a warrior land whose great shields and confining helmets, flashing in the Mesopotamian sun, gave them a frightful demeanor.

These were Greek hoplites. More than 10,000 strong, they hailed from throughout the Greek world, selling their skill in arms for a portion of Cyrus's war chest. To the Persians on both sides, these bronze-clad bruisers would not have seemed unfamiliar. Hoplites in close ranks called phalanxes—densely packed formations that sacrificed mobility for defense and striking power—helped defeat the Persian Empire's attempt to conquer Greece back in the reign of Xerxes during the first two decades of the fifth century BCE. Since then, hoplites—who probably derived their name from the large round shield, or *hoplon*, they carried—had become one of the chief exports of the Greek lands, their battle-winning tactics and armament finding plenty of buyers in an ancient world full of clashing dynasts. Cyrus, a Persian prince, was staking his bid for the crown on their spear points.

He was right to do so, though he could not know how close the Greek mercenaries were to the cancellation of their contract. In fact, by the end of the battle, the hoplites stood alone in defiance amid the ruin of the cause for which they had marched so far from home. Cyrus was dead, his army mostly scattered. Artaxerxes now decided the fate of his vanquished foes—but not of the "Ten Thousand," as history would come to know these indefatigable Greeks.

OUT OF ASIA AND INTO HISTORY

The denouement of Cunaxa offers one of history's most intriguing curiosities. In the course of the savage fighting, Cyrus was cut down, his army—with the exception of his Greek freelancers—routed. As the dust settled, the Ten Thousand came to understand their predicament: Though undefeated tactically, their employer was dead, along with any hope of remuneration for their services. Nevertheless, the hoplites occupied a choice piece of ground, defeating all attempts by their much more numerous antagonists to break them. This was the strength of hoplite tactics writ large—a challenge that Persia, with all its resources and genius for administration, never managed to answer satisfactorily.

A bizarre impasse had been reached. Though deprived of their cause and far from their hearths, the Greeks remained unbroken on the battlefield over which their side had lost control. Artaxerxes's legitimate claim to victory stood awkwardly alongside his impotence in the face of a huge Hellene phalanx. Neither camp could force a resolution.

The adventure that ensued, recounted for posterity by its most famous participant, soldier and writer Xenophon, put Greek resourcefulness and tenacity in bold relief. Eager to get home, Xenophon and his 10,000 comrades marched north out of the heart of the Persian Empire to the shores of the Black Sea, deprived of their officers and hounded all the way by hostile Persian forces bent on foiling their deliverance. "The sea, the sea!" they cried upon seeing the sun-girded waves after emerging from Anatolia (Asia Minor). Though still quite far from home, the very sight of water after so many trials through the wilderness of Asia was enough to remind them of Greece—a land defined as much by its coastlines as by its mountains and plains. Many challenges still lay ahead, but they would ultimately make it back to the Greek world that had seemed impossibly remote on the dusty plain of Cunaxa.

The so-called March of the Ten Thousand became a fixture in the ancient Greek ethos. Since throwing back Xerxes and his awesome military juggernaut, Greeks had defined themselves in opposition to the Persian colossus as caretakers of an Aegean civilization representing everything that Asiatic tyranny supposedly denigrated. Against this background, the triumph of the Ten Thousand seemed like a supreme act of vindication—an exemplar of superior Greek military virtues over Persian fecklessness. A phalanx of hoplites had managed to extricate itself, against all odds, from the very heart of Persian territory. What further proof was needed of Greek superiority?

None, according to many who thought Greece's time had arrived. By the middle of the fourth century BCE, a movement was well afoot to unite Greece's infamously fractious city states behind a league capable of projecting force deep into Persia. Chief among the idea's advocates was the esteemed orator Isocrates, who envisioned a united Hellenistic world hurling itself against the eastern barbarian in righteous vengeance.

As for the question of who would lead this pan-Hellenic crusade, Isocrates was unambiguous: Philip II, king of Macedon, was the only ruler capable of roping Greece's fiercely independent city states into a workable alliance. Located north of Greece, between the plain of Thessaly and the rich hills of Thrace, Macedon had traditionally been disparaged as a barbarian land by its neighbors to the south. But Philip, a man of prodigious ambition and ability, had wormed his way into Greek auspices even as he built himself a military machine like no other on Earth. While Greece debated, Philip acted—and ultimately used his newly minted army to force the city states into a league under his control. By 336 BCE, he was ready to take on his cherished dream: an invasion of the Persian Empire. He fell to an assassin's blade before making it happen.

Two years later, Philip's son, Alexander, took up the crusade that seemed to have found a momentum all its own. What was about to break on the Persians was a re-imagined version of the phalanx menace that had frustrated them for generations—a new form of warfare incorporating traditional and not-so-traditional elements of Greek-style combat into a mobile mill for the grinding of lives. Persia probably never had a chance against the leap in military thinking that came storming out of the West. But if there were any doubts, the Battle of Issus put them to rest.

THE CHANGING FACE OF WAR

The fourth century BCE was a time of change in Greek warfare. During the Peloponnesian War (431–404 BCE), Sparta and her allies clashed with the Athenian maritime empire over control of the Greek world, immersing their city states in a long agony of fire, brutality, plague, and murder. Desperation to deliver a killing blow through the interminable stalemate forced a consideration of new ideas, shaking the old foundations of hoplite warfare.

In the decades following Athens's defeat, these new ideas took root. Gone was the unquestioned supremacy of the old ways, in which proud landowners donned their heavy panoply, briefly left their wives and slaves, and settled affairs on the flat field of honor in a clash of serried shields. For one thing, the hoplites of old were amateurs, and proud of it—bravery, a large enough purse to afford arms, and love of *polis*, or one's city-state, were all they had ever needed to take their place in the phalanx. They were farmers and citizens, not landless hirelings. But now professionalism had crept into the picture. Once only Sparta, whose earthly needs were provided by a nation of slaves, had cared to support a population of full-time slayers practicing their craft to the exclusion of everything else. Now virtually every city state took the time to school their young men in fighting.

Nor were hoplites the only show in town anymore. Their former domination of the battlefield, the result as much of their cherished place in Greek tradition as their solid tactical effectiveness, had been undermined by the loosening of conventions. Light infantry, *peltasts*, had become just as necessary, as had trained cavalry. Those foolish enough to fight only with hoplites were likely to see their heavy infantry whittled down by swift, maneuverable formations of javelin throwers, slingers, or disciplined horsemen. The heavy phalanx remained; but it could no longer secure victory on its own.

Tactical innovations abounded in a land that had replaced ritualized combat with hard pragmatism. In 371 BCE, Epaminondas of Thebes dealt the Spartan phalanx a devastating defeat by massing an unprecedented fifty ranks of hoplites on his left wing, their immense pushing power concealed from Spartan eyes until it was too late. Iphicrates, an Athenian commander of mercenaries who acquired legendary status by routing a column of Spartan hoplites solely with fleet-footed peltasts, committed his progressive ideas to parchment, one of which espoused the creation of a new type of infantryman with a longer spear and lighter armor. And up north, in the wilds of Macedon, an implacable king was building a new type of army using ingenuity, discipline, and the bellicose passions of his rough-hewn countrymen.

Like Thessaly to its south, Macedon was a land dominated by warrior elites whose retinues enforced localized power in the crags and valleys. To bend his waspish nobles to his will, Philip channeled their equestrian inclinations into a corps of cavalry units, their competition with one another used to hone their skills in maneuver warfare. They soon became formidable, wielding great lances in attacks delivered with explosive violence—not to harass or weaken, but to smash. Not even in Thessaly, renowned for its hard-galloping horsemen, had anyone seen their like. Charging from the wings, they were intended to punch holes in the enemy line and drive its broken fighters onto Philip's other ingenious invention: the Macedonian phalanx.

Like Iphicrates, whose ideas may have influenced him, the Macedonian king favored lightly armored infantry in the phalanx. Wearing open-faced helmets, they advanced with a smaller shield slung over the neck and one shoulder, freeing both hands to wield a relatively new weapon that Macedon's foes would learn to fear and respect: the *sarissa*, an enormous wooden pike nearly eighteen feet (5.5 m) in length. The sarissae multiplied the hitting power of the phalanx dramatically, allowing the first five ranks to present the points of their weapons to an enemy.

THIS STATUE OF A GREEK HOPLITE, A HEAVY FOOT SOLDIER, WAS CREATED IN 1900 AND PROBABLY HELD A SPEAR AT ONE POINT. HOPLITES PROBABLY DERIVED THEIR NAME FOR THE LARGE ROUND SHIELD, OR HOPLON, THEY CARRIED.

Getty Images

The effect of this new phalanx, rolling forward like a great spiny beast, could be awesome as long as the ranks maintained formation and performed according to orders. Philip's new tactics could not be mastered overnight. To ensure proper discipline, Philip professionalized his army. Though recruited into regional battalions, the men drew a wage from the king himself. Constant drilling, the king's infectious élan, and the promise of glory in a competitive culture all conspired to build an army of unusual cohesion and ability. These men bore little resemblance to the hoplites who had humbled Xerxes a century and a half earlier. Philip was relying not on civic duty to win him victories, but on the skills of his 30,000 to 40,000 expert butchers. They would lust for the kill, but fight as one on the field.

Despite his sweeping innovations, Philip retained the spirit of old Macedon. Brilliance, charisma, and ruthlessness had given him unprecedented authority. But to those who fought for him, he was more a first among equals than a remote monarch. Sharing in the trials of campaigning, the king knew the men under his command as "Companions"—a label that spoke volumes about the warrior culture from which this terrifying host had arisen and the customs to which it clung.

BEYOND THE HELLESPONT

Such "leading from the front" habits took their toll on Philip, who died one-eyed, hobbling, a disfigured beast from some tragic myth. But Alexander, still in his early twenties, was not to be outdone. As the ships transporting his army approached the far shore of the Hellespont, which divided Europe from Asia, he leapt first into the water, just as Protesilaus had done as the Achaean fleet converged on the Trojan beach in Homer's *Iliad*. The year was 335 BCE, and one of the greatest odysseys in history was about to begin.

The keen young king was, in a real sense, following his father's lead. Philip had already sent soldiers into Asia before his death two years earlier to prepare the way for the main invasion, now being led by Alexander. However, Philip's preliminary force was able to achieve little beyond ensuring the safe arrival of Alexander and the main army, foiled as it was by the efforts of Memnon, a Greek general in Persian service. Once Alexander and his 40,000 or so men were ashore, Memnon advised a scorched-earth policy to deny the invaders any forage. But the local Persian governors, or satraps, to whom he answered blanched at the prospect of torching so much of the revenue on which they relied, and opted for battle instead. At the Granicus River, Alexander proved the worth of his vaunted military machine, routing the satraps and their forces in a bold assault across the stream. The young Macedonian king, personally leading the elite Companion cavalry on the right wing, fought savagely in the fray and nearly lost his life.

The great adventure had begun. Alexander proceeded south down the coast of Asia Minor, liberating the Greek cities of Ionia as he went, then made his way east. By the summer of 333, he had forced his way through the Taurus Mountains at the Cilician Gates, leading his army south into Syria. He then divided his army, giving part of it to his most trusted general, Parmenio (or Parmenion), to secure the Mediterranean coast while he himself headed inland to intercept the expected Persian counterattack from King Darius III.

But Darius had other plans. By the time Alexander and Parmenio had reunited after failing to engage any large enemy forces, a Persian army nearly 100,000 strong had stolen a march north of the Macedonians and encamped on

Alexander's line of communication back to Greece. The Great King had not been idle, having mustered his forces during Alexander's long path of conquest, relying on the immense distances of his empire to buy him time. That time now paid off: Alexander wasn't just outnumbered; he had been outmaneuvered. Since disbanding his navy after liberating Ionia, his only line of supply led overland to the Hellespont and into Europe. Either he turned around and defeated Darius, or his men would be reduced to foraging for food in a hostile country with autumn well under way.

This was the only coup Darius ever achieved against his young nemesis. Driving his point home, he descended on the village of Issus, where Alexander had left his wounded to be cared for, and slaughtered them to a man. The brash Macedonian had brought this upon himself—let there be no mercy for the invader. Darius, unchallenged sovereign of a realm too large for most Macedonians even to comprehend, had arrived personally to destroy this insolent whelp.

THE BANKS OF THE PINARUS

Seven miles (11 km) southeast of Issus ran the Pinarus River, emerging out of its defile in the Amanus Mountains to cut the shallow coastal plain at the far northeast corner of the Mediterranean basin. It was here, in November 333 BCE, that Darius chose to receive the Macedonian attack he knew was coming.

Though the Persian king had played his hand well, his situation was not without its perils. To be sure, he had forced a fight with his enemy on his own terms, posing the sort of threat to Alexander's logistics that required the Macedonian to make an attack on ground of Darius's choosing. Nevertheless, the Great King needed a victory, and soon. Alexander's invasion had been met with desultory resistance, to say the least, allowing a penetration of the empire the like of which had never been seen before. Much of Anatolia was gone, its ancient and wealthy Ionian cities with it. How much more of this could Darius's reputation take?

Interestingly, it was a situation similar to that faced by his ancestor, Xerxes, on the eve of Salamis. Vast armies like the one that now prepared to face Alexander the Great came with a hefty price tag. Nor could they be raised quickly, so large were the distances and bureaucratic challenges. For these reasons, as well as his standing at court, Darius had to force a resolution or squander the energy, resources, and momentum that had gone into this concentration of military might. And with winter coming on, he was running out of time.

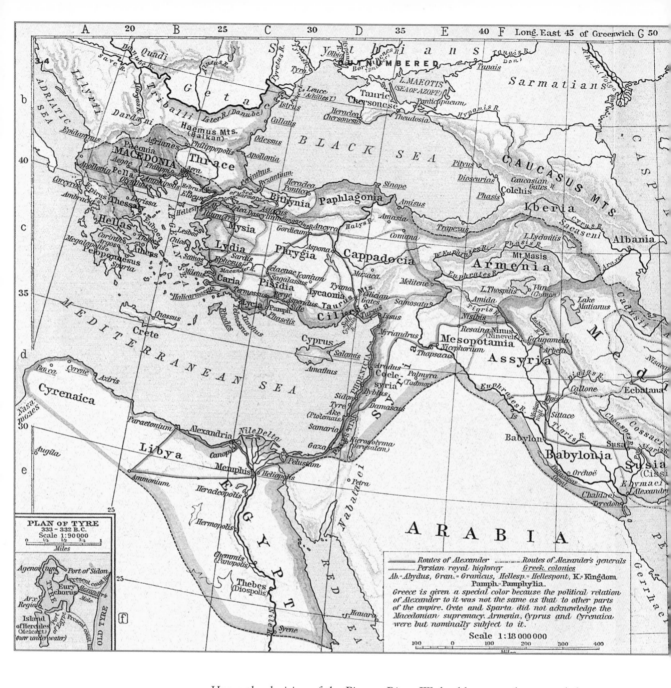

Hence the decision of the Pinarus River. Wedged between the sea and the mountains, the coastal plain on the Pinarus—just one and a half miles (2.4 km) in width—lacked the sort of elbowroom Darius would have preferred to exploit his much greater numbers. But he had to grapple with his enemy *now*, and Alexander was hugging the coast. The two armies were relatively close, ensuring Alexander's imminent appearance, but still allowing Darius enough time to prepare his position on the riverbank. And so the die was cast.

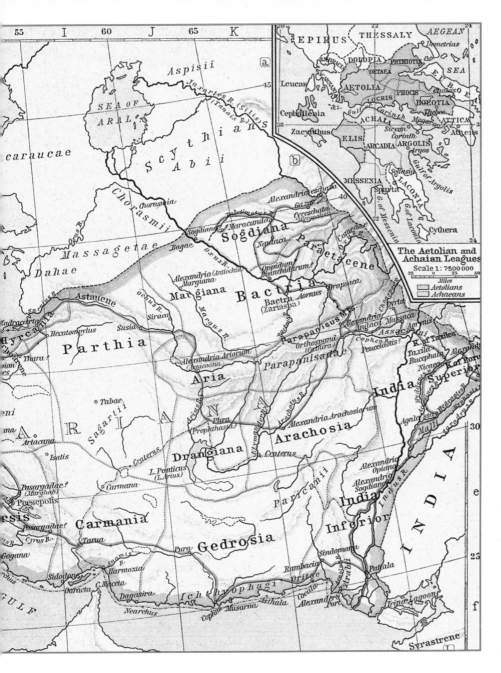

A MAP OF THE MACEDONIAN EMPIRE SHOWS HOW THE SEA JUTS INTO THE VILLAGE OF ISSUS, JUST NORTHEAST OF CYPRUS. IN HIS CAMPAIGN TO CONQUER PERSIA, ALEXANDER LEFT HIS WOUNDED IN ISSUS TO RECOVER; DARIUS LATER DESCENDED UPON THE VILLAGE AND SLAUGHTERED THEM.

The shahanshah was no doubt confident. The Pinarus was more a sluggish mountain stream than a proper watercourse, but its presence before his concentrated ranks would definitely pose a problem for advancing enemy troops.

Besides, the Persian army was a force of nature unto itself. Darius's cavalry, drawn overwhelmingly from the nobility, rode into battle with bows, spears, and an equestrian tradition that went back to the roots of Indo-European civilization. His infantry, mustered from many lands, was similarly armed, capable of showering the enemy with arrows and dealing with all but the toughest infantry. First among the Great King's soldiers were the Ten Thousand Immortals, functioning as both imperial guard and shock troops. With few exceptions, both cavalry and infantry were more lightly armored than Greek or Macedonian types, representing a tradition that relied on the bow, favored the feint, and drew on manpower pools an order of magnitude larger than anything in Europe. Numbers, archery, and speed of horse had been the military underpinnings of an empire two centuries old, and there was little reason for Darius to doubt their effectiveness now.

Still, he hedged his bets. With wicker shields, loose caps instead of helmets, and a skirmishing tradition, much of the Persian infantry lacked the staying power necessary to defy a Greek-style phalanx. To remedy this, Darius happily relied on his considerable resources to hire a phalanx of his own. Its numbers remain uncertain, but a mass of mercenary hoplites definitely formed the heart of the Persian line. Surrounding Darius at the center, these adventurers filled the front ranks of the Persian host. They were Greeks, some peltasts as well as hoplites, who were happy to cash in on their hatred of Macedonian oppression. Hiring them was easier for Darius than bending the martial traditions of his subject peoples to create an equivalent.

This was the army that arrayed itself on the north bank of the Pinarus. Numbering perhaps 100,000, it manifested the power of an empire like no other at the time. On November 5 its masses looked south across the river and spied Alexander's approach, his columns coming on in near perfect order to fill the plain.

THE AGGRESSORS

As he approached the battlefield, Alexander took in his opponent's dispositions and no doubt felt a surge of nervous excitement. This was not the poorly arrayed muster of Granicus before his eyes, but an enormous royal army, its eclectic colors and raiment making a fantastic spectacle to men such as he who had never seen warriors of Gedrosia, Hyrcania, or the myriad other exotic lands that swore obeisance to the King of Kings. Should the Macedonian ruler defeat this magnificent host, he must surely be a god.

Darius's preparations were exemplary. At Granicus, the Persians had put their cavalry in the front line, but here Darius massed all 11,000 of them on his right wing against the Mediterranean shore, clearly hoping to force the Macedonian flank. Greek hoplites held the center, their concentrated, heavily armored ranks intended to act like an anchor while their mounted colleagues on the right delivered a killing blow. Masses of archers to either side of the Hellenes would rain murder down on Alexander's troops should the latter force the Pinarus. Though Asiatic infantry stood ready at the flanks of the Greek mercenaries, the majority of Darius's foot levies formed a huge reserve stretching behind the phalanx. The shahanshah himself stood in his chariot at the center, surrounded by the 3,000 peerless horsemen of his royal guard.

Alexander had not anticipated the Persian decision to concentrate cavalry on the seaward wing. Knowing the skill of the Persian horse, he deftly arranged to redeploy his own Thessalian cavalry to support his left, where previously only the allied Greek horsemen had been stationed. This maneuver was kept from Persian eyes by sending the Thessalians behind the Macedonian phalanx, whose forest of sarrisai concealed the redeployment.

AS HE APPROACHED THE BATTLEFIELD, ALEXANDER TOOK IN HIS OPPONENT'S DISPOSITIONS AND NO DOUBT FELT A SURGE OF NERVOUS EXCITEMENT. SHOULD THE MACEDONIAN RULER DEFEAT THIS MAGNIFICENT HOST, HE MUST SURELY BE A GOD.

This done, the units of Alexander's army assumed their positions south of the Pinarus according to a plan that, broadly speaking, rarely changed throughout its leader's brief career. To the right of the Greek and Thessalian cavalry stood missile troops, archers, and javelin men, from Thrace and Crete. Then came the great Macedonian phalanx, its six battalions of foot Companions arranged, left to right, in order of increasing prestige based on performance. To the right of these were the *hypaspists*, or "shield bearers," the elite of Alexander's infantry, chosen for their impressive physiques and equipped, unlike the *phalangites*, to deploy quickly wherever their shock tactics could exploit a breakthrough or fend off disaster. Rightmost of these were the foot *agema*, the elite of the elite, recruited from nobility and charged with guarding Alexander with their lives. The Companion cavalry came next, deployed in seven squadrons and commanded personally by Alexander and the cavalry element of his agema. Also on the right, closest to the rising mountain spurs, was a contingent of Agrianians—Balkan allies who formed the elite of Alexander's light footmen, principally as javelin men. Greek hoplites were held in reserve.

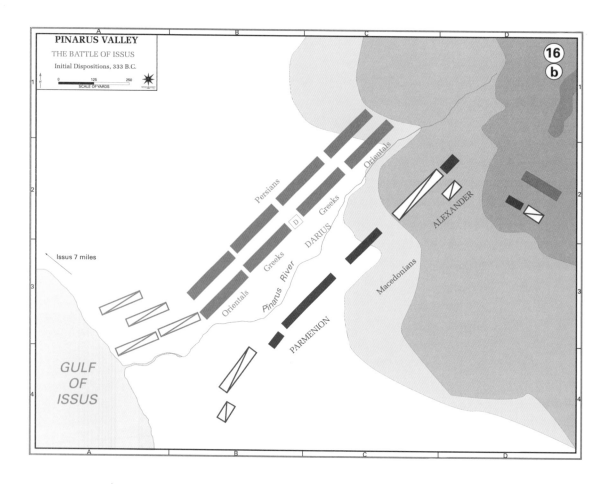

PINARUS VALLEY

THE BATTLE OF ISSUS

Initial Dispositions, 333 B.C.

SCALE OF YARDS
0   125   250

Issus 7 miles

GULF
OF
ISSUS

THE BATTLE OF ISSUS, 333 BCE:
ALEXANDER MEANT TO STRIKE
WITH THE BEST OF HIS CAVALRY
ON THE RIGHT WHILE PARMENIO,
SPELLED PARMENION HERE,
HELD AT ALL COST ON THE LEFT.

United States Military Academy

While Alexander commanded the right, he entrusted the left to dependable Parmenio, including four battalions of the phalanx. The general's task, as always, would be to hold at all costs while Alexander charged on the opposite flank.

After sending a mixed force of foot and horse to chase away a detachment of Persians on the high ground behind the Macedonian right, Alexander straightened out his line and advanced slowly toward the Pinarus. Greek hoplites and two squadrons of Companion cavalry were also sent to further reinforce the right, whose uncertain condition had become a concern to the young king.

He had, in total, slightly more than 40,000 combatants under his command, of which fewer than 6,000 were cavalry. The odds were long, to say the least. And Alexander, possessed of a confidence that would one day take him beyond the snow-capped borders of the known world, pressed for attack into the bristling ire of an empire.

OUTDOING ACHILLES

Between the looming brown peaks to the east and the blue-gray expanse of the Gulf of Issus, the carpet of Persian soldiery moved in a subtle commotion, alive with the anticipation that hung over the crowded plain. Their numbers, Alexander knew, made the Persian deployment deep. His own line stretched to span the field. Alexander may have thought of Leuctra at this point, where Epaminondas's Thebans had dashed Spartan invulnerability with sheer depth of ranks. Philip, Alexander's father, had known Epaminondas. The battle must have featured prominently in the boy's education.

But Darius was no Epaminondas, and the Persians were not fighting like the city states of old. Depth of deployment mattered, but so did generalship. Alexander now ranged across the front of his army, exhorting his officers and calling attention to those men, some of them common soldiers, who had distinguished themselves. This was the bond of king and Companion, a relationship as real to the men at Issus as the weapons with which they unhesitatingly killed. Nation, army, king, and subject were all blurred in a martial endeavor to which all were attached as surely as a fighter to his greaves. Alexander's throne had become a saddle, his state a military camp, and all those who soldiered with him shared in an adventure that made a home out of battlefields.

But it wasn't enough to merely assemble, direct, and encourage his men. Alexander needed, like every Greek and Macedonian, to embody the ideals of Homeric heroes, to live as they lived. Alexander needed to channel Achilles, finest of warriors, as much as he needed to acquire the Persian Empire. The one ensured the fulfillment of the other.

Once back in the company of his Royal Horse Guard, Alexander personally launched the charge. He had done the same at Granicus, and nearly gotten himself killed. Now he unhesitatingly did it again, spearheading the Companion cavalry across the riverbed toward the archers and infantry of Darius's left flank, the hypaspists following close behind. Arrows had already begun to fall on the Macedonian ranks, lending urgency to Alexander's thrust—the quicker he and the supporting elements of his assault got across the river, the quicker they would be able to drive away or even slaughter Darius's archers.

As Alexander's elements—two battalions of the phalanx, the shield bearers, and the Companion cavalry—moved forward to support the king's attack, Parmenio received the fury of Persia's finest. Darius's 11,000 cavalry stormed

ALEXANDER M.DARIVM VIC. SVPERAT
CÆSIS IN ACIE PERSAR. PEDIT.C.M.EQVIT
VERO.M.INTERFECTIS. MATRE QVOQVE
CONIVGE.LIBERIS.DARII REG.CVM M.HAVD
AMPLIVS EQVITIB. FVGA DILAPSI.CAPTIS.

through the riverbed in thundering glory, clashing with the Thessalians and Greeks, and forcing Parmenio back. Alexander's army quaked with the impact; the Macedonian phalanx, barely holding on the left and pushing forward on the right, ran afoul of the riverbed, the terrain and tremendous violence disrupting their orderly deployment. Seeing an opportunity, Darius's Greek mercenaries at the center exploited the chaos, punching holes in the Macedonian battalions with shield and spear. The muddy dross of the Pinarus soon splashed with gore.

Parmenio had his own problems, which is why he had been given the job—Alexander knew the old hand could handle himself under duress. But this was precisely the problem with Alexander's modus operandi: He himself was unaware of Parmenio's situation at this critical moment, given his own preoccupation with going into harm's way to deliver, as modern German strategists would call it, the *schwerpunkt*—the point of maximum, concentrated effort. One could not be hero and general at once. So as his vaunted phalanx wavered under the punishment, and his left wing fought savagely to hold its ground, he busied himself with the killing thrust—which, fortunately for him, came soon enough. Relying on the eagerness of his elite cavalry and shield bearers to close with enemies who lacked the same hitting power in a melee, Alexander forced a gap through the Persian left wing with thrusting brutality and sent it flying in retreat. He then regrouped his forces and exhorted the hypaspists to turn left, into the tender flank of the enemy Greek infantry, with the Companion cavalry in support.

The issue was still in doubt on the seaward flank when the king of Macedon decided matters on the opposite end of the line, beneath the glowering mountains. Darius's Greek center, grappling with the long Macedonian pikes, had no energy to spare for a stab in the ribs from Alexander's shield bearers and cavalry, smashing their way in from the direction of the mountains under their wild-eyed king. The Greek hoplites and light infantry fought desperately under the crunch, then collapsed beneath the swords and lances of Macedon's elite.

The *schwerpunkt* had been exploited. Alexander made for Darius, slashing and stabbing like a man possessed, his retinue slaughtering those closest to the Great King, including his Royal Guard and generals. Darius saw his situation undone, and fled in his chariot behind the screen of the fighting.

Rout raced through the Persian ranks at the sight of Darius's flight. On the bloodied shore, Persia's cavalry wheeled and ran while the center of the battle descended into a maelstrom of infantry brawls, the Greek mercenaries losing

THIS SIXTEENTH-CENTURY PAINTING DEPICTS THE BATTLE OF ISSUS, ALSO ENTITLED "THE VICTORY OF ALEXANDER THE GREAT." ALTHOUGH THE BATTLE TOOK PLACE CENTURIES PRIOR, THE PARTICIPANTS ARE SHOWN IN SIXTEENTH-CENTURY ARMOR.

Albrecht Altdorfer

their cohesion before the stabilized and advancing phalanx. The real butchery soon began, with Alexander's men everywhere in pursuit of desperate and fleeing throngs, cutting them down like grain.

Defeat and humiliation had come to the world's greatest empire.

ONE EMPIRE LOST, ANOTHER GAINED

Thousands died that day between Issus and the Pinarus, the overwhelming majority of them on the Persian side. Alexander's booty was precious indeed: Darius's family, left in the rout, including his wife and mother. The Macedonian ruler insisted they be treated in accordance with their royal status, offering a glimpse at his future plans. For Alexander meant to assume the throne of Persia as its rightful king, requiring compliance and acceptance of the Persian nobility.

Issus had offered proof of the superiority of Macedonian arms. The sarissa-armed phalanx, the elite hypaspists, the ferociously effective cavalry, and the combined arms approach that made them all work in concert proved too much for the Persian host, whatever its awesome size. Why hadn't the throngs of Persian archers been able to make a difference? Because Alexander's assault had closed the distance too quickly. How could Darius's immense corps of elite cavalry along the shore fail to deliver the sort of decisive breakthrough that Alexander had made? As swift and skilled as these horsemen were, Parmenio's combination of Thessalians—perhaps the equal of their Persian opposites in the saddle—and phalangites were able to hold on just long enough for matters to decide themselves on the other end of the battle line. As for the center, where Darius had massed his Hellenic mercenaries, their weapons were all but doomed against the probing sarissai of Alexander's phalanx, even during the latter's difficulty maneuvering over the riverbed while under attack.

Two years later, Alexander drove the point home at the Battle of Gaugamela, where Darius's army outnumbered him by an even greater margin—indeed, the Persian line is supposed to have dwarfed Alexander's by over a mile (1.6 km). The result, however, was the same. The Macedonians had produced a matchless formula for battlefield victory, backed by a general with tremendous charisma, raw talent, and luck in abundance.

The rise of this formidable military machine and its unleashing in Asia spelled the end of the Achaemenid dynasty, one of the ancient world's most successful clans of empire builders. In its place came a Hellenized world ushered in by Alexander's awe-inspiring, and destructive, campaigning. From the Mediterranean to the Indus River in India, Alexander built his own heroic immortality on a foundation of corpses. What followed was one of the most culturally complex periods in ancient history—an ornate amalgam of Near Eastern and Greek/Macedonian elements known to us today as the Hellenistic Age.

THE ALEXANDER MOSAIC DEPICTS ALEXANDER THE GREAT AND HIS ENEMY, DARIUS III, SHOWN OPPOSITE IN HIS CHARIOT, CONFRONTING EACH OTHER ACROSS THE FIELD DURING THE BATTLE OF ISSUS. THE MOSAIC WAS CREATED DURING THE FIRST CENTURY AND WAS A REPRODUCTION OF A PAINTING. IT WAS FOUND IN 1831 ON THE FLOOR IN THE LARGEST HOUSE IN POMPEII AND IS MADE OF A MILLION TESSERAE, OR SMALL TILES.

CHAPTER 3

CANNAE
216 BCE

HANNIBAL'S MASTERPIECE THRASHES
ROME AND CREATES A LEGEND

55,000 CARTHAGINIANS VERSUS 80,000 ROMANS

AS HE LOOKED OUT AT THE RANK UPON RANK OF ROMANS, Hannibal Barca might have wondered if anyone had seen so great a force since the heyday of mighty Persia. And yet he had eagerly offered battle rather than avoid this collision. Near a hill town called Cannae, his army now faced the fight of its life because he had *wanted* to grapple with this mammoth rectilinear host now arrayed against him, had come by way of the Alps on a journey more perilous than that of Odysseus (if not nearly as lengthy) specifically to kill as many Romans as he could. And now they had obliged him.

He had not come by such confidence easily. But he had already defeated the Romans on several occasions in the epic struggle that posterity would know as the *Second Punic War*. And he had at his disposal one of the finest, most professional armies in the known world—an army forged from men from many peoples who responded with lightning efficiency to a single commander.

In the distance, the Romans came forward in a sublime spectacle of walking shields. Soon the killing would begin, and the Romans would understand why their own numbers had become a burden rather than an asset.

Looking to the officers who directed his peculiarly efficient military machine, he may well have recalled that day, long ago, that had set him on this fateful course.

THE SACRIFICE

According to the Greek historian Polybius, Hannibal's education in war began before a temple of Zeus. Carthaginians did not sacrifice to the father of the Greco-Roman gods, so we can assume the act was committed on ground sacred to Baal Shamin or Melqart. We can imagine Hamilcar Barca and his little boy as they smelled the split flesh of the animal they slaughtered together, the pooling blood offered in good faith to a capricious deity.

The man, his graying hair belying a vigor feared by numerous enemies, had asked his son whether he wanted to come along into the danger of conquest. Across the narrow sea in Spain, an empire awaited to be built with swords and oaths. The boy, just nine years old, could barely contain his enthusiasm. How often had he yearned for this moment? The man agreed to bring his eager son along on one condition: that the youth swear an oath, there and then on the suffering animal before them, to never be a friend of Rome.

Hamilcar Barca, Hannibal's father, lived from 275 to 228 BCE; a legend in his own time, he had brilliantly led men in battle against the hated Romans, only to see his victories in Sicily thrown away for a shameful peace in 241 BCE. Now, with so many of his ancient city's possessions stolen by Rome, he meant to build a new empire in Spain—an empire from which, someday, the war against Rome could be renewed.

His son took the oath that day in 237 BCE, and proved as good as his word. Grown to manhood in the shadow of his father's Spanish enterprise, Hannibal became nothing less than the scourge of Rome—and a legend so huge that his name survives, some twenty-two centuries later, as a byword for military brilliance. He performed feats of leadership that nobody thought possible, and nearly brought Rome to her knees. But nothing he ever achieved on behalf of his embattled city state quite compares to the victory he secured, against formidable odds, near a place called Cannae.

A MIGHTY STATE LAID LOW

The origins of the conflict that locked Carthage and Rome in a generations-long death grip lay in Sicily. Founded in the eighth or ninth century BCE by settlers out of Tyre in the Levant, Carthage began life as a Phoenician outpost and quickly grew to become a great power in its own right. From her strategic location on the northern coast of what is today Tunisia, Carthage manifested the ancient Phoenician

urge to trade by building a maritime empire in the western Mediterranean. Her navigators even sailed beyond the Pillars of Hercules to trade along the Atlantic coast of Africa and, evidence suggests, distant Britain. In this vast marine enterprise, the Carthaginian thalassocracy came to look on the control of nearby Sicily, a large island at the heart of the great sea, as absolutely necessary.

But Sicily defied domination by any one power. Greeks, the equal of their Phoenician rivals at sea, had settled the island early in their colonizing period, founding great city states like Syracuse. Though as fractious and divided as their mainland Greek counterparts, these city states fought fiercely against Carthaginian encroachment, ensuring a centuries-long struggle between opposing cultures.

It was against this background, in 264 BCE, that Rome became involved in the Sicilian cockpit. Carthage, whose glory days had begun when Rome was little more than a gaggle of hardscrabble farmers on the Tiber River, had never faced a foe worthy of her own wealth and abilities. That long record now came to an abrupt and violent end.

Carthage was a state born of the Near East and its ancient kaleidoscope of civilizations. Phoenicia's Semitic language had given birth to the Greek alphabet, her mariners had been serving warlords as far back as the Assyrians, and her kings had fought for and against some of Egypt's greatest pharaohs. Representing the far western manifestation of that storied tradition, Carthage was a satellite of antiquity's birthplace.

Rome, by comparison, was a newcomer. Heavily influenced by ancient Greek and Hellenistic civilizations, she nevertheless retained an Italian complexion that made her stand apart from the powers she would eventually topple. From the Roman republic's founding in the sixth century BCE, she expanded outward to take control of the Etruscans, Latins, Samnites, and a host of other Italian peoples, building a centralized league of "allies" whose allegiance to Rome was codified in treaties. Rome's success lay in her willingness to extend the considerable benefits of citizenship, or its approximation, to conquered peoples willing to play nice. The result was less an empire and more a union of Italian peoples lured to cooperation by Roman leadership skilled in the subtle interplay of carrot and stick.

Rome's payoff for this farsighted approach was straightforward enough: manpower. While Carthage—a traditional city ruled by wealthy elites who ran their state like a corporation and jealously guarded the benefits of enfranchisement— had to rely on foreign mercenaries to supplement her paltry pool of conscripts, Rome could rely on a relatively large coalition of agricultural peoples obligated by treaty to provide soldiers in time of war.

Rome relied on this manpower as the basis of her effort against Carthage in the First Punic War. (The word *Punic* comes down to us from the Roman word for "Phoenician.") Drawn into Sicily by a request from Italian adventurers for support in their struggle over the northeastern corner of the island, Rome hoped for an easy stepping stone to overseas empire and got, instead, a lengthy and devastating war against the Carthaginians. The Romans reinvented themselves as a naval power, building whole fleets from scratch and defeating the Mediterranean's foremost maritime state in a war whose greatest clashes occurred at sea.

Sicily became a province of the Roman republic's new empire after the peace treaty of 241 BCE, and Carthage was reduced to a second-rate naval power. With the seizure of Sardinia soon afterward, little of the Punic city's imperial domain remained beyond the coast of Africa, leaving her with few options—one of which lay in Spain. There, under the auspices of Carthage's most dynamic bloodline, war with Rome was rekindled.

A FAMILY AFFAIR

When Hamilcar Barca began his Spanish campaign in the 230s BCE, Carthage's presence there was limited to the coast. He planned to extend the empire's influence inland, establishing either direct or indirect control over the region's considerable resources.

What emerged over the years was a Barcid enterprise, enriching the family as it added territory to Carthage's domain. Hamilcar and his successors absorbed most of southern Spain into a Carthaginian possession whose extensive mining operations and agricultural hinterland proved central to Carthage's comeback after the disastrous war with Rome.

Upon Hamilcar's death in 228, the conquest fell to his son-in-law, Hasdrubal. By this time the old Roman enemy was growing anxious at Carthage's success in Iberia, prompting diplomatic exchanges that settled on a limit to Carthaginian expansion at the Ebro River in the north. This left plenty of territory for Carthaginian expansion, which proceeded through aggression, diplomacy, and bribery of locals.

By the time Hannibal took over the family business in 221 BCE on the death of Hasdrubal, he had acquired an unmatched education in war and diplomacy. Still in his twenties, he inherited an army of singular experience and loyalty—professionals from Africa, the Balearic Islands, and Spain, who had fought for years under the Barcids and their cadre of Punic officers.

And Hannibal meant to take them into harm's way. He adopted a more aggressive stance than his two predecessors, launching bold strikes into central Spain and securing allies wherever he could through equally energetic diplomatic overtures. By 219, one of those allied tribes had become embroiled in a conflict with Saguntum, a city on the eastern coast. What ensued has been somewhat confused over the intervening centuries. But if the precise sequence of events is unknown, the immense impact they ended up having on the course of history is all too clear.

The citizens of Saguntum seem to have sent overtures to Rome for protection against Hannibal. Though the city was well south of the River Ebro, that didn't stop the Roman Senate from exploiting a promising opportunity. Saguntum was soon

STOKING THE FIRES OF VENGEANCE: A YOUNG HANNIBAL ACCEDES TO HIS FATHER'S REQUEST AND SWEARS ETERNAL ENMITY TO ROME ON A SACRIFICIAL ANIMAL.

Private Collection / © Agnew's, London, UK / The Bridgeman Art Library International

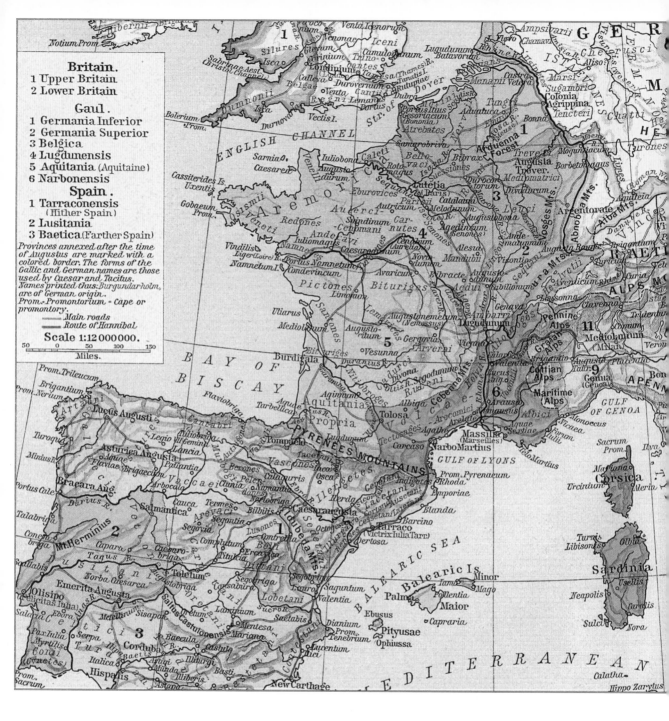

adopted as a "friend" of Rome, essentially putting it under Senatorial protection. Hannibal laid siege to it anyway, honoring his allies (whose tribal name remains lost to history) and, perhaps, deliberately goading the Romans, who did nothing to help their new "friends" beyond sending outraged emissaries to Carthage. They were rebuffed, and Saguntum fell in 218.

The question remains: How much of the Saguntum affair was driven by Hannibal, and how much by his ostensible superiors in Carthage? Did the general drag his state into war on the belief that he had already hatched a scheme to win it? Or were his actions merely the result of a larger Carthaginian plan to grab all of Spain and flaunt Roman power? In any event, the vast majority of Carthage's leadership was quick to choose defiance over a condemnation of their general's actions. The Second Punic War, or "Hannibal's War," as the Romans would know it, was on.

THE ROMAN WAY

The Roman state that prepared to confront Carthage for the second time in a generation was a republic governed by annually elected magistrates. Typically dominated by the state's wealthiest families, these offices served as a means of funneling good talent to the top, with the lowliest positions preparing young men to run for magistracies higher up the ladder. Most powerful of all were the consuls, only two of which were elected each year. Competition was fierce for this coveted pair of spots, each of which manifested something approaching monarchical power.

The Senate, having originated as a sort of royal council in Rome's distant past, had morphed into the senior advisory body of the state. Though it could not pass legislation per se, it could strongly influence the course of such efforts in the popular assemblies, and maintained a traditional control over foreign policy. Its members represented the cream of society—the wealthy, as well as former office holders with leadership experience.

War was a public affair to Romans. Unlike every other great state of the ancient Mediterranean world, Rome eschewed the use of professional troops, opting

A MAP OF THE LATER ROMAN EMPIRE SHOWING THE ROUTE (IN RED) HANNIBAL TOOK INTO ITALY. THE FIVE-MONTH JOURNEY TOOK AN INCREDIBLE TOLL, REDUCING HIS INFANTRY ALONE FROM 90,000 TO 20,000 MEN.

instead to place the burden of fighting on citizen landholders who could afford
their kit and weaponry. Bravery and stoicism, so deeply inculcated in the Roman
psyche, were believed to compensate for any want of long-time experience and
drill. Armies were invariably disbanded at the end of a campaign, losing the cohesion and esprit de corps that they had developed during their shared experience.

All of these factors stood in stark contrast to the Carthaginian way of war,
which brooked no illusions about the abilities of amateurs. While the Punic elite
ruled in Africa through aristocratically controlled councils and two *suffetes* who
operated as rough equivalents of Rome's consuls, the army they relied on for
defense was mustered from warlike peoples holding second-class status in the
empire: Libyans, Numidians, Iberians, and others. But they were paid to fight from
year to year, and trained by their Carthaginian officers under a system that built
and preserved unit cohesion, loyalty to superiors, and fighting efficiency. What
these couldn't provide, Carthage was willing to buy in mercenaries from Greece,
Gaul, and other locales.

One other major factor separated Rome from its Punic rival. Roman officers,
especially consuls, were expected to achieve glorious deeds on the battlefield; martial achievement was the only real currency in senatorial circles. But they were
given a mere year to do it, as their terms lasted only that long. (Compare this with
Hannibal, whose whole life was given over to leading men in battle.) Such pressures, combined with a complete lack of formal training, ensured at least the occasional military disaster.

Against an enemy like Hannibal, it ensured a whole slew of them.

SHEER SLAUGHTER

Given all these curious liabilities, how had Rome won the First Punic War years
earlier? While Carthage waged war by balance sheet, Rome fought to win at any
cost. The image we get of Carthage through the sources is a state geared toward
profit; war was tolerable only so long as it didn't jeopardize the imperial revenues
that supported the Punic status quo.

Rome, by contrast, understood victory in war as life. Defeat, however cost-
efficient, was so execrable to the typical Roman citizen as to make it intolerable.
Setbacks were understood as inevitable; ultimate victory, however, was as necessary as bread or wine. Backed by the tremendous resources and manpower of the
league of subservient allies at its doorstep, as well as a willingness to adapt and

improvise, this philosophy of killing purpose proved overwhelming in the First Punic War. Roman popular culture abhorred the absence of triumph in war the way nature abhors a vacuum.

Against this truculent enemy, Hannibal had only his own wits and a well-trained army of professional killers. They proved more than enough.

Nobody had ever attempted an undertaking as hazardous as the one on which he now staked the future of his state. Hannibal meant to lead a huge host out of Spain, into Gaul, across the Alps, and into Italy. Once there, he hoped to exploit Celtic hatred of Roman colonization along the Po River into ready recruitment, and unleash his reinforced army into the heart of the Roman Empire itself.

By 218 he had completed preparations and mustered a massive army for the march: 90,000 infantry, 12,000 cavalry, and thirty-seven war elephants. Though many of these men must have been fresh recruits from throughout the Punic Empire, Hannibal built his huge force around the cadre of veterans whose long experience under the Barcids would now prove crucial to forging a cohesive and effective military machine.

NOW LOOSE IN ROME'S BACKYARD AND TWICE UNDEFEATED, HANNIBAL BARCA PREPARED TO SET ALL ITALY ABLAZE.

They were soon tested to their limits. Though Hannibal's embassies had contacted tribes along the route, not all responded positively. Only through bloody campaigning beyond the Ebro was the young general able to secure northern Spain. Then it was across the Pyrenees Mountains, into Gaul and across the Rhone, a huge undertaking in its own right. By this time Hannibal had lost his weakest troops through desertion and thousands more to garrison the gains in northern Iberia. The Alps proved even more unforgiving. Negotiating the mountain passes in winter, Hannibal's freezing men were forced to grapple with hostile mountain peoples barring his passage.

By the time his battered army descended onto the Lombard plain toward the end of 218, the five-month journey had taken a dreadful toll. Just 20,000 infantry, 6,000 cavalry, and half the elephants remained.

Despite this, Hannibal quickly scored his first major victory against Roman arms at the Trebia River in December 218, severely mauling a larger army under the consul Tiberius Sempronius Longus. What followed was the fulfillment of Hannibal's greatest hope: thousands of Gauls, eager to strike a blow against their longtime Roman adversaries, flocked to the Carthaginian standard. With their help, Hannibal ambushed another enemy army along the banks of Lake Trasimene the following summer, reaping a ghastly harvest in Roman lives.

Now loose in Rome's backyard and twice undefeated, Hannibal Barca prepared to set all Italy ablaze. The gamble, it seemed, had paid off.

ALARM BELLS

Rome shook from the Punic impact. Unaware that Hannibal would even attempt such a move until he had already advanced well into southern Gaul, the Roman Senate scrambled to mount a defense. Armies, however, were not made overnight.

Under the circumstances, it is hardly surprising that Rome appointed a dictator. This was precisely the sort of crisis for which such a provision was created, requiring bold, centralized action.

But Fabius Maximus wasn't bold—indeed, he defined his tenure as dictator by avoiding bold action precisely because it had already cost Rome two armies and around 40,000 lives. Fabius represented the practical streak that ran through Roman society parallel to the aggressive one. Realizing that Hannibal's logistical situation was his weakness, the dictator opted to shadow him, rather than clash openly with him, hampering his supply efforts and goading him to act recklessly.

Whether this original "Fabian strategy" worked was beside the point; in time, the Roman people and their bellicose Senate clamored for something more direct. More than Roman pride was at stake. With an enemy army ranging freely throughout the peninsula, Rome stood a real chance of losing face with its Italian allies, threatening the very system that ensured Roman greatness. Fabius's tenure was not renewed, allowing elections to proceed apace.

By 216, the city had worked itself into a war fever. Reflecting the mood, voters elected two consuls who pledged to act assertively in the mounting crisis. Lucius Aemilius Paullus had been consul once before, in 219, and brought shrewd experience to the post. His colleague, Gaius Terentius Varro, was a "new man" with no family background in leadership and only his innate abilities to recommend him. Though not as seasoned as Paullus, he must have been an extraordinary figure to have won a consulship without any family connections.

To take on Hannibal, the Senate decided to give their new consuls command over an army of unprecedented size: eight legions, four times the size of the typical consular army. Because Roman legions always went to war with an equivalent number of *alae*, or legions raised from the Italian allies, this constituted a truly impressive host. At more than 5,000 infantry and 300 cavalry apiece—larger than the typical legion due to the emergency posed by Hannibal—the total number of troops raised came to more than 80,000 men.

In another breach with tradition, Paullus and Varro marched together, each assuming command on alternate days. By mid-summer, the two consuls were headed east to rendezvous with the remnants of the old army, which had been shadowing Hannibal's move south along the eastern coastal plain of Italy. They then proceeded in the footprints of their Carthaginian quarry, who had taken over the Apulian Plain hilltop town of Cannae as his headquarters. Though abandoned, the Romans had maintained Cannae as a supply dump, giving Hannibal's men plenty with which to fill their stomachs.

Toward the end of July, the massive Roman army, its columns throwing up clouds of dust in the summer heat, caught up with Hannibal, who observed its approach from his hilltop fastness. The massive size of the Roman host, clearly much greater than previous armies, must have given Hannibal pause. He quickly came to observe, however, what his consular foes already knew: The Carthaginians, despite their much smaller numbers, possessed an advantage in cavalry. On the second day of the Romans' approach, he unleashed a corps of these excellent horsemen, supported by light infantry, to harass the enemy, which resulted in a long but inconclusive skirmish.

By this time, the two consuls had begun to seriously disagree over strategy, the sources tell us. Paullus, experienced and leaning toward Fabian caution, worried that fighting here, on the broad plain beneath Cannae, played into Hannibal's hands with his better cavalry. Varro, by contrast, is universally portrayed as impulsive to the point of recklessness. For him, dawdling only worsened Rome's precarious situation, and the relatively level plain offered excellent ground for the heavily armed legions of infantry to advance in good order.

Paullus, assuming command the following day, seems to have accepted the inevitability of a battle now that the two opposing armies were in such close proximity, and prepared his legions for a fight. Between Cannae and the Roman position flowed the Aufidius River, a slender ribbon of blue cutting through squares of orchard and farmland. Paullus made two camps—the main one, with perhaps two-thirds of the army, and a smaller one on the opposite bank with the rest of his force.

The location of these camps remains as controversial to scholars as the site of the battle that was soon to follow, and has much to do with the course of the river, which may have shifted significantly in the two millennia since August 216 BCE. What seems certain is that Paullus built two camps to most effectively take advantage of the local terrain. While the majority of his army prepared for battle at the primary camp, foraging parties could operate out of the secondary one with a modicum of security, expanding the reach of Roman influence on the plain while still offering battle to the Punic enemy from two mutually supporting strongpoints.

Hannibal's reaction to this was prompt and unambiguous. On the very same day, he moved his army from its camp on the heights around Cannae to the plain below, taking up positions on the same side of the Aufidius as the Roman main camp. Clearly the consuls were going to have their battle.

CHESS ON THE APULIAN PLAIN

In an age when pitched battle was virtually impossible unless both sides agreed to it, the series of maneuvers and countermaneuvers that invariably preceded every clash amounted to a sort of grand chess match between sparring commanders. Each was keen to draw his opponent into a fight on ground of his own choosing while still maintaining order, cohesion, and morale in his own camp—factors that became increasingly challenging with the passage of time, especially for green troops whose heightened anticipation while in sight of the enemy could lead to desertion or, just as dangerous, an impulsive need for action.

Hannibal, still on the heights, could easily have stayed put. Thanks to the largesse of Cannae, his men were unlikely to feel the pangs of hunger for quite some time. Nevertheless, the food was sure to run out eventually—and while his cavalry could always outmatch his Roman enemy in the hit-and-run game of raiding and foraging, the Roman situation could only get stronger with time. This was their country, after all. In time more men would come, and more supplies.

Hannibal had come to deal death in battle, not wander in perpetuity. To inspire Rome's allies to abandon her before it was too late, the Carthaginians needed to wreck Roman arms as completely as possible. Reason favored a fight.

The Carthaginian made his move. The following day, August 1, he marched his army out and deployed in preparation for battle. Arrayed in splendor within sight of the Roman ramparts, the Punic forces taunted Roman manhood by their very presence. No assault against the prepared defenses was possible; but by his offer to fight, Hannibal sent a powerful message to the weary hearts of his enemies: *Here we are. Will your consuls rise to the challenge?*

Paullus, in command, refused. Given his level-headed reputation and renowned courage, he probably had good reason to delay. But his decision risked undermining the efforts of the largest army Rome had ever mustered. When dawn broke the following morning, Varro acted, leading his army out of the main camp and crossing the river to form in front of the smaller camp. To defend the larger encampment, he left some 10,000 men, roughly two legions' worth.

By crossing the river before deploying to offer battle, Varro gave his enemy a choice: Either attack the main Roman camp and risk being outflanked while doing so, or come and fight on ground of Varro's choosing.

Hannibal, clearly unfazed by the jockeying, crossed the stream in two columns at a good distance from the Roman lines. With so few cavalry, the Romans could not hope to hinder the enemy crossing. The Carthaginians formed up and prepared for battle.

PLANS IN DEPTH

The Roman legion of the third century BCE bore little resemblance to its counterpart in the later empire, whose uniformed, homogeneous ranks have become a staple in film and literature. In lieu of a standing army of professionals, age and economic status dictated the composition and even the tactics of the *legion*—a word whose origins lie in the old Latin word for "levy."

Four types of infantry filled the ranks at Cannae. Out front were the *velites*, recruited from the poor and those men of quality too young to join the older ranks. Typically armed with small shields, swords, and javelins, they acted as loose-order skirmishers to harass and hinder the enemy. Behind them came the *hastati*, composed of landed men in their early twenties. In addition to a large, oval shield and bronze helmet, they carried a short thrusting sword and two *pila*—heavy javelins with specially shaped points designed to puncture enemy shields and render them useless. Next came the *principes*, men in their late twenties who were armed very similarly to the hastati. And bringing up the rear were the *triarii*, who were older men of experience. They were heavily armored, with helmets, large shields, short swords, and thrusting spears. Excepting the velites, all were arranged in groups called *maniples* that could include between sixty and 160 men each, depending on circumstances. How did these four lines perform and interact in combat? Nobody knows for sure. Certainly the three lines behind the velites, all of whom were heavily armed and armored, staggered their maniples so that those in the second line covered the gaps in the first line, and so on.

Cavalry, recruited exclusively from the wealthy equestrian class, typically guarded the wings of Roman armies against flanking attacks. Rome's allies always provided a disproportionate number of horsemen—Varro had more than 6,000 cavalrymen at Cannae, 4,000 of which were allied Italians.

At Cannae, Varro and Paullus bet everything on their formidable infantry. Though deployed in the center as always, the seven legions and accompanying alae were packed in by lengthening the depth of the maniples. (This is minus the two legions' worth left to guard the main camp.) The result was an immense fist of legionaries unlike any that had gathered before. The four lines of the legions remained—velites, hastati, principes, and triarii. They had just been arranged along a narrower front relative to their unprecedented numbers. Through sheer depth of force, the consuls hoped to launch an unstoppable mass through the enemy center, delivering a death blow. All the cavalry on the wings had to do was hold long enough to allow the infantry to do its job.

As events would prove, that was a tall order. The Romans, who outnumbered their foes by a good 30,000 combatants or more, surrendered the possibility of outflanking Hannibal's line. This may have been due to the terrain. Depending on

ROMAN DICTATOR FABIUS MAXIMUS, PICTURED, EARNED THE TITLE "THE DELAYER" BECAUSE OF HIS ABILITY TO AVOID BOLD ACTION.

Getty Images

F. D. Meys, Inv. et Del.   *Patas, Sculp.*

FABIUS ELU DICTATEUR.
An de Rome 535.

Après s'être livrée pendant quelques jours aux transports de la plus vive douleur, Rome ne s'occupa plus que des moyens que lui prescrivait une sage politique pour écarter les dangers dont la menaçait un ennemi puissant et formidable. On pensa que dans une aussi grande extrémité un homme revêtu du pouvoir suprême pouvait seul sauver la République. L'Intrigue et la cabale se turent cette fois devant l'image de la patrie éplorée, et Q. Fabius Maximus est créé Dictateur.

Aussitôt que Fabius eut rassemblé ses troupes, il partit pour rejoindre l'Armée. Arrivé près du Camp, il apperçoit le Consul qui venait à sa rencontre à Cheval, suivi de ses licteurs et de ses principaux Officiers. Sur le champ il lui envoie dire de mettre pied à terre de venir le trouver sans suite et sans licteurs. La prompte obéissance du Consul et le respect avec lequel il aborda Fabius, rendirent aux Citoyens et aux Alliés cette haute idée de la Dictature, que le tems avait presque effacée.

Persuadé qu'avec des troupes peu aguerries, qu'a ferait trembler le seul nom d'Annibal, il étoit dangereux d'attaquer ouvertement un ennemi si redoutable, Fabius crut ne devoir lui opposer qu'une sage lenteur ; seul moyen de consumer ses forces, et de rendre par des succès partiels, mais répétés, la confiance à ses propres Soldats.

Mais une conduite aussi mesurée ne pouvait manquer de déplaire à un Peuple léger, qui s'était flatté de voir bientôt dans ses murs Annibal enchaîné au Char du Dictateur triomphant. Elle était tout en butte aux déclamations du Général de la Cavalerie, Q. Minucius Altier, vain, présomptueux il versait sur Fabius le ridicule et le mépris ; le traitait de temporiseur (surnom que la gloire a depuis consacré) et promettait aux Romains la défaite entière d'Annibal, si son courage n'était pas enchaîné par la faiblesse d'un timide vieillard.

Déjà prévenu contre le Dictateur, le Peuple reçoit avec avidité des discours qui n'auraient dû exciter que son indignation. Il applaudit en aveugle aux traits lancés contre le Héros qui sauve la Patrie, et ne craint pas de violer les loix en accordant au téméraire Minucius une autorité égale à celle de Fabius.

where the river actually flowed at the time, Varro may have been anchoring one of his flanks on its banks while depending on the heights around Cannae to anchor the other, accounting for his contracted front. Barring this, he may simply have opted for a depth of ranks based on a belief in massed pressure that went back to Epaminondas and the famous Battle of Leuctra.

The Roman deployment, at least, was certainly sound. Everybody on the battlefield that hot August day knew the Punic army suffered from a paucity of infantry relative to the Romans, and that heavy infantry in particular could win victories through its ability to occupy and defend ground against lighter troops.

Certainly Hannibal knew this. And yet he unhesitatingly offered battle.

THE DUST SWIRLS

Dexterous, redoubtable, and adaptable, the army Hannibal led at Cannae—just 55,000 strong or thereabouts—relied on a supple interplay of cavalry and infantry that revealed years of instructive service. Numerous different warriors, from different lands and speaking different languages, took orders from the Barcid command structure that day and performed heroically. Only professionalism and long experience could account for this.

Like all ancient generals, Hannibal deployed his cavalry on the wings. (His elephants had all died by this point.) But unlike the Romans, he intended to use them for more than placeholders. On the right were the Numidians, bareback riders who wore virtually no armor and relied on volleys of well-aimed javelins to break up their enemies. The left wing was comprised of heavy cavalry—Spanish and Gallic riders, the wealthier of them wearing mail shirts, who rode hard into battle in close order. Much more numerous than their Numidian comrades, these fearsome riders were entrusted to Hasdrubal, one of Hannibal's most trusted lieutenants, who meant to shatter the Roman right wing.

But what about the center? Here Hannibal would have to receive the full force of around 80,000 legionaries. Some 24,000 close-order infantry spanned the middle of the Carthaginian line between the cavalry wings, the overwhelming majority of which were allied Celts recruited from the Po Valley. The rest, perhaps 8,000, were Spanish, armed with large oval shields and wielding an array of spears, javelins, and short thrusting swords on which the Romans would ultimately base their famous *gladius*. Among the Celts, only chieftains could afford a mail shirt and helmet, and they would have stood out amid their shirtless underlings—fierce warriors armed with large shields, spears, and heavy slashing swords as much as three feet (0.9 m) in length. Out in front of the close-ranked Celts and Spaniards ranged skirmishers from all the nations in Hannibal's army, though their numbers cannot be known.

With so few infantry to receive the expected Roman onslaught in the center, Hannibal made a decision that would echo down the ages as inspired. He ordered them to bulge forward in a crescent shape, with the very center forming a blunt point behind which the remaining units ranged outward *en echelon*. Behind the wings of this convex formation lurked two phalanxes of Libyan infantry. These were Hannibal's finest, now sporting Roman arms and armor captured from enemy dead. Five thousand strong each, they anchored the whole line.

In the ritualized nature of ancient warfare, skirmishers, crowds of them preparing for battle in front of both armies, were the first to clash. They now tested each other on the plain, hurling missiles and occasionally closing to exchange blows. If either force were to have an impact on the coming battle, one of them would have to be pushed from the field. At Cannae, no such triumph seems to have occurred, resulting in a stalemate that gave way to the movement of regular troops.

Hasdrubal, preparing his heavy cavalry on the Punic left wing for an imminent charge, saw the Roman infantry start to advance and made his move. The Celts and Spaniards, many of them nobles in their tribal cultures and resplendent in mail and plumed helmets, thundered across the field, directing their accelerating mounts into the Roman right wing. There, cavalry under Paullus himself awaited their arrival with what must have been mounting dread. In addition to being outnumbered on this part of the line, the Romans had yet to best Punic cavalry in a fight, and must have anticipated a vicious struggle.

It came soon enough. Once in among each other, the two sides clashed in a maelstrom, the sources implying that many were pulled from their mounts and continued fighting on foot. The Romans were outmatched, and soon fled for their lives, those on foot either falling to Punic spears or—as Paullus himself did—making their way to the infantry to continue fighting there.

On the Carthaginian right, the Numidians wrangled with the Roman left wing, whose horsemen fought under Rome's supreme commander that day, Gaius Terentius Varro. Less numerous than their Gallic and Spanish colleagues on the opposite end of the line and also incapable of closing decisively, they wheeled and turned, hurling volleys of javelins against Varro's cavalry. An impasse had been reached, with neither side willing or able to sweep the other from the field.

The center, by contrast, surged with savage collisions. Here the Roman legions had at last reached their destination, striding into the violence with the confidence of numbers. At the apex of the Punic crescent, Gauls and Spaniards fought desperately against the enemy, only to fall back before the punishing pressure of the hastati and principes. Before long, their cause seemed hopeless, and the bulge began to collapse. The tremendous Roman numbers, it seemed, were telling.

TRAPPED

The plight of the Carthaginian center belied Hannibal's understanding of the situation. By forcing his line outward to begin with, he had ensured that the Roman infantry would be pulled almost inexorably into the Punic center as it fell back like a collapsing bubble. Hannibal had intended to use the Romans' own momentum against them, and it was working.

But it was the cavalry that made the next decisive move. Having regrouped and rested his heavy cavalry after driving Paullus's wing from the field, Hasdrubal launched his horsemen clear across the rear of the Roman center to clash headlong into Varro's cavalry, still sparring with the Numidians. Varro, engaged on two sides and now wildly outnumbered, broke and wheeled in abject flight.

He never saw the climactic developments in the center that he had helped set in motion. As Hannibal's Gauls and Spaniards gradually gave ground and then broke altogether before the Roman juggernaut bearing down on them, the inversion of Hannibal's line pulled the Romans in as if by suction. By the time the legions were smelling blood and reveling in the chase, they were already well inside a trap that had been carefully laid for them.

Soon the Libyans, as yet unengaged and fresh, closed like a vise on the flanks of the oncoming legions. Roman cohesion had in all likelihood become a sham by now, as hastati, principes, and triarii all pushed forward with a mass of warrior energy. Resistance against the oncoming Libyans, deliberate and grim faced behind their captured helmets, was no doubt fierce at first but confused. Many in the Roman ranks now clearly understood the scale of their predicament, sending a wave of subdued panic through the masses. They had been corralled like cattle.

Those at the front of the corral had no idea what was breaking on the rear. Hasdrubal, having vanquished both Roman wings with his corps of hard-driving cavalry, now proceeded to savage the Roman rear as it advanced clumsily forward. The trap was closed.

Once Hannibal's retreating center rallied and turned on its embattled pursuers, the Roman army—still close to 80,000 strong—found itself hemmed in from nearly every direction. Hannibal may well have hoped for this outcome, but the completeness of his triumph was probably beyond even his wildest dreams.

He still had a huge enemy to subdue. And Romans were not in the habit of laying down their weapons in times of mortal crisis—quite to the contrary, in fact. This partially explains what followed: a drawn-out, exhausting horror show of slaughter between two foes who had long since embraced the idea of war without quarter. Despite Hannibal's penchant for taking allied prisoners and treating them well in the interest of breaking their ties with Rome, the fury of Cannae had gone too far to permit restraint. The Libyans in their thrusting phalanxes, the Gallic and Spanish infantry with their tribal war bands, and Hasdrubal's pounding horsemen, all killed their way into the center against legionaries fighting desperately in a thousand separate melees whose participants were incapable of comprehending the totality of the calamity closing in on them.

Given the size of the disaster, the bloodletting must have proceeded throughout most of the day. Rome's loss screams out to us still: 50,000 dead, a figure so conspicuous that historians have mulled over it ever since. Polybius, whose writings remain a primary window into the military affairs of the Republic, gave a figure of 70,000 dead. Livy, a Roman historian writing during the first century BCE, offers a figure of 50,000, which has acquired the weight of orthodoxy over the years, not least because it is simply more comprehensible. Nobody in the records gives a smaller figure.

This is simply staggering. Cannae's death toll (Punic losses were between 6,000 and 8,000) sounds more like plague mortality. No army in antiquity had likely suffered anything like this, amounting to a near-gutting of Rome's military-age manhood. Descriptions of the battlefield are graphic even for ancient sources, conjuring images of a plain packed with eviscerated dead and dying, the survivors lingering in a kind of hell.

"Some they found lying with their thighs and knees gashed but still alive," writes Livy, "these bared their throats and necks and bade them drain what blood they still had left. Some they discovered with their heads buried in the earth, they had evidently suffocated themselves by making holes in the ground and heaping the soil over their faces."

As far as anyone knows, no general had ever performed a maneuver of such perfection before Hannibal's uncanny achievement. It remains the exemplar of double envelopment today, studied by aspiring military geniuses around the world. Norman Schwarzkopf claimed to have relied on the lesson of Cannae in his execution of Desert Storm.

In the event, it did Hannibal little good. This is perhaps the greatest indictment of his efforts. Though unmatched in tactical expertise, the famous son of Hamilcar had only a myopic vision of how victories on the battlefield could decide events. More to the point, he misunderstood the nature of his enemy.

Rome fought on — an achievement as astounding as Hannibal's at Cannae. Some of Rome's southern Italian allies defected to the Punic cause, but Rome held on to most of the loyalties that allowed her to field such enormous armies. In the end, Hannibal would become little more than a glorified brigand in the Italian countryside. Rome, utterly unyielding, drew Hannibal out of Italy by threatening his North African homeland. The war ended in 201 BCE with a string of Roman victories.

Cannae remains a perfect example of the worth of superior generalship over superior strength. Assured of his abilities before the fight even began, Hannibal delivered a coup de grâce that had been planned as soon as the opposing armies formed up for combat. For this, as much as his legendary crossing of the Alps, Hannibal remains a fixture in the popular imagination.

CHAPTER 4

CARRHAE
53 BCE

ROMAN ARMS BECOME TRAPPED BETWEEN THE SCORCHING SUN AND THE WRATH OF PARTHIA

10,000 PARTHIANS VERSUS 40,000 ROMANS

T HE BURDEN OF EMPIRE BORE DOWN ON ROME LIKE A forge's heat on metal, gradually transforming it into something all but unrecognizable to the ghosts of Cannae. With the Punic Wars, the Romans had set themselves on a course that seemed like destiny—but that put pressures on their cherished republic that even the likes of Hannibal had been powerless to summon. Far-flung provinces needed armies capable of staying longer than a campaign, officers who paid more attention to conquest abroad than to reputation at home, and tools of government that lost none of their efficacy over huge distances. In time the government, designed to run a city state, proved woefully inadequate for a multinational empire.

The long-revered customs of statecraft, once preserved by Roman conservatism, frayed. Scandal and violence replaced oratory in the Forum, rushing into public life through the chasm left by the inadequacy of tradition. Into the lurch strode the only figures capable of offering an alternative: aristocratic strongmen.

Legionaries had long since become professional soldiers whose reward was a wage and a promise of land. Gone were the days of the public levy, based on men whose propertied status in the census obligated them to serve as a form of honor denied the landless mob. Such were the needs of the empire that the

mob itself became fair game for recruitment. With the offer of a modest homestead as reward for years of soldiering, land became the inducement rather than
the qualification for military service—a reversal that quickly politicized armies,
with long-serving soldiers coming to view their commanders as patrons in whose
hands lay the promise of future reward. This peculiar relationship was galvanized by the duration and ferocity of imperial campaigns, during which men
and their commanders—increasingly given longer stints of service to perform
their craft—forged relationships that competed with other loyalties. With the
triumph of force over reason, military calculations and relationships now framed
Roman politics.

Against this backdrop of instability, brinkmanship, and demographic shift,
men with enormous power and ambition found few obstacles to thwart their abuse
of the system. They could mobilize old military connections, buy off or intimidate
voting blocs, or threaten subversion to get their way. By the 60s BCE, three such
"entrepreneurs" vied for dominance of the Roman republic and its empire: Marcus
Licinius Crassus, Gnaeus Pompeius Magnus ("Pompey"), and Gaius Julius Caesar.

Each had the ability to shape the course of political events. Pompey, one of
Rome's foremost war heroes, had risen to power by refusing on several occasions
to disband the legions under his command and using the threat of violence to
advance his own position. Crassus, his arch-rival, was the richest man in Rome
and one of the richest in the known world. And Caesar, youngest of the three, was
a longtime protégé of Crassus whose considerable connections straddled the gulf
between the city's elite and common people.

Tired of opposing each other for minimal gain, the three formed an unoffi-
cial triumvirate—a political bloc, initially secret, whose purpose was to dominate
Roman affairs utterly through a pooling of resources.

The result was a sort of three-way tyranny in which each member of the trio
was given what he most desired. Pompey, eager to cash in on his years of hard campaigning, received control of Spain—an office he exercised through legates while
he enjoyed the pleasures of the capital. Caesar, hungry to build a reputation on the
backs of vanquished foes, got a military assignment in Gaul that would earn him
immortality. And Crassus was awarded a proconsulship of Syria.

Crassus, well into his sixties, was eager for glory. While his two fellow triumvirs were military heroes, his own martial successes had become a distant memory.
Accordingly, he made a decision that ended up having severe repercussions for

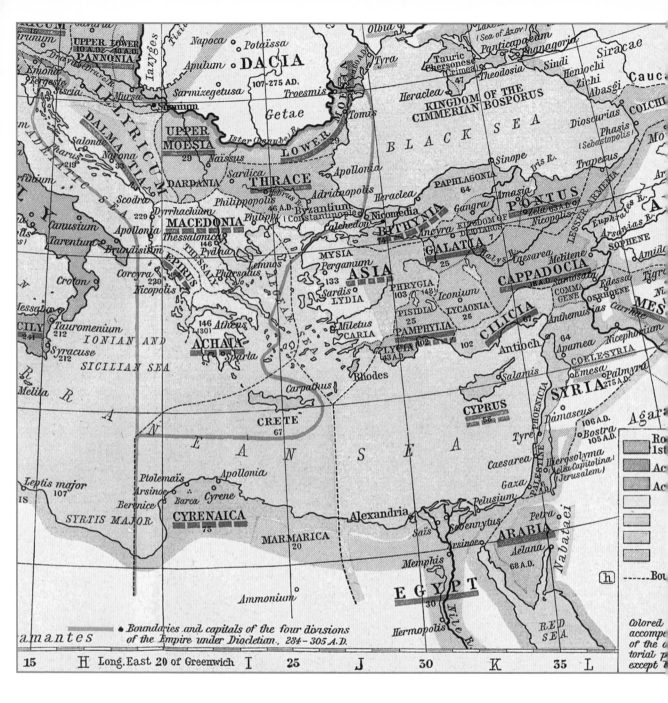

both him and his state. Once in Syria, Crassus picked a fight with the only other power in the ancient world capable of standing toe-to-toe with Roman arms: the Parthians. And, against remarkable odds, they dealt old Crassus—the man who had crushed the slave rebellion led by Spartacus twenty years earlier—one of the most complete and ignominious defeats in Roman history.

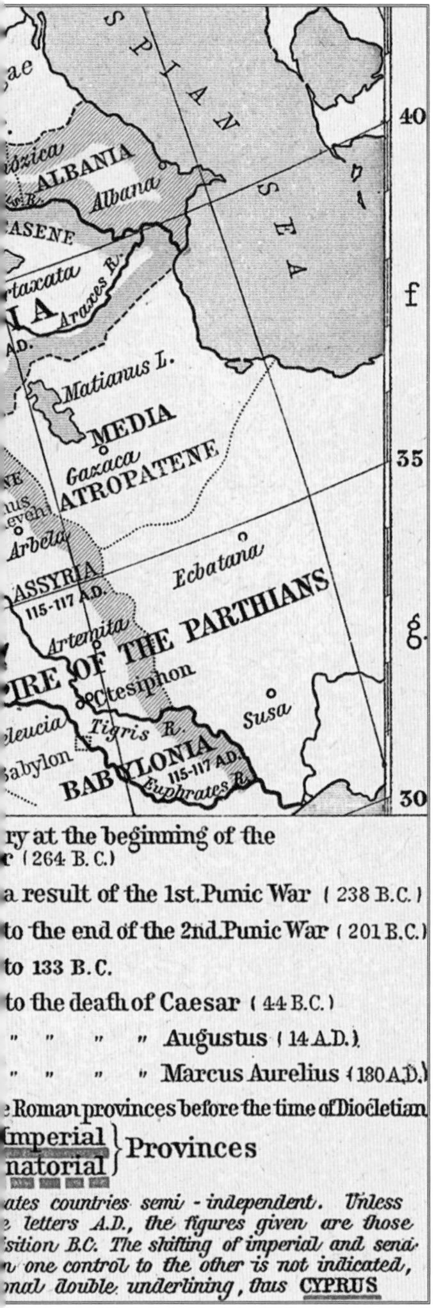

The map on the left shows place names including:

ALBANIA, Albana, Matianus L., MEDIA, Gazaca, ATROPATENE, Arbela, ASSYRIA 115–117 A.D., Ecbatana, Artemita, EMPIRE OF THE PARTHIANS, Ctesiphon, Seleucia, Tigris R., BABYLONIA, Babylon, Susa, Euphrates R., 115–117 A.D., CASPIAN SEA

Legend fragments:

...ry at the beginning of the
...e (264 B. C.)
...a result of the 1st. Punic War (238 B.C.)
...to the end of the 2nd. Punic War (201 B.C.)
...to 133 B.C.
...to the death of Caesar (44 B.C.)
" " " " Augustus (14 A.D.)
" " " " Marcus Aurelius (180 A.D.)
...e Roman provinces before the time of Diocletian
Imperial } Provinces
natorial }
...ates countries semi - independent. Unless
...e letters A.D., the figures given are those
...sition B.C. The shifting of imperial and sena-
...n one control to the other is not indicated,
...nal double underlining, thus CYPRUS

WARRIORS OF THE STEPPE

The origins of the Parthian Empire went back to the Hellenistic Age. In 245 BCE the Parni, horsemen hailing from the Eurasian steppe, took advantage of a revolt by the satrap (governor) of Parthia in northeastern Iran against the Seleucid Empire, largest of the successor states to form in the wake of Alexander the Great's conquests. In the ensuing chaos, both the satrap and his Seleucid masters failed to prevent the Parni from consolidating control over Parthia and using it as a base for expansion.

Though ostensibly answerable to the Seleucid kings in Mesopotamia and Syria, the new masters of Parthia—known as the Arsacid dynasty, after a progenitor named Arsaces—continued to grow in strength and territory, ultimately displacing the old Hellenistic empire as supreme in Asia. In 141 BCE, five years after Rome took Carthage by storm and razed it to the ground, Parthian armies took the Seleucid capital at Seleucia, confirming their control over an empire stretching from the Indian frontier to the Fertile Crescent.

Purveyors of war in the saddle, the Arsacid Parthians relied on their outstanding cavalry to spearhead the attacks that won them an empire. They were warrior lords, unaccustomed to bureaucratic sophistication and slow to learn its lessons. What emerged was a vast empire unlike the Seleucid or Acheamenid Persian states that preceded it—an overlordship that, though borrowing some of the administrative organs of the past, relied mostly on feudal relationships to bind subject kingdoms to the Parthian center. This status quo was enshrined in a stratified society in which everyone, from royalty down to shepherd, knew his or her place and how to stay there.

FROM ARMENIA TO SYRIA, THE FRICTION BETWEEN ROME AND PARTHIA GUARANTEED GENERATIONS OF WARFARE IN THE ANCIENT COCKPIT OF EMPIRES. CARRHAE SITS IN THE NORTHWESTERN CORNER OF MESOPOTAMIA.

The king's armies were similar to the feudal hosts that dominated the European Middle Ages. Royal power rested on the clannish relationships between great families. Nobles, like their ancestors going back generations, maintained a retinue of warrior retainers at personal expense, and it was on these that Parthian armies relied in times of war. As masters of a vast and diverse empire, the Parthian leadership could call on a variety of soldiers and mercenary bands. But the horsemen of Parthia's nobility formed the vanguard of the king's striking power.

By the time the so-called First Triumvirate dominated Roman affairs, the Arsacid dynasty had little to fear from anyone save its own nobility, whose constant intriguing always posed a threat to royal sovereignty—a consistent issue for Iranian kingdoms. In 57 BCE, King Phraates III was murdered by his own sons, Mithradates and Orodes II, who soon fought each other for sole possession of the throne.

The courtly chaos did not go unnoticed in Rome, where the triumvirs schemed to take advantage of Parthian civil strife. Mithradates, unpopular among the nobility and branded a rebel after the majority of them supported his brother, established his power base in Mesopotamia. Accepting Roman backing, he became a means for the triumvirs to insert their influence into the Parthian Empire.

Crassus raised an army and headed for Syria in November 55 BCE, his departure from Rome stalked by controversy over a war that some in the Senate thought unnecessary. In fact, friction between the two empires had been a reality since Pompey's military ventures extended Roman control up to the Euphrates River the previous decade. Since then Parthia and Rome had eyed each other across a long, sandy border.

Back in 95 BCE, the two powers had signed a treaty of friendship. Now, more than forty years later, that "friendship" was about to disappear like a mirage in the desert.

FIRST MOVES

The treaty of friendship had always been a temporary measure—a cynical expression of mutual respect between two predatory powers that knew better than to completely rule out a future test of strength. Now, enticed by a civil war, Rome's power-hungry triumvirs meant to grab as much of the shaken Parthian realm as possible.

Crassus was no fool. Mithradates was as expendable as he was useful, his efforts in Mesopotamia more a diversion to keep the Parthian state off balance than anything else.

Rather more was expected from Armenia to the north. Once a Parthian vassal and now a client of Rome, Armenia was the only other power in the region capable of wielding considerable force. But King Artavasdes wished to maintain as great a degree of autonomy as possible, and saw the continuing animosity between Rome and Parthia as a crucial means to that end. Crassus certainly expected cooperation from the Armenian ruler—but how much? And how dearly purchased?

Crassus would find out soon enough. In the meantime, he saw to the subjugation of enemy lands with characteristic Roman thoroughness. Having arrived in Syria in 54 BCE, he headed his army due east, directly into Parthian territory, rather than opting for the longer route through friendly Armenia. The source of debate by historians ever since, the move seems to have been an attempt to make the most of what remained of the campaigning season—time was of greater import at this late hour than the addition of Armenian forces to his army.

Once across the Euphrates River, Crassus entered ground zero of the Parthian civil war, and quickly took advantage of the bedlam. His army, more than 40,000 strong, swept aside the forces of the defending satrap, then occupied and garrisoned the local cities, most of which—with large Greek populations—welcomed the conquerors as liberators. At Zenodotium, in modern Syria, a contingent of his troops fell to treachery, earning the city Crassus' special attention. The place was stormed and sacked, its surviving citizens sold into slavery.

Now that northern Mesopotamia was under his control, Crassus left a garrison of 8,000 men and retired to Syria for the winter. He had indeed made much of the year's campaigning: Not only had he extended the limits of Roman authority, he had given his army of raw recruits invaluable on-the-job training. With further drilling through the winter months, they would be ready to face the Parthian response they all knew was coming.

With the winter rains came news and visitors. Crassus's son Publius, a Roman officer in his late twenties on loan from Julius Caesar, arrived with 1,000 tough Gallic cavalry under his personal command, and was no doubt given a warm greeting. Less welcome was King Artavasdes of Armenia. Though he came with 6,000 cavalry, his message was not a helpful one. More men were ready to come to Rome's aid, insisted the king, as long as Crassus invaded Parthia through Armenia. Obviously a ploy by Artavasdes to get Roman protection from an expected Parthian invasion of his country, it served only to grate on Crassus's nerves as further proof of Armenian inconstancy. The meeting ended poorly, with the king of Armenia heading home along with his cavalry.

Another embassy showed up in the early spring as snowmelt swelled the tributaries of the Euphrates. Led by one Vagises, it came from Orodes II, king of kings, amid news of the death of Mithradates and his cause. Precisely what transpired that day between Crassus and his Parthian guests is not known, though it appears to have been the final chance for peace between two empires in the midst of a collision. Mithradates, having been cornered in southern Mesopotamia around the same time in 54 BCE that Crassus was retiring into winter quarters, had been executed. Orodes, still weak politically from the fractures that had riven his empire's noble houses, preferred peace.

Crassus would not have it. He had already seen his destiny laid out for him on the Syrian roads that now dried under the vernal sun, beckoning him eastward. By the time the summer heat had baked them hard, they would bear the sandals of seven legions on their dusty courses. The time had come, everything was in preparation, and glory—the only kind of glory that mattered to a Roman—lay within his grasp.

Vagises was sent packing. The die was cast.

TWO FRONTS AND A GAMBLE

King Orodes had almost as much as Crassus to be thankful for as the spring of 53 BCE dawned. The first Roman invasion of Parthian territory had been endured without terrific loss even as Mithradates and his cause were extinguished. Though dealing with two crises at once, the court of Orodes must have realized that matters could have been much worse.

Parthia and Rome were birds of a feather: upstart powers, relatively new on a very ancient scene, which had snatched their lofty positions through carefully orchestrated aggression. But the similarity ended there. Unlike their horse-heavy Parthian opponents, the Romans favored war on foot, with its solidity, geometry, and inexorable push of shield and sword. Siege warfare came naturally to the Romans, who warmed to the methodology of engineering and its application of focused, maximum violence. The ballista, for example, an engine utilizing torsion to hurl a stone or bolt accurately at great distance, was typical of the sort of sophisticated, direct-fire, long-range weapons that exemplified Roman siege craft. For this reason, the Parthians feared an onslaught by Roman armies, whose deliberate approach to war had consumed the Mediterranean basin on three continents.

Moreover, the Parthians—unlike the Near Eastern powers that came before and after them—possessed a conspicuous lack of siege craft beyond the basics of investment. This was unfortunate, if only because the Parthians' other martial abilities were so formidable. With every city that Crassus occupied in Mesopotamia, the chance of Orodes reclaiming the region became more remote.

Both empires, then, sought a battle in the open: Crassus because his age and political mandate demanded a swift reckoning with the enemy, and Orodes because pitched battle, which favored Parthian mobility in this part of the world, was the only real chance of dealing the invaders a decisive blow.

Orodes moved with impressive celerity. He faced a double threat: In addition to throwing back a tenacious invader, he needed to shore up his shaky reputation after being raised to the throne on the shoulders of patricide and fratricide—hardly an enviable scenario for any untried monarch. He would never have pulled it off were it not for a man known to history as Surenas.

Or Surena. Or Suren. All we know, given the paucity of Parthian records, is that he was from the Suren, an extremely powerful clan in the Parthian world. Leaders of the Suren were

POMPEY THE GREAT, A MEMBER OF THE TRIUMVIRATE, OVERSAW SPAIN, AN OFFICE HE EXERCISED THROUGH LEGATES WHILE HE ENJOYED THE PLEASURES OF THE CAPITAL.

Getty Images

charged with placing the crown on the emperor's head, revealing their profound significance in the wider affairs of the empire. The Suren were the most powerful in a circle of powerful families, their lords elevated to the most important generals in the realm.

And none were more important than the so-called Surenas who now acted on behalf of Orodes. According to the sources, he had been instrumental in ousting Mithradates and backing Orodes, placing him at the very heart and soul of the Parthian Empire. Surenas later defeated Mithradates and brought him to the court of Orodes for summary punishment. The historian Plutarch described him as "the foremost Parthian of his time, besides having no equal in stature and personal beauty." Whatever the truth about his physique, Surenas certainly had courage and cunning—both of which were now placed at the disposal of Orodes.

SIEGE WARFARE CAME NATURALLY TO THE ROMANS, WHO WARMED TO THE METHODOLOGY OF ENGINEERING AND ITS APPLICATION OF FOCUSED, MAXIMUM VIOLENCE.

The Parthian king of kings settled on a wise if unconventional strategy, showing his capacity for quick thinking in a crisis. Armenia was the key: Orodes would head that way with a huge royal army to ensure the country's subjugation and remove it as a front in the war with Rome. With Armenia knocked out of the war, Parthia could concentrate its forces on Roman Syria and the threat from Crassus. All that was needed was a spoiling force to occupy Crassus until Orodes was finished humbling the Armenians.

That task naturally fell to Surenas. A high noble of the Empire, he could raise more than 10,000 men with his own resources and connections. Those men—in effect a private army attached to Surenas like family—would be used to buy time for the man whom Surenas had helped put in power.

All Orodes wanted was a delaying action. What his general gave him was an upset victory of historic proportions.

ON THE MARCH

Crassus marched east in the late spring of 53 BCE, foregoing conquest of lower Mesopotamia with its teeming urban centers and heading straight for a clash with the Parthian foe. The forces at his command had changed markedly in the years since Rome had embarked on the imperial enterprise. A series of sweeping reforms, usually attributed to Gaius Marius, consul in 107 BCE, had created a more professional, flexible army. Gone were the three lines of the legion based on property qualifications and age. Under the reforms, legionaries were all equipped with the same armor and weapons: upper body armor, a great shield, a 34-inch (86-cm) thrusting sword (the deadly *gladius hispaniensis*), and a pair of *pila*, or heavy javelins.

Moreover, each legion was divided into ten "cohorts" of around 480 men each. Composed of six "centuries" of eighty men each, the cohort had become the basic tactical unit of the battlefield, replacing the smaller maniple of earlier days. Capable of acting alone or in concert with other cohorts in a detachment from the legion, it afforded much greater flexibility to commanders, who could cater their deployments to different circumstances.

Just as important, the average legionary was no longer a man of means. Poorer citizens now filled the ranks, equipped uniformly by the state and often serving for years, even decades, overseas.

An army devoted overwhelmingly to infantry warfare, the Romans relied almost exclusively on allied peoples for cavalry and other auxiliary units such as archers. Crassus marched east with only around 4,000 cavalry in his army. Of these, 3,000 were allies, almost certainly recruited in Syria after he had arrived. Though we know little about them, these easterners would probably not have been heavily armored. The rest were Publius Crassus's Gauls, 1,000 strong and, no doubt, veteran fighters. As was customary for the Gauls, the majority of them would have been very lightly armored. Only the chieftains would have been sporting a mail shirt or helmet, and we cannot know how many of these rode with Publius.

It was on the infantry that Crassus pinned his greatest hopes. Some 4,000 auxiliary infantry accompanied his army, about which little is known. They may well have included skirmishers, archers, even slingers, depending on where they had been recruited. The heart of the army, however, was the seven legions raised in Italy. Altogether, they must have numbered just under 34,000, all citizens of the Republic and well-trained to fight in classic Roman fashion. Though mostly raw recruits who had been raised specifically for this campaign, they had had more than a year to drill and acquire experience. Crassus, a cautious commander by nature, had doubtless taken care to prepare them as best he could for what lay ahead. During the late 70s BCE, he had brought Spartacus to heel only after seeing to the thorough instruction and preparation of the troops under his command.

Boasting of 40,000 tough legionaries, the army of Crassus expected another easy defeat—a replay of the battle it had won the previous year in western Mesopotamia against the forces of the local satrap. On June 9, 53 BCE, the forward cavalry scouts of his force clashed with Parthians near Carrhae, on the Belikh River, a tributary of the Euphrates, and took a beating. Streaming back to Crassus, they reported the presence of an enemy force waiting just across the Belikh.

It was afternoon under a Near Eastern sun, and his men had been marching for hours. The enemy, however, had been fixed. How could Crassus be sure they would still be there tomorrow?

In a move of uncharacteristic impulsiveness, Crassus chose to close out the day with a general engagement. The scouts, though mauled by the enemy vanguard, reported only that a small force of enemy cavalry had formed up ahead. There seemed nothing to fear from this, given the impressive size of Crassus's army. Advised by one of his officers, Cassius Longinus, Crassus deployed the army along a broad front so as to avoid being surrounded by the Parthian horse.

At some point, however, Crassus changed tactics. According to Plutarch, our best source for the battle, the commander listened to his own judgment and opted for a radically different formation. With the rapidity of well-drilled professionals, the legions formed themselves into a giant square, with four sides of close-ranked legionaries around a hollow center. Each side received a detachment of cavalry for mobile protection. Thus prepared for a threat from any direction, the army advanced like a moving fortress over the sandy plain.

SHOCK AND AWE

Surenas saw the Romans coming on and chose not to wait for them. He had assembled an extraordinary force and prepared it for just this encounter. Now he would show these vainglorious Romans what the men of the East were really capable of.

As the second most powerful leader of the empire, Surenas had enormous resources at his disposal. The host that stood with him that day under the blinding June sun was typical of Parthian armies in that it had been raised by its noble leader from his own estates. But unlike most Parthian armies, this one—around 10,000—had been specially prepared to take advantage of Roman weaknesses.

Seeing the Romans come steadily onward, Surenas, joining his fellow heavy horsemen in the front rank, gave the order to attack. Across the hot plain, Crassus and his men heard an unearthly cacophony unlike anything they had encountered. While most nations of the ancient Mediterranean went to war with the sound of trumpets, the Parthians advanced to the rumble of great kettledrums, hundreds of which now boomed over the dust like thunder from Hades.

Surenas and his fellows in the vanguard trotted forward beneath the din, their forms wrapped tightly against the scorching desert sun. To the Italian eyes that saw them emerge from the swirling dun clouds, they made a weird sight: riders in close order, dressed strangely for a fight in the Mesopotamian desert. Though drawn out in an impressive line of battle, they looked no different from the light horsemen that were ubiquitous in this part of the world, and no more threatening.

A MERE 1,000 OF THE PARTHIAN FORCE WAS COMPRISED OF CATAPHRACTS; THE REST, SOME 9,000, WERE MOUNTED ARCHERS, ALL OF WHOM NOW BEGAN UNLEASHING CLOUDS OF WHISTLING DEATH INTO THE ROMAN RANKS FROM ALL QUARTERS.

Then Surenas gave another order, and the cavalry transformed before their Roman spectators. Spurring now to a gallop, they pulled their raiment away in a flash of movement, revealing the glint of armor beneath. These were the dreaded cataphracts—Parthian gentry who rode hard into battle with lances leveled. Their armor, fashioned from metal scales sewn into an overlapping pattern, covered them from neck to shin—a fact that Surenas had cleverly concealed for as long as possible beneath furs and linens. A cataphract's mount was similarly armored, presenting a mounted warrior unlike any in the ancient world.

Riding hard now like a wall of onrushing metal scales, Surenas and his fellow cataphracts headed straight for the front of Crassus's formation. But the Romans would not be so easily turned. Locking their shields into a makeshift wall, the legionaries stood firm, exemplifying the merits of their infantry doctrine. The cataphracts veered off in a cloud of dust, their attack breaking harmlessly on the Roman line.

But this was a mere appetizer; Surenas now served up his carefully prepared main course, which came galloping in the wake of the cataphracts and flowed like two streams of a parted river around the Romans, meeting up behind Crassus's formation to complete its encirclement. Unlike the heavy cataphracts, these horsemen rode unarmored. They were horse archers. Recruited from the serfs of Surenas's estates and trained from youth to loose arrows from the saddle, they wielded the dreaded composite bow, the defining weapon of the Asiatic steppe. Fashioned from bone and wood and curved at both ends, this deadly accurate weapon proved nightmarishly effective—especially in massed numbers.

A mere 1,000 of the Parthian force was comprised of cataphracts; the rest, some 9,000, were mounted archers, all of whom now began unleashing clouds of whistling death into the Roman ranks from all quarters. Soon the Romans, who responded on all four sides by forming the *testudo*, or "turtle" formation that made good use of their large shields, began suffering sporadic wounds. It immediately became obvious that these Parthian arrows pierced harder and farther than most; the Romans could count on their shields for protection, but their armor was apparently useless against the missile that got through.

Despite the cries of his wounded and the mounting frustration of his men, Crassus cannot have found this situation entirely surprising. After all, he had known about the Parthian penchant for mobile war with missiles. But he satisfied himself with the knowledge that this barrage of arrows could not go on indefinitely. With Roman discipline and grit, he and his men could endure this humiliation until the Parthians ran out of ammunition, at which point the legions could be unleashed on the unarmored horsemen, who would of necessity withdraw— or succumb to Crassus's own cavalry, which were better trained for close-quarter melee. Either way, he would walk away from this experience a winner, with his men having blooded themselves decisively against the Parthian foe.

Before long, however, Crassus or one of his officers spied the last great surprise that Surenas had in store. Pulling into view just behind the roving throngs of horse archers, a long caravan of camels loped easily over the sandy ground. Each beast was laden with cargo, the precise nature of which was revealed when Parthian archers began riding over to fill their quivers.

Surenas had brought hundreds of thousands of extra arrows with him, promising no end to the barrage that already was becoming hellish. Crassus and his men had become a huge target to be slowly savaged in the afternoon heat.

IN THIS SCHEMATIC, THE DILEMMA OF CRASSUS AND HIS LEGIONARIES IS MADE STARKLY CLEAR. THE SQUARE ROMAN FORMATION IS SURROUNDED BY THE OUTSTANDING PARTHIAN CAVALRY, SHOWN AS ARROWS. THE PARTHIANS APPROACH THE ROMANS, UNLEASH THEIR ARROWS, AND REVERSE DIRECTION TO AVOID CONTACT AND REFILL THEIR QUIVERS BEFORE REPEATING THE PROCESS. PARTHIAN CATAPHRACTS, HEAVILY ARMORED CAVALRY, COULD THWART ANY ATTEMPTS BY THE ROMANS AT BREAKING OUT OF THEIR FORMATION.

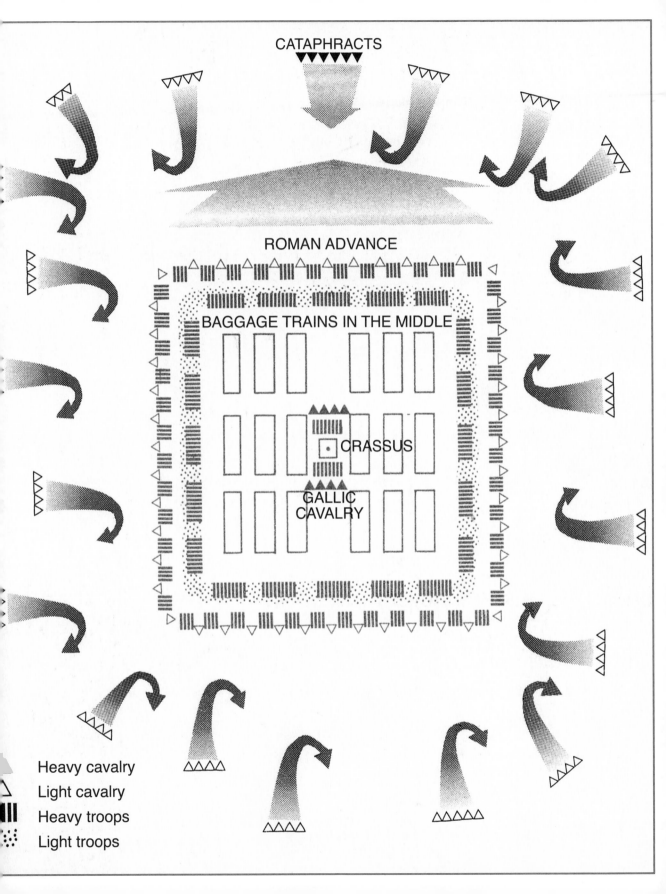

DESPERATE VALOR

Crassus saw the writing on the wall and hatched a desperate plan. He could not stand firm and watch his command whittled into oblivion. Only one option presented itself: A breakout must be made, taking advantage of Roman combined arms to break the Parthian cavalry and force a different sort of battle, hopefully on Crassus's terms. Under the constant hail of arrows, with shields overhead like makeshift roofs, the old consul conferred with junior officers. Soon a runner was sent looking for Publius, the old man's son, to lead the attack.

Publius was ideal for the task. A darling of the Roman aristocracy, he was widely regarded as a perfect exemplar of Roman virtue. No less a citizen than Cicero praised the younger Crassus as having "dignity without arrogance and modesty without sloth." He was now called upon to remedy his father's disastrous position by an act of bold leadership.

Publius hastily tapped a mixed contingent for the job: In addition to his own 1,000 Gallic cavalry, he assumed command over an additional 300 horsemen, as well as eight cohorts of legionaries and a supporting force of 500 archers. Once assembled, he bravely led them headlong into a stretch of the encircling wall of Parthian horse archers, who quickly retired.

CRASSUS AND HIS ARMY DIE IN THE MESOPOTAMIAN DESERT, 53 BCE. CRASSUS, LURED INTO A PARLEY WITH THE ENEMY, WAS MURDERED, ALONG WITH THE OFFICERS WHO ACCOMPANIED HIM.

©Mary Evans Picture Library/ The Image Works

Believing that they had scored a breakthrough, Publius and his men followed, only to be lured into a trap. Once out of view of the rest of the Roman army, Publius's force found themselves confronting a wall of cataphracts, behind which gathered the archers who had just recently made a hasty retreat.

In came the arrows, arching over the protective wall of cataphracts and sending Publius's men pitching into the dirt. The Romans charged, crashing headlong

into the cataphracts in an eruption of horse-borne violence. Sheathed in coats of metal, the knights of Parthia thrust mercilessly with their heavy lances, dealing grievous wounds among the Roman allies, who grappled in vain against their armor-clad opponents. The Gauls, notoriously implacable, took to pulling cataphracts off their mounts and even rolling under enemy horses to stab their vitals from below.

Publius and his men fought savagely, but to no avail. Losing men by the minute, they retired to a nearby hillock, bringing as many of their wounded with them as they could carry. There, unseen but not forgotten by their Roman comrades in the square, across the swirling battlefield, Publius and his forlorn command fought against Parthia's finest. They formed a circle of shields and endured the arrows beyond number, the mighty onslaught of charging cataphracts, until hope had all but gone.

Who now, father or son, was going to save whom?

THE CREEPING END

As his son battled for survival, Crassus led a fighting withdrawal of his force onto sloping ground. There he sent out messengers to Publius to ascertain what he could about the breakout operation whose outcome remained a mystery to him.

One of them managed to get through and return with a heart-rending message: Publius had been corralled onto a bit of high ground and was fighting for his life.

Crassus, personal and professional grief crashing in on him, decided—not without considerable deliberation—to join up with his beleaguered son and make a combined last stand. There were plenty of sound reasons not to do this, not least of which involved risking what remained of his embattled force in a link-up that was sure to commit them to an interminable battle against mobile adversaries. Should he not cut his losses and run? Perhaps. But how would that look back in Rome, once the facts had been skewed in the rumor mill? And his son was out there fighting.

The Parthians soon forced a change in events. Through the crowd of horse archers, the Romans on their higher ground spied a cloud of galloping horsemen, who eventually made their way to within shouting distance of the Romans. A horseman hurled a parcel into the Roman lines, which immediately revealed itself to be the head of Publius Crassus.

The Romans groaned collectively in grief. Crassus, struggling against his own overwhelming sorrow, apparently gave as rousing a speech as he could under the circumstances, exhorting his men to vengeful wrath.

For their part, the Parthians were relying on more than words to ensure victory that day. Surenas resumed the pressure, corralling his enemy with cataphracts and punishing him with steady, maddening missile fire. Hour after hour the attrition continued, until the setting sun forced an end. The Parthians were not willing to fight in darkness, and Crassus was given a night's reprieve. Half of his force lay dead from the day's long anguish.

The next morning, the Parthians found some 4,000 Roman wounded left behind in Crassus' withdrawal to western Mesopotamia. They were all slaughtered. What followed was a pathetic chase across the desert between Crassus's army, broken up into fleeing contingents, and Surenas's cavalry, which spread out in the hunt to destroy what remained of their quarry. In the end a fraction of Crassus's men made it back to safety. The Roman commander himself was trapped in a stretch of foothills and duped into a parley with Surenas, partly because his own accompanying legionaries, tired of the chase, insisted that he go. Once in the presence of the enemy, he was murdered, along with the brave officers who dared to accompany him.

Parthia, in its first war with Rome, had dealt Crassus a complete and utterly humiliating defeat—against four-to-one odds. Though hardly rash, Crassus had nevertheless ventured into cavalry country with a paucity of good horsemen. He had also been outgeneraled by a cleverer opponent who knew the Roman dependence on infantry tactics and how to exploit it. In addition, the Romans had nothing to counter the awesome combination of heavily armored cataphracts and swift horse-archers. Though Rome would eventually learn from this disaster, as it did from all its military setbacks, it was Parthia that had the bragging rights in the first-century-BCE Near East.

CHAPTER 5

ALESIA
52 BCE

CAESAR SHOWS HIS ENEMIES THE MEANING OF ROMAN TENACITY

50,000 ROMANS VERSUS MORE THAN 200,000 GAULS

T HE ROMANS COULD NOT SEE THE GAULS IN THE DARKNESS, but knew they were closing fast by their war shouts, piercing the night like the howl of wolves. Darts, sling stones, and javelins whistled unseen through the air, many of them thudding menacingly into the wooden beams of the towers and others forcing a grunt from the throat of some wounded legionary.

Soon the Gauls were on them, having scaled the wall with ladders and hooks, now slashing with their longswords and bellowing in the blood sport. The Romans, however, fought furiously, regrouping in closed ranks and advancing on the infiltrators with discipline, forcing them back only to receive another threat from a new quarter in the black chaos.

Then, just in time, came a rushing column of reinforcements, brought from another part of the wall by Mark Antony. Destined to make the history books as a lover of Cleopatra and enemy of Octavian, first emperor of Rome, Antony now reveled in the role he probably would have preferred to play until the end: a courageous Roman officer and lieutenant of Caesar, the *other* great Roman to share Cleopatra's bed.

Now, fighting to defend the walls that Caesar's genius had inspired, Antony and his men struggled just to stay alive in the wilds of Gaul, so far from home.

But the bloody business of this night, like all the other fights around Alesia, only served to prove the Roman way of war—and its frightful effectiveness when waged by a man like Gaius Julius Caesar.

CONQUERING GAUL

"All Gaul is divided into three parts," begins Julius Caesar's *Commentaries on the Gallic Wars*, a phrase that has welcomed legions of students to the Latin language over centuries. Written by Caesar himself in the third person, the *Commentaries* follow their author's trials and victories in Gaul, and quickly became an exemplar of spare, late Republican Latin prose. They also open a window on one of the most captivating moments in ancient history.

Caesar went to Gaul to become great. To do this, he meant to fully subjugate a free, populous, and warlike people through cunning and force of arms, and make them subservient to the will of Rome. By the time he finished this bloody enterprise, he had added most of modern-day France to the burgeoning Roman Empire. It was a campaign of conquest for conquest's sake, born of one man's implacable ambition, and punctuated by moments of utter savagery. Yet the sheer scale of his undertaking—a Herculean endeavor that overcame immense adversity through relentless determination and imagination—never loses its capacity to impress.

The people he chose to subdue were Gauls, part of the Celtic culture that had dominated Europe for centuries. They were an agrarian people who traded widely, facilitating the spread of Mediterranean goods and ideas to the north. Living on the periphery of antiquity's great urban civilizations, they dwelt in concentrated, fortified settlements that were not quite towns or cities but more than villages. They were also fierce fighters, with a warrior ethos and skill in metalworking that made them frightful adversaries and valuable allies.

As the first line of his *Commentaries* intimates, Caesar meant to base his campaign on the ancient stratagem *divide et impera*—"divide and conquer." To defeat the Gauls, a people divided by tribal loyalties, this was a sound approach. But it also risked sowing enough discontent to inspire pan-Gallic resistance against the Roman invader. When this happened on a grand scale, Caesar responded with a campaign that remains legendary. Alesia, the most spectacular military achievement of the man whose very name became a synonym for "ruler," is a paradigm of victory against greater numbers.

MAN OF THE PEOPLE

Long before his epic adventure in Gaul, when Caesar was still in his twenties, he sailed for the Greek island of Rhodes to study rhetoric under the esteemed teacher Apollonius Molon. En route, his vessel was set upon by pirates operating out of Cilicia, in present-day Turkey, and he was taken captive.

The pirates informed him that he was to be ransomed for twenty talents of silver. Caesar scoffed, reminding his captors of his value as a member of Rome's governing class, and told them to ask for fifty.

For the next forty days, the arrogant young aristocrat entertained the corsairs with his own poetry, drank and commiserated with them, and never failed to act in their presence like a man of breeding who was due a fulsome portion of respect. He also took care to remind them between bouts of laughter around the fire that he was going to kill them all someday.

Once the ransom was paid, Caesar used his freedom to assemble a private force of avengers, with whom he tracked the pirates down and captured them. He appealed to the governor of Asia to punish the villains properly, only to receive an indifferent response. So he had them executed himself. After they were strangled to death, their corpses were crucified.

Self-confident, haughty, calculating, driven, ruthless—these qualities, so clearly evident in the incident with the Cilician pirates, helped to make Gaius Julius Caesar a man to be reckoned with.

Historical contingency did the rest. He was neither rich nor physically impressive, but he came to manhood in an age rife with possibility for those willing to act boldly. As the social forces born of imperial expansion began changing the Roman status quo, ambitious young men like Caesar found numerous opportunities in the ever-shifting world of power brokering.

Born to a patrician family in 100 BCE, he acquired a typically excellent education and, after emerging unscathed from the brutal proscriptions issued by the dictator Lucius Cornelius Sulla in 81 BCE, worked his way up the *cursus honorum*, the ladder of elective offices through which all men of the Senatorial class were expected to climb. By 60 BCE he had served with distinction as an army officer, filled for a time the office of Pontifex Maximus (chief priest of the state religion), and governed part of Spain, where he became a military hero fighting native contingents. He had earned a reputation as a gifted speaker, shrewd litigator, and a

THE PAINTING SHOWS ALESIA SURROUNDED BY A FEAT OF ROMAN ENGINEERING—TWO NEARLY IDENTICAL CIRCUITS OF WORKS THAT INCLUDED WALLED DITCHES, FORTS, RAMPARTS, GUARD TOWERS, AND SLOPES BRISTLING WITH SHARPENED STAKES. ONE CIRCUIT FACED THE CITY; ITS TWIN GREETED ATTACKERS APPROACHING FROM THE OUTSIDE.

Alte Pinakothek, Munich, Germany / Lauros / Giraudon / The Bridgeman Art Library International

QVANTA STRA
GE VIRVM SVBLI
MIS ALEXIA CESSIT
CÆSAREIS AQVI
LIS, PICTA TABEL
LA NOTAT

politician skilled in the art of manipulating the masses. At the age of forty, he won election to consul, highest of Rome's magistracies.

His term of office was a turbulent one, to say the least, marked by an excess of bribery and intimidation. Climaxing a trend that had been accelerating in Roman politics for decades, the corruption of Caesar's year as consul was backed by the power of the First Triumvirate he had formed with Marcus Licinius Crassus and Gnaeus Pompeius Magnus ("Pompey")—a pooling of resources to control politics for mutual benefit (see chapter 4).

What was it all leading to? Caesar's ultimate goals at this point cannot be known, but he clearly leveraged the power of his alliances and office to pave the way for his future. All consuls were granted the opportunity, upon the conclusion of their terms, to assume a "proconsulship" as governor of one of the provinces. Through political cronies and allies, Caesar had legislation passed that granted him governorship of Cisalpine Gaul, Illyricum, and Transalpine Gaul as soon as his consulship was concluded. Moreover, the legislation stipulated a term of five years.

The benefits to Caesar were obvious. Having racked up enormous debts through his tumultuous career (one of the reasons he befriended wealthy Crassus in the first place), he needed the access to extortion and corruption that governorships in the provinces typically offered. He also needed protection from his political enemies for his consular abuses, and proconsular governorships extended the immunity to prosecution that was a consul's privilege—in the case of Caesar, for five long years.

But Caesar's proconsulship offered him something even more important than these. Illyricum, along the Baltic coast of the Adriatic, Gallia Cisalpina (literally "Gaul this side of the Alps," or northern Italy), and Gallia Transalpina (Gaul on the far side of the Alps, officially known as Gallia Narbonensis) all offered potential for military glory. Gallia Narbonensis in particular seemed ripe with opportunity, standing guard on the empire's frontier with barbarian Gaul and its tribal politics. With five years' dispensation from political obstacles, he was bound to be able to scare up a victory great enough to compensate for his corrupt reputation and pave the way for his triumphant return to Rome.

The product of limitless aspiration and political excess, his plan was ambitious in the extreme. The risks, moreover, were colossal—Gaul and its defiant people were to prove worthy adversaries indeed.

THIS MAP SHOWS THE EXPANSION OF ROME THAT AVOIDS THE ALPS, THE THIN WEDGE BETWEEN ITALY AND GAUL (MODERN-DAY FRANCE). CAESAR GOVERNED CISALPINE GAUL, ILLYRICUM, AND TRANSALPINE GAUL–AREAS THAT ALLOWED HIM THE POTENTIAL FOR MILITARY GLORY AND THE EXTORTION OF FUNDS TO PAY OFF HIS ENORMOUS DEBTS.

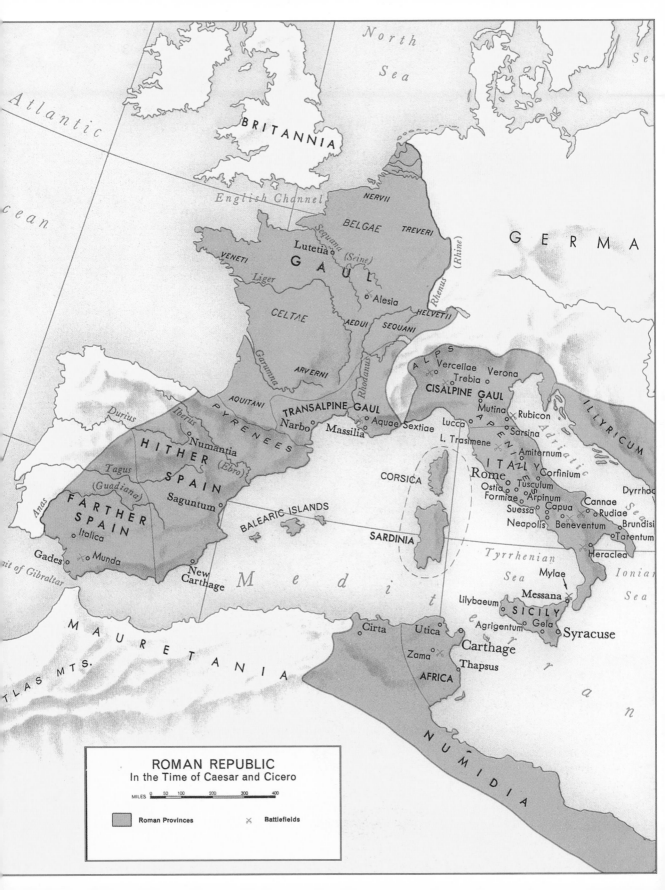

North
Sea

Atlantic

cean

BRITANNIA

English Channel

NERVII

BELGAE   TREVERI

GERMA

Lutetia   *Sequana (Seine)*

GAUL   *(Rhine)*

VENETI   Alesia   *Rhenus*

Liger   HELVETII

CELTAE   AEDUI   SEQUANI

Garumna   ALPS   Vercellae   Verona
                             Trebia
ARVERNI   CISALPINE GAUL   ILLYRICUM
AQUITANI   Mutina   Rubicon
         PYRENEES   TRANSALPINE GAUL   Sarsina
                    Narbo   Aquae Sextiae   Lucca   *Adriatic*
                        Massilia   L. Trasimene   Amiternum
HITHER   Numantia   I T A L Y   Corfinium
Iberus (Ebro)   CORSICA   Rome   Tusculum   Dyrrha
SPAIN   Ostia   Arpinum
Tagus   Saguntum   Formiae   Cannae
(Guadiana)   Suessa   Capua   Rudiae
FARTHER   Neapolis   Beneventum   Brundisi
SPAIN   BALEARIC ISLANDS   Tarentum
Anas   Italica   SARDINIA   *Tyrrhenian*   Heraclea
Gades   Munda   *M e d i*   Mylae   Ionian
Strait of Gibraltar   New   *Sea*   Messana   *Sea*
                    Carthage   *t*   SICILY   Syracuse
                                Lilybaeum   Gela
MAURETANIA   Cirta   Utica   Agrigentum
                         Zama   Carthage
ATLAS MTS.   AFRICA   Thapsus   *r*
                                              a
                    NUMIDIA   *n*

ROMAN REPUBLIC
In the Time of Caesar and Cicero

MILES 0 50 100   200   300   400

▨ Roman Provinces   ✕ Battlefields

DIVIDE ET IMPERA

As luck would have it, Caesar's opportunity to involve himself militarily in Gallic affairs came as soon as he assumed his proconsulship. The Helvetii, a tribe located in modern-day Switzerland, were suffering from years of depredations at the hands of marauding Germans on their northeast border. They decided to migrate to new lands, burning their settlements to leave nothing to German invaders and embarking on a path that, unfortunately for them, took them across the Roman province of Narbonensis, modern-day Provence.

Caesar used the plight of the Helvetii and his duty to prevent trespassing on his province as a casus belli, routing their warriors in a pair of clashes that established the daunting reputation of Roman arms in the region. Next to fall were the Suebi, a Germanic people whose king, Ariovistus, had involved his people as mercenaries in the region's tribal tensions. Caesar saw them as a threat and smashed them with his legions in 58 BCE. His Germanic border secured, he marched north against the Belgae the following year, defeating a coalition that had warred on peoples allied to Rome. The turn of the Veneti came in 56. Located in Brittany, they were a seafaring people, which required Caesar to build a fleet. Victory, though costly, was achieved.

Though acting ostensibly on behalf of the Roman state, Caesar was out on a limb. None of his campaigns was sanctioned by the Senate, many of whose august members harbored deep suspicions about him, and his efforts assumed the character of naked opportunism. Though granted command over four legions, he ultimately raised four more without Senatorial authorization, further enhancing the private nature of his army and its achievements. (A legion at this time typically included 3,000–5,000 men.) With the help of his fellow triumvirs, he even managed to extend his proconsulship for another five years. Caesar had become a rogue warlord in all but name.

His awesome achievements, however, had become the talk of Rome, restoring his heroic stature among the people—the sort of thing Senators ignored at their peril. Particularly striking were his bold expeditions into Germania and Britain. These near-mythical regions, standing at the very fringe of the known world, captured the Roman imagination. By 54 BCE Caesar had twice bridged the Rhine to terrorize German foes, and launched two punitive expeditions across the English Channel to fight the fearsome Britons in their war chariots. It seemed as if nothing was beyond his grasp.

But if much of Gaul now squirmed under the Roman sandal, some natives welcomed the arrangement. Caesar had always managed to wage war by making peace—to play Gallic nations against each other, some of whom happily joined his army as auxiliaries. Celtic cavalry, in particular, was valued by the proconsul to compensate for his infantry-heavy legions. At no point had enough disparate tribes joined forces to pose a massive threat to Roman forces, a possibility that probably haunted Caesar in his nightmares. That changed in 52 BCE.

Early that year, the heart of Gaul erupted in defiance to Roman domination. The movement, initiated by the Carnutes, took inspiration from an uprising two years earlier by the Eburones that managed to wipe out an entire legion. But this time numerous peoples would join the fray, offering the first pan-Gallic resistance to Caesar's string of brutal victories.

One of these peoples was the Arverni, who elected as their king a man in his early thirties named Vercingetorix. Charismatic, cunning, and implacable, Vercingetorix ultimately assumed leadership over the whole movement, becoming the personification of a desperate attempt to purge Gaul of the Roman curse.

A COUNTRYSIDE ABLAZE

When Caesar hastened to Gaul from business in Italy, the late winter snows had yet to melt. But the fires of war were already filling the countryside with pillars of black smoke.

Vercingetorix had long studied Roman tactics. He also understood the scale of the stakes involved, and fought like one possessed by a cause whose failure would mean the end of all he had known. Given total control over the combined Gallic contingents, he placed primary importance with the cavalry, knowing the ease with which they could outpace Caesar's legions, and enacted draconian rules of conduct for the army, understanding the need to impress every Celt with the grave importance of the struggle at hand.

The odds were with him, not least because Caesar had overreached his army's capacity to police a vast landscape. Those tribes that remained loyal to Rome under the blackening sky played right into the hands of Vercingetorix, who either defeated their warriors outright or simply despoiled their territory.

The effect was the same: Rome, unable at first to rush to the aid of her friends, looked like a weak ally, further swelling Vercingetorix's army with desperate and disaffected countrymen. As his scorched-earth policy swept the countryside, Rome's enemies grew in strength and determination.

Caesar soon faced a complete breakdown of the status quo he had striven so mightily to create—and that sustained his campaign of political aggrandizement. He saw his Gallic allies abandon him and watched Gaul slip through his fingers as his Roman base in Narbonensis suffered invasion.

The struggle raged back and forth through the spring and summer of 52 BCE. Though making headway against the enemy on a handful of occasions through the sheer tenacity of his loyal legions, Caesar suffered a terrific setback at the Arverni capital of Gergovia.

In the wake of that bloody battle, during which both sides lost many valuable warriors, Vercingetorix raised fresh troops and clashed once again with Caesar while his legions were on the march. Repulsed after a hard fight, the Gallic army retired to Alesia, capital of the Mandubii, in what is today north-central France.

Located atop a steep hill between two rivers, Alesia offered ideal ground for defense. Vercingetorix sent his numerous cavalry out into the countryside to raise a relief force while he and his 80,000 infantry awaited investment with the town's inhabitants. He had no desire for a fight in the open, as the discipline of Caesar's legions had proven all but unbreakable, so accepting a siege was not unpalatable to him—especially with the arrival of help that he knew was imminent.

Caesar, interestingly, was just as eager to embrace the current situation. With nearly all of Gaul up in arms against him, his only hope lay in defeating the main Gallic army. Here he had managed to fix it in one place and surround it with his legions. Alesia may have appeared formidable in the extreme, but its ramparts and throngs of defenders were infinitely preferable to an endless guerilla fight. Besides, the Roman way of war favored spade work.

And there was soon more than enough of that to go around. Accustomed, like all legionaries, to building a fortified camp every night before bedding down, the men in Caesar's command took to moving earth as easily as they did to slaying foes. Caesar had somewhere between 50,000 and 55,000 soldiers at his disposal, some 5,000 of which were Germanic mercenary cavalry. The rest, legionaries and their supporting auxiliary troops, began working the landscape around Alesia like ants, gradually turning it into one of the most impressive force-multipliers in the history of ancient warfare.

ENGINEERING A VICTORY

In the July heat of 52 BCE, Julius Caesar faced the gravest crisis of his career. Looking up at the heights of Alesia, with its busy forges and cook fires sending streams of smoke into the sky over central Gaul, he must have felt the press of history bearing down on him. This verdant countryside would bear witness either to his crowning achievement or his utter annihilation.

With Vercingetorix and his army surrounded, this was clearly the time and place to fight. But Caesar already faced superior forces inside the enemy encampment, and had every reason to expect another numerically superior force to arrive any day. The numbers arrayed against him were potentially staggering.

To compensate, he needed to rely on the unique thing he possessed in abundance: Roman engineering. Over the ensuing days, the Gauls in their plateau fastness watched with horror as Caesar and his dedicated men deliberately and rapidly enveloped Alesia in an embrace of wood and earthen fieldworks of unprecedented sophistication. After securing the perimeter with makeshift forts, they dug a ditch: twenty feet (6 m) wide, with perpendicular walls, extending some eleven miles (18 km) or more around the circumference of the hill upon surrounding terrain above the river valleys that in some places was equal in elevation to Alesia. The Romans backed this first ditch with two more, each measuring fifteen feet (4.5 m) deep by fifteen feet wide (4.5 m), one of which was flooded with water diverted from the rivers.

THESE MUST HAVE BEEN TENSE DAYS INDEED WITHIN THE GALLIC TOWN AND WARRIORS' CAMP, AS THE BESIEGED AWOKE EVERY MORNING FROM A FITFUL SLEEP TO SEE THE ROMAN NOOSE DRAWN A LITTLE TIGHTER.

The excavated soil was immediately put to good use, forming a rampart behind the ditches, its slope bristling with sharpened stakes and its summit crowned with a twelve-foot- (3.5 m)-high palisade featuring battlements. Guard towers, two or three stories high, were constructed every eighty feet (24 m) along the palisade's entire length.

Though Alesia's defenders made repeated sallying attempts against the laboring legionaries, they soon had to contend with more than the wall and its formidable ditches. Caesar had fields of booby traps laid to further hamper approaches to the palisade, including clusters of covered pits with sharpened stakes at the bottom, rows of sharpened tree trunks sunk into the ground to allow just their burnt points to protrude, and logs with attached iron hooks. Work was completed under the supporting fire of engines such as *ballistae*, essentially giant crossbows employing the torsion of animal sinew to loose missiles, whose strategic location in the forts and guard towers allowed the Romans to sweep the approaches with deadly bolts in case of attack.

When completed, Caesar's eleven-mile (18 km)-long circumvallation of Alesia formed an impenetrable barrier that ensured the starvation of the town's defenders unless relief came. But it was only half of Caesar's fortification effort. Incredibly, he built a supporting line of contravallation facing outward to welcome attackers from the countryside—a longer circuit of works, nearly identical to its inward-facing opposite. The result was a double barrier around Alesia, within which Caesar's army, divided into seven distinct encampments and supported by no fewer than twenty-three forts, gathered a month's worth of provisions. Consuming perhaps a month's work of toil, it must have been an awesome sight.

Vercingetorix and his men certainly thought so. With food stockpiles in the town running low and no way of knowing when help might arrive, some of the Gallic leadership started making drastic suggestions, including, it has been said, cannibalizing those who weren't fit to fight.

Like his Roman opposite, Vercingetorix was a gambler. He had sent away the most formidable part of his army, the cavalry, both to ease his supply situation in Alesia and alarm the countryside through speed of horse. But there was no way of ensuring that the decision would pay off. These must have been tense days indeed within the Gallic town and warriors' camp, as the besieged awoke every morning from a fitful sleep to see the Roman noose drawn a little tighter. The Gauls knew Caesar and his fellow Romans well enough to understand their perseverance in the face of a challenge. This would not end without a great deal of bloodshed.

Initial attacks to upset the Roman engineering effort had been in vain. Now it was a colossus of diabolical genius, its slat walls mocking in a crenellated grimace, threatening a slow death. With the rumble of empty stomachs in their ears, the Gauls opted for a desperate course, ejecting from their midst all those—old, young, female—who could not fight.

Caesar would not take them. Indeed, they represented his greatest asset— their mouths had been the basis for building the wall in the first place. Now

Vercingetorix would have to live with his decisions. Whatever the gods might think, Caesar could certainly live with his.

Begging to be taken in by the Romans, even as slaves, the throng was turned away. Presumably many of them died beneath the walls of Alesia from starvation and exposure.

Not long after this, word reached Caesar of the appearance of large Gallic contingents mustering on a plain to the southwest. The relief army had arrived.

"NEITHER A BRAVE NOR COWARDLY ACT COULD BE CONCEALED"

Vercingetorix's gamble had paid off, if only in the nick of time. Commius, king of the Atrebates, had been placed in supreme command of an army that included contingents from numerous peoples—some of them erstwhile allies of Caesar's. They had raced to Alesia as soon as they were able under the circumstances.

Their numbers were huge. Even if Caesar's estimate of 250,000 infantry and 8,000 cavalry is inflated (as many historians accept), less than half of that would have made the Roman situation precarious in the extreme. The day after camping less than a mile (1.6 km) from the Roman lines, they mustered for an attack, mak-

ROMAN BALLISTAE, OR GIANT CROSSBOWS, WERE BASED ON ANCIENT GREEK TECHNOLOGY THAT USED TORSION TO THROW MISSILES WITH DEADLY ACCURACY. A TWO-MAN BALLISTA COULD HURL EITHER A 3-4 LB (1.4-1.8 KG) STONE OR A WOODEN BOLT WITH A SHARPENED IRON HEAD OVER SEVERAL HUNDRED YARDS.

ing an impressive show for the defenders of Alesia watching from their lofty vantage. Vercingetorix and his men succumbed to elation and quickly prepared to hit the Romans from the other direction in concert with their fellows.

The resulting battle tested the Roman preparations to their limits. As Caesar describes it, the melee unfolded in the open for all to see, with Gauls from the heights and ranks of Commius's force jeering their Roman foes and calling encouragement to each other—a struggle in the round in which "neither a brave nor cowardly act could be concealed."

Perhaps eager to test the enemy sooner rather than later, Caesar dispatched his cavalry to give the oncoming relief army a hot reception even as his army did its best to hold the sallying fighters from Alesia at bay. As usual, the Gauls supported

their hard-riding horsemen with groups of light infantry and archers. The battle dragged on until, just before sunset, Caesar's German cavalry made a concentrated charge, dashing Gallic morale and sending Commius's men streaming back to their camp. Dispirited, Alesia's defenders retired to their fortified summit.

Not for the first time (and certainly not for the last), Rome's allied cavalry units proved decisive in a long and bloody fight. Caesar probably patted himself on the back for the missions he had made across the Rhine to impress potential German mercenaries.

For their part, the Gauls rested a day before assaulting the line again in the dead of night. Commius sent his men in silence up against the Roman defenses under darkness, many of them carrying an array of scaling ladders and other siege-work paraphernalia. At a predetermined signal, they laid into an all-out attack, the noise inviting a supporting effort from Vercingetorix amid the bellow of *carnyces*, the Celtic war trumpets that Romans had learned to fear. Bloody chaos raged in the darkness. Roman machines dealt death from the towers while Caesar and his officers, hurting for reliable intelligence, filled holes in the line where they could and exhorted the men to their best in the swirl of moon-lit faces.

LIONEL NOEL ROYER'S FAMOUS PORTRAIT OF VERCINGETORIX THROWING DOWN HIS ARMS AT THE FEET OF CAESAR. AFTER LANGUISHING IN A ROMAN PRISON FOR FIVE YEARS, HE WAS EXECUTED, PROBABLY BY STRANGULATION.

Musee Crozatier, Le Puy-en-Velay, France / Giraudon / The Bridgeman Art Library International

The elaborate Roman defenses held, if barely, sending the Gauls skulking off at dawn to leave heaps of dead and dying in the morning haze. With food running out in Alesia and casualties rising on all sides, the next attack they made would in all likelihood be the last.

It came on the other side of the line. To the northwest, the Roman works had a weakness where a prominent hill reached close to the Gallic position. There was uneven terrain too close to the defenders of Alesia to fortify properly, and Caesar

had been forced to leave it all but undefended, its encampment of Roman soldiers sticking out for their lack of immediate support.

Out in the Gallic relief camp, Vercassivellaunus, a relative of Vercingetorix, was put in command of 60,000 picked men to attack the Roman line opposite this breach in the circumvallation. Moving in the darkness of night, they positioned themselves on the heights above the Roman contravallation and, at midday, commenced a furious attack, inviting a corresponding effort by Vercingetorix.

It came soon enough, sandwiching the exposed Roman camp between two waves of fierce assault. The men of Alesia used the naked hill to their advantage, swarming over it with warriors howling bloody murder, their deadly longswords hacking cruelly at the faltering Roman line of shields.

For the first time since the siege had begun, Caesar's hard-pressed army teetered on the brink of collapse. Hungry for a breakthrough, cognizant of having surprised the enemy at his weakest, and able to reinforce their losses at a rate the Romans had long since lost, the Gauls reached a tipping point of effort.

Ferocity drove them forward. This was a fight they could win, allowing them to bring individual warrior prowess to the fore—a custom that typically hindered them in the open against hardened Roman discipline, but that favored them here on the rocky knoll that gave onto the soft side of the Roman barricade. Coming on with spear and sword, and pushing the enemy back with their great oval shields, the Gauls sent a flitter of panic through the Roman ranks even as they got in and around the defenses that had held them at bay for so long.

As the fight surged back and forth at the weak point, Gallic attackers kept the pressure on at other locations along the wall. Advancing under cover of shields, filling in the trenches with soil and debris, and loosing storms of missiles at the exhausted Roman defenders, the Gauls brought Caesar's army to its knees.

The contested hill became a hive of furious activity. As attacks and counterattacks raged back and forth, Caesar found himself organizing new ad-hoc cohorts to reinforce crumbling points of the line, only to watch advancing Gauls pulling down Roman works with huge grappling hooks. Caesar kept pulling men from other points on the wall to reinforce the maelstrom near the hill, but ultimately led the last full measure himself with what few reserves remained. Drawing attention with his conspicuous red cloak, he inspired his own men even as he convinced the Gauls that victory must be at hand.

Caesar had sent his cavalry around the rear of the driving Gauls. These appeared presently, causing a terrific stir in the Gallic ranks and driving many of them into rout. The close-in slaughter on the hill, in the very midst of which Caesar now found himself, reached a ghastly peak, finally breaking the Gallic effort altogether. With breathtaking swiftness, after a long afternoon of butchery, the battle was over. Caesar's lines had thinned to the breaking point, but held. Alesia would not be relieved.

A WARLORD'S TRIUMPH

Vercingetorix surrendered to his nemesis, delivering himself into a long and humiliating demise. After languishing in a Roman prison for five years, he played a leading role in Caesar's triumph through Rome as a vanquished barbarian king, followed by an ignominious execution, probably by strangulation.

Alesia marked the end of organized resistance in Gaul to Roman rule. It also galvanized Caesar's political preeminence. With the death of his daughter, who had been married to Pompey, and the slaughter of Crassus by the Parthians (see chapter 4), the First Triumvirate fell apart. Caesar came out of Gaul a conquering hero, his troops bound to him by ties of shared victory against the barbarian. Only Pompey stood in his way for control over Roman politics, setting the stage for a civil war that would consume the empire for years. Pompey would lose to Caesar; but Caesar, overreaching in the dictatorship given to him by the Senate and people of Rome, succumbed to assassination on the ides of March, 44 BCE.

His descent into reckless political aggrandizement has always tainted the memory of Caesar, as if his considerable talents were used—against the culture in which he had been raised—purely for personal gain. By any standard, however, the victory at Alesia remains an almost incredible achievement—and a testament to the Roman way of war that Caesar perfected.

CHAPTER 6

TRICAMARUM
533

BYZANTIUM'S FINEST TAKE ON THE
GERMANIC CORSAIRS OF NORTH AFRICA

15,000 BYZANTINES VERSUS 45,000 VANDALS

See the emperor in his twilight years. Loneliness, plague, and the long decades of intrigue have taken their toll. Where once dark eyes shone with vision and authority, now sunken orbs shift uneasily in a face haggard with stress. A shadow stalks him, ever present but barely seen—the specter of what could have been.

He has outstayed his welcome on this earth. His beloved wife is gone many years now, taken while still in her youth by the reaper. Her death fell like drought on the fields, taking the promise of an heir with it. Now, as the purple finery loses its luster and the palace drafts bite harder, he cannot even rely on the comfort of children to ease his passing. He is alone.

Outside, the anger in his capital is palpable. Constantinople is no longer what it once was. Only twenty years have passed since the great plague, a pestilence unlike anything since some calamity out of scripture. Bodies beyond number had littered the streets, verily choking the city with a press of overwhelming mortality, a heaven-sent punishment for imperial hubris. For had not the emperor himself been stricken with the sickness? Even now the scars of his ordeal remain, along with a wasting fatigue that saps his defiance of old age. Perhaps he has really been dying ever since.

But the people in their common misery, hardened by the hell of plague and war and piracy, have no stomach for their emperor's suffering. Their taxes are too high, his demands are too many, and the preoccupation with theological matters that gives him peace of mind only widens the gulf between himself and his people.

Things were not always so. Once—it seems so long ago now—he had been a ruler for the ages, feared and adored by his subjects in equal measure. He had put down revolts ruthlessly, summoned great minds to better the intellectual heritage of civilization, and built the most glorious structures in Christendom. He had been an emperor whose name— Justinian—would one day rank with those of Augustus, Trajan, Marcus Aurelius, and mighty Constantine.

More importantly, he had reconquered the eternal city of Rome itself, as well as much of the old empire that had been lost to petty kings and barbarian invaders in the West. Under his reign, for the first time in more than a century, the Roman Empire was mighty once more, reunited from Constantinople.

This was all thanks to the one man he has feared more than any other during his time on the throne. The greatest general of his age, Belisarius has received little from his emperor beyond jealousy and suspicion, a fact that haunts Justinian's conscience. But how could it be otherwise? For men who fight with such brilliance and courage seem ever to covet what their masters receive from God himself: absolute power. Would any sane man view Belisarius as anything but a rival?

Nevertheless, those were better days, when Justinian's dreams seemed always within reach, and Belisarius worked miracles to regain territory stolen from the empire. The emperor turns his mind's eye there once again, leaving the dreary march to death's door, the burden of tragedies, returning to the old days of triumph—the reclamation of imperial dominion that began with the first of Belisarius's campaigns: Tricamarum and the reconquest of Africa.

T HROUGH THE FIRST SEVERAL CENTURIES CE, ROMAN administration gradually proved unequal to the sheer expanse of empire it was charged with governing. A bifurcation between the empire's halves seemed all but inevitable, with the older, more densely populated East proving more resilient to internal and external pressures than the West, with its lack of concentrated urban wealth and long borders with the barbarian Germanic tribes. When Justinian's predecessor Constantine (272–337 CE) established his new capital at Byzantium in 330, formally rechristening it Constantinople, it accelerated this gradual shift of the Roman axis from West to East.

While the Eastern half, or Byzantine Empire, carried on as if little had altered its deep connection to the imperial past, the West underwent a series of convulsions that morphed it into a collection of Germanic kingdoms that owed their legal existence to the Roman penchant for outsourcing security to migrating Gothic nations the empire could no longer defy militarily.

These "invaders" were all closely related culturally, spawned of a single Nordic past that originated centuries earlier along the shores of the Baltic. But generations of migration and conflict had sundered them into separate tribes and, eventually, kingdoms, producing a kaleidoscope of Teutonic identities to bedevil the increasingly embattled Roman state.

Of these, the Vandals were neither the most numerous nor the most infamous. But they went far in the *Völkerwanderung,* or Germanic migration, that made a shambles of Roman authority, migrating all the way to southern Spain. During the early fifth century CE, under King Geiseric, they crossed the Straits of Gibraltar and looted their way along the rich North African coast. Carthage fell in 439, becoming the Vandal capital from which squadrons of swift raiders preyed on the Mediterranean for booty and plunder. Soon Sicily, Corsica, Sardinia, and the Belearic Islands fell to Vandal invaders, becoming incorporated into a Germanic maritime empire, threatening the entire Mediterranean balance of power.

As Arian Christians whose creed had been formally condemned by Christian orthodoxy at the Council of Nicaea in 325, the Vandals found themselves lords of a hostile land. African Catholics and clergy viewed their Vandal overlords as heretics, and the Vandals returned the favor—Gaiseric and his henchmen persecuted and disenfranchised countless non-Arians, immersing their newly won empire in strife.

In Justinian, who ascended the Byzantine throne in 527, the hope of restoring the empire found its most ardent champion. Justinian was a man of outsized ambition and self-importance, but one whose fanciful attachment to the Roman past compelled him to find a legal approach to the fulfillment of his desires. He didn't have long to wait.

Hilderic, King of the Vandals, proved vulnerable in his religious tolerance and lack of warrior prowess. In 530 a rebel sect with widespread backing raised his cousin Gelimer as rightful monarch, overthrowing the court and damning Hilderic to a dungeon. Justinian, having established ties with the erstwhile king, feigned outrage at these illegal proceedings while in all likelihood cheering the

A MOSAIC OF JUSTINIAN I (483-565). JUSTINIAN, A VISIONARY AND INDEFATIGABLE RULER, OBSESSED OVER THE GLORIES OF THE PAST AND HIS ROLE IN RESURRECTING THEM.

San Vitale, Ravenna, Italy / Giraudon / The Bridgeman Art Library International

opportunity for intervention he'd been waiting for. With a renegade prince at the helm of Vandalia, few could find fault with a Byzantine invasion.

Preparations were made in due haste. But Justinian's choice of men to lead this most important long-range military operation proved interesting indeed: a man of conspicuous youth whose humble origins were bound to raise more than a few eyebrows in Constantinople's privileged castes. In fact, as the Vandal–Carthaginian court was imploding under its own fractiousness, Belisarius, Justinian's young dynamo, was already making a name for himself in the sandy wastes of Byzantium's Near Eastern frontier.

DARA

Tall, charismatic, every inch the aristocratic officer, Flavius Belisarius hailed from minor Thracian nobility. He was still quite young when he became part of Justinian's entourage, impressing the future emperor with his intelligence and bearing. In 527, the same year war broke out with Sassanid Persia, Justinian assumed the throne and began seeking a peace between the empires that proved elusive. Within three years his protégé—still in his early twenties—was appointed Master of Soldiers on the Persian frontier to await the onslaught that seemed all but inevitable.

Belisarius concentrated his modest army of 25,000 at Dara, a fortified community commanding the road from Persia into Roman Mesopotamia. When an army almost twice that size came to destroy him and prepare the way for invasion, Belisarius opted to fight rather than await a siege.

This was a remarkable decision given the disparity in numbers, which eventually grew even greater with 10,000 Persian reinforcements. The Byzantine general had three mutually supporting trenches dug, with the center ditch slightly behind the other two, each of which stretched outward toward the higher ground that flanked the valley. Belisarius massed his infantry, many of whom were recent recruits whose battle worthiness was in question, behind the center trench. His cavalry massed along the length of the flanking trenches, their forward movement afforded by crossing points spaced at intervals. All were within sight of the walls, offering supporting fire from engines and archers.

Through three days of attack, the Persians failed to do more than minimal damage to the Roman line. Belisarius was able to protect his men behind the trenches when needed, attack over them to disrupt enemies as they retired, and even outflank them by positioning cavalry behind the hill to his far left. Though hard-pressed at times, the Romans never came close to collapse or rout.

The victory at Dara marked the first time in many years that Roman arms had delivered a defeat to the Persians. It also marked the arrival of a general in Byzantine service who could make the most out of Justinian's limited resources. Belisarius had lived up to his emperor's expectations. His reward would be considerable: command of the emperor's dream to rebuild the Roman Empire.

AS THE VANDAL-CARTHAGINIAN COURT WAS IMPLODING UNDER ITS OWN FRACTIOUSNESS, BELISARIUS, JUSTINIAN'S YOUNG DYNAMO, WAS ALREADY MAKING A NAME FOR HIMSELF IN THE SANDY WASTES OF BYZANTIUM'S NEAR EASTERN FRONTIER.

THE EAST GOES WEST

By the reign of Justinian (527–565), with the entire western half of the empire (including Italy) lost to Germanic overlords, the Byzantine state centered on Constantinople could look in virtually every direction and see only enemies. But Justinian, a visionary and indefatigable ruler, obsessed over the glories of the past and his role in resurrecting them. Rome had once conquered a realm that overtook the ancient lands of the East, including Byzantium. Now the East would return the favor.

With his casus belli in place against the fractured Vandal Empire, Justinian put into motion a deeply ambitious operation to attack Africa and Carthage. His border with the Persians was at last secure, thanks in large part to Belisarius's victory at Dara, which allowed Constantinople to negotiate a treaty with the Sassanids dubbed (rather optimistically) the "eternal peace."

Everything was in place by the early summer of 533. Formally blessed by the city's patriarch, Justinian's fleet set sail from Constantinople in June. The emperor, who watched the armada make its way slowly out of the harbor from the walls of his palace, must have been impressed and hopeful of so great a show of force.

In fact, it was barely up to the task assigned to it. The Byzantine state was no military juggernaut, nor were its resources so abundant as those that Justinian's predecessors might have commanded. To transport a Byzantine army of even modest size across the Mediterranean, properly escorted by fighting vessels capable of thwarting the infamously powerful Vandal fleet, required an operation the like of which no emperor had undertaken in recent memory. Justinian had gathered around 600 vessels, only 100 of which were naval ships. The rest were charged with carrying the finest spearhead Constantinople was capable of producing: some 5,000 cavalry and 10,000 infantry. With these, it was assumed, Belisarius was supposed to bring a mighty and warlike nation to its knees and occupy its capital.

Belisarius, commanding with his wife Antonina at his side, worried most about running into the Vandal fleet. In 468, a Byzantine fleet sent to punish Geiseric for the hell he had been raising throughout the Mediterranean had met with complete destruction at the hands of Vandal war galleys.

Luck, however, was with Belisarius. Gelimer had a revolt in Sardinia to wrestle with, and had sent the bulk of his fleet there. Moreover, he apparently knew nothing of the Byzantine expedition. Belisarius gradually made his way west and south, stopping at Sicily and Malta, and finally reaching the African coast, five days' ride from Carthage and due south of the fortified city.

After an uneventful disembarkation, the Romans made off for their target, the Vandal capital, marching north at a good clip along the coast road. At "Ad Decimum"—the tenth mile marker (16 km) from Carthage—Vandal forces clashed with the vanguard, resulting in the death of Ammatas, Gelimer's brother. Another Vandal column ran afoul of 600 of Belisarius's mercenary Huns, who smashed their unfortunate opponents with characteristic speed and ferocity. Though the Vandal king himself, commanding a third column, managed to rout the cavalry Belisarius sent up to reinforce

THE GERMANIC KINGDOMS OF THE SIXTH CENTURY SHOWING THE EXTENT OF THE VANDAL EMPIRE. DURING THE EARLY FIFTH CENTURY, UNDER KING GAISERIC, THEY CROSSED THE STRAITS OF GIBRALTAR AND LOOTED THEIR WAY ALONG THE RICH NORTH AFRICAN COAST.

The Germanic Kingd
East Roman Emp
The headship of Theodoric and the
Goths is indicated by underlining the
The colorings of the district occupi
intended to show how checkered t
district the area bordered in green
that of the later duchy of Franconia
Scale 1:30000
100   0   100   200   300
Miles

the Roman van, the sight of his slain brother threw him off track. Belisarius then struck with his regrouped cavalry while Gelimer dithered, sending the Vandals flying west to Numidia.

Carthage now lay vulnerable to Belisarius like the throat of a sacrificial lamb. Within the walls, the Vandal minority found themselves exposed without Gelimer and his enforcers. Catholic rage drove the Arians into their churches for sanctuary, and the doors swung wide to welcome Belisarius and his Roman liberators.

Soon the bold general was warming Gelimer's throne with his Thracian behind and negotiating the transfer of power in Carthage with the city's elite. He had eluded the Vandal fleet, sent their king packing after a glorified cavalry skirmish, and captured the jewel of Africa without a siege—all with just 15,000 combatants. Justinian would be pleased indeed.

Gelimer, however, was hardly beaten. He had been caught off guard and outgeneraled, a mistake that had cost him his capital. But his army was still intact. More important, word had been sent to his brother Tzazon in Sardinia to bring his formidable army home. Together, they would make a force large enough to make even Belisarius panic.

In the meantime, the throneless Vandal king did what he could to discomfit the Roman occupation of Carthage and its environs, including offering a bounty for every Roman head brought to him in his camp west of Carthage. With loyalties outside the city walls favoring the Vandals, Gelimer soon had a very impressive collection of desiccating craniums. He also sent agents into the city with orders to bribe Belisarius's mercenaries. And the Huns, in particular, seemed ready to do business.

Perhaps Belisarius would meet his end in Africa after all.

IN OR OUT?

Carthage had been neglected for many years under its erstwhile owners, and Belisarius had his hands full hastily repairing the walls and defenses in preparation of a siege by Gelimer. But the general had even greater issues to worry about.

To begin with, he was in charge of a conquering force whose men were at risk of getting swallowed by the vast city they had occupied. Things had cooled since the warm reception the Romans received at the gates, and while Belisarius's men were strictly forbidden from taking advantage of the locals, friction inevitably grew as Arian and Vandal elements gradually found the courage to organize against Roman government.

Outside, Gelimer's heavily reinforced army ranged freely, cutting an aqueduct to make things even harder on the Romans. And inside, Belisarius's Hunnic cavalry treated with Vandal elements. After word reached the general of their growing perfidy, he demanded an oath of loyalty from them and promised a bigger chunk of booty. But his trust in them was forever compromised.

From his headquarters in Gelimer's palace, Belisarius could sense the growing danger of his situation. Winter had begun raking the Mediterranean with storms, making reinforcement from distant Constantinople all but impossible under the circumstances. And with Gelimer and his throngs making trouble beyond the walls, food shortages were all but assured. The Roman fleet, safe in the city's harbor, was nevertheless trapped—Vandal squadrons, no doubt stationed on local shorelines in preparation for any enemy action, would pounce on Belisarius's ships.

Time had become Gelimer's ally. Belisarius needed to strike before it was too late.

An older general may have put his trust in the walls, opting against something brash that could precipitate a defeat unnecessarily. But Belisarius understood what his men were capable of—and that fighting sooner was better than later. After all, how long could he depend on the Huns? How long before Gelimer's peddlers infiltrated other units of his army? Better to risk a fight now, while he was still in near-total control, than wait while the Vandals grew stronger.

OF ALL OF THE HORSEMEN UNDER BELISARIUS'S COMMAND, THE MOST VALUABLE WERE THE *BUCELLARII*, OR "BODYGUARDS," WHO ACTED AS ELITE SHOCK TROOPS WHEN NECESSARY.

The Byzantine army was an eclectic one for its compact size. The dominance of Rome's heavy infantry legions was a distant memory by this time. Hard lessons from the likes of the Huns, Persians, Arabs, Moors, and Celts—along with the burden of defending a vast empire with limited resources—had instilled in Roman strategists an abiding love of the horse and its mobility. Consequently, Belisarius's most important troops were mounted. Six hundred of these, as we have seen, were Huns armed with deadly composite bows. These were some of the finest horse archers in the world, also capable of close-in fighting with spears and swords. Another 2,000 were regular Roman horsemen sporting armor and bows, probably recruited from the empire's nobility.

The rest of Belisarius's army, however, reflected the complex ethnic relationships Constantinople had forged with peoples within and without its borders. As the empire's citizens were not required to serve in the military, the court relied on professionals recruited in warlike communities and on mercenaries. Around 2,500 of Belisarius's horsemen were *foederati*, recruited from warrior peoples settled within the boundaries of the empire in exchange for martial service. Of various nationalities, they were heavily armored and fought with spears. Another 400 heruls served in Africa—mounted Gothic warriors from outside the empire bound by treaty to the court and fighting under their tribal nobility. But of all the horsemen under Belisarius's command, the most valuable were the *bucellarii*, or "bodyguards," at least 300 of which typically accompanied every Roman general in the field. Like members of a lord's personal retinue, these heavily armored cavalrymen acted as elite shock troops when necessary. Taking into consideration the bodyguard units of every major officer in his command, Belisarius had at least 1,000 of these formidable brutes with him in Africa, and probably many more.

At 10,000 strong, infantry formed the bulk of the Byzantine force. Though neither as esteemed nor as powerful as their earlier legionary predecessors, Byzantine regular infantrymen—most of whom were well armored with mail and shield—still fought in tightly packed formations that could take and dominate ground with ease if under the right leadership. The gladius had been replaced by a stout thrusting spear, lending an ancient Greek aspect to the appearance of their ranks. Though still vital to every army, these units now supported their mounted comrades in a fight rather than the other way around—a reversal of the tactics that had taken Roman law and culture to the edges of the known world.

With these men, all of whom made a living from fighting the emperor's enemies, Belisarius meant to take the fight to Gelimer before the season ran out. In December, with the weather still moderate, he led them out of Carthage's protective walls, hoping to score one last miracle.

"BY VALOR OF SOUL"

Procopius, a retainer of the great Roman general, was an eyewitness to the events in Africa and one of the early Byzantine era's most important chroniclers. To him, Belisarius was an icon of Roman virtue and an exemplary leader of men.

Through Procopius, Belisarius's exhortation to the army acquires a heroic dimension. "Now as for the host of the Vandals, let no one of you consider them," cries the great Thracian. "For not by numbers of men nor by measure of body, but by valor of soul, is war wont to be decided."

The Roman army issued from Carthage in good order, with the vast majority of the cavalry under an officer named John the Armenian leading the column.

Belisarius followed with the infantry and 500 cavalry, probably his bodyguard. The Huns, whose loyalty was still in question, hung back like spectators in the train, waiting to see how events unfolded.

Alerted to the Roman advance, the Vandals rode out from their camp at Bulla, encountering John and his cavalry near Tricamarum, eighteen miles (29 km) from Carthage. The two forces camped at a distance from each other, a creek bed dividing the plain between them down the middle.

The following day around noon, Gelimer left the women and children within the encampment's stockade and rode out with his warriors, virtually all of whom were mounted, to form up on the near side of the creek bed. Divided into three wings, the broad Vandal lines must have made a formidable sight. Outnumbering Belisarius's entire army by perhaps three to one, Gelimer's men, many of whom were armored in mail, carried shields and spears in the saddle. On this occasion, however, the king had ordered them to pitch their spears and draw swords, all of which now glinted menacingly in the North African sun. This was going to be a mean and desperate fight at close quarters.

John the Armenian answered the challenge, bringing his cavalry up in three squadrons to match the enemy across the watercourse. Gelimer, although clearly outnumbering his foe, refused to charge, preferring to await an attack that could falter on the banks of the creek bed, offering an opportunity. Belisarius soon arrived with the rest of the cavalry and the infantry in tow, having come forward quickly upon learning of the standoff.

Using John as his instrument, the Thracian general meant to probe the enemy line for signs of weakness. This was going to be a purely mounted battle, as the Roman infantry had yet to come up and Belisarius wasn't in a mood to wait. We must assume his confidence in his men was high, as he was about to take on a huge throng of well-armed enemies whose insistence on maintaining the defensive could multiply with terrain the advantage it already possessed in numbers.

John cut loose at the head of a picked force, galloping over the bed and hitting the Vandals right up the middle. Tzazon, who lately lead the struggle over Sardinia, commanded here, no doubt conspicuous in his helmet and mail. With some support from both flanks, he poured fury onto the Romans, his men crowding onto the Byzantines with swords slashing. John's horsemen buckled and then retired, falling back to the Roman lines.

Though attacking up the bank of a rivulet and wildly outnumbered, John's men had exposed the haphazard reaction of the Vandals to his assault. Belisarius at least seems to have spotted some telling weakness, and sent his lieutenant into the enemy center once again, this time with more picked men. But Vandal numbers and skill proved too much once again, sending John trotting back across. On neither occasion did the Vandals follow up their rebuff with a counterattack, preferring instead to maintain their cohesion and wait on events.

The third time John went across the creek bed, it was with Belisarius's standard flying overhead and yet more of the Roman army's finest cavalry—according to Procopius, "almost all of the guards and spearmen." In the fighting that ensued, Tzazon himself was killed, news of which immediately filtered through both armies. Encouraged by this turn of events, the whole Byzantine line went forward, crashing into Vandal ranks that wavered and grew disorganized with the death of their prince. The coup de grace, however, came from an unlikely quarter: The Huns, sensing the change in the wind, rediscovered their loyalty to Belisarius and charged the Vandals mercilessly. The fight that ensued could not have lasted long, perhaps only fifteen or twenty minutes, by which time the superior Byzantine cohesion began to tell.

Gelimer, undone by the loss of another brother and watching his people fold before the onslaught, bolted from the battlefield. His cause was lost.

THE END OF AN ERA

Once the Roman attack built into a Vandal rout, no hope of maintaining resistance against Byzantine occupation remained. Though a brief attempt was made by Gelimer to make a stand within the stockade, the arrival of Belisarius's infantry outside the barricade undermined his nerve, and he fled into the desert. Abandoned by their king, the warriors and people of Vandalia made a desperate exodus westward, variously ending up as corpses or prisoners as the Roman cavalry rode them down. The day's losses, as reported by Procopius, were almost incredibly small: 800 Vandals and 50 Romans.

Belisarius's conquest of Africa—a campaign that broke the back of the Vandals and ended forever their identity as a distinct kingdom—must rank as one of the most economic acquisitions in history. Much of this is due to the character of Belisarius himself, who commanded boldly and thoughtfully, and to his lean army, whose professionalism and coherence represented the best that a wealthy empire could produce at the time.

But Vandal weakness also played a major role in Gelimer's downfall. Twice Vandal armies had clashed with Byzantines in Africa, and twice a prince had fallen, throwing the Vandal line into disarray. By the time he was flying westward to appeal for help to the Moors, Gelimer had lost as many brothers as he had battles—and his mighty kingdom, to boot. Bad luck had conspired with the ancient Germanic custom of leading from the front to deprive the Vandal ruling house of its vital fighting men. Had Belisarius and John gambled all on attacking the center at Tricamarum because they knew Tzazon commanded there and hoped to win by taking his life? Probably not. But it may have been a possibility, knowing as they did the decisiveness of Gelimer's undoing upon seeing the bloody corpse of Ammatas at Ad Decimum.

Then there was the atmosphere of despair that must have hovered over the battlefield that day in late 533. By the time they were facing down the Romans at Tricamarum, swords drawn like doomed heroes in a Teutonic myth, the Vandals had lost their honor and their capital. (Why else had their king ordered them into battle with only swords, as if they were preparing for a fight to the knife?) The knowledge that the enemy general before them had fate and an uncanny confidence on his side may have featured prominently in their defeat, as well—an unnerving thing to ancient fighting men. The very passivity of Gelimer's tactics—awaiting action and receiving attacks despite his overwhelming numbers—speaks volumes. The king was still reacting to events rather than deciding them. Despite Belisarius's dangerous hiatus within the walls of Carthage, he had never truly surrendered the initiative to his Vandal adversary.

The young Thracian became a legend. Back in Constantinople, his emperor granted him an ancient and treasured reward: the right of a triumph through the city, parading majestically at the head of his prisoners, the booty of a vanquished and plundered kingdom trailing behind in wagon after groaning wagon. But Justinian's Constantinople wasn't Rome during the glory days of the early empire. Gelimer, making his appearance in the general's triumph as a belittled enemy to be mocked by the masses, would have been ritually strangled in the old days. But Justinian granted him an estate in the Galatian countryside on which to spend his days in comfortable retirement—a gilded cage for a magnificent prize.

Belisarius was granted no such preferred treatment. His triumph was a shiny reward meant to appease the general's vanity in lieu of trust. For making a mockery of the Mediterranean world's most notorious rogue state with only a token force, Belisarius had earned the undying jealousy of his master. Two years after Tricamarum, the general would spearhead Justinian's treasured invasion of Italy, once more outsmarting his enemies with limited men and resources, only to be recalled once again to keep him within arm's length. It was a pattern that would replay itself in the future: Justinian, facing a dreadful military crisis on some frontier, would turn to his martial magician, only to reward his brilliant success with more suspicion and a forced retirement.

For Justinian, the risks paid off, at least for a time. For a gleaming moment in history one empire claimed sovereignty over virtually the whole of the Mediterranean seaboard, recalling greater days of Roman grandeur. Belisarius had been a crucial part of that reconquest. But in 542 a plague struck the Byzantine

Empire, and ultimately its neighbors, that proved devastating enough to threaten everything Justinian had accomplished. Possibly a relative of the Black Death that devastated fourteenth-century Eurasia, this sixth-century pandemic—sometimes referred to as the Plague of Justinian—claimed as much as sixty percent of the population of some regions. Much of the world of late antiquity simply collapsed.

Though catastrophic in its own right, the plague was only the worst of Justinian's problems. His hyper-ambitious military campaigns exacted a terrific tax burden on the populace, pushed the Byzantine military system to its limits, and committed certain regions—Italy chief among them—to decades of warfare that proved ruinous for generations to come. Rome, after changing hands numerous times between Byzantine forces and their Gothic enemies throughout the wars of the period, became an underpopulated dystopia—a supreme irony given the pretensions of the man whose vision unleashed those wars in the first place.

CHAPTER 7

AGINCOURT
1415

**FRENCH CHIVALRY ENDURES THE FLIGHT OF
THE BODKINS ON ST. CRISPIN'S DAY**

6,000 ENGLISH VERSUS 30,000 FRENCH

UNDER A PAVILION OF GOLD CLOTH, THE KING OF ENGLAND
sat on his camp throne and awaited the approaching defeated—burgesses and knights, men accustomed to comfort and deference. Here, on the long walk uphill to the king and his retinue, they would find neither.

Behind them was the ruin of Harfleur. This was their town, once a mighty port on the Norman coastline. Now its walls showed ugly gaps in the masonry and its fine houses smoldered, victims of indiscriminate bombardment by English guns and catapults. Defiant in their miserable state, the vanquished leaders of the community proceeded out of Harfleur's Leure gate, walking up the hill between rows of muddy-faced Englishmen toward the warrior-monarch who had engineered the town's downfall and now received its formal capitulation.

Coming before the king, the unarmored men fell to their knees and handed their conqueror the keys to Harfleur, in whose defense they had lately labored so desperately. Their trial was over—chivalry had demanded of them all their bodies could bear, and now they were to be rewarded in their defeat with a feast at the table of the very man who had pummeled their hamlet with stone and iron.

That man was King Henry V. Son of a usurper, he had come to France to reclaim what he believed was rightfully his—great swaths of France over which the magnates of northwest Europe had been warring for generations. After making an uncontested landing, he had marched his army to the gates of Harfleur with the intent of seizing it and turning it into an English-held port—a continental bridge-head like the one that already existed in English Calais to the northeast.

The siege, however, had taken more than a month, foiling Henry's plan for a quick campaign. As he sat in splendor surrounded by his leading nobles and house-hold retinue, gazing down on the gentlemen who groveled before him, the English sovereign must have appeared implacable. But even then, in his moment of tri-umph, hard facts were doubtless occupying his mind.

The theatrics of victory belied an English camp that suffered dreadfully. Dysentery was killing Henry's men faster than his clerks could register their deaths on the rolls. Autumn was fast approaching, decreasing his options with every sun-set. And he now had a port to occupy—one of France's finest, and dearly won. To keep it, he needed to parse his shrinking army even further to provide a garrison large enough to defy any counterattack.

Despite all these daunting dilemmas, he could not call an end to the campaigning season of 1415. As difficult as Harfleur had been to take, its subjugation alone was hardly enough to warrant the enormous effort Henry had undertaken to raise an army and transport it across the English Channel. All Europe was watching—and wondering what this new king was really capable of.

No, he would have to strike one more blow against his enemies before returning home. That meant going on a march with an army that had already endured much. But with that army, depleted from malnutrition and sickness, he would win one of the greatest upsets in medieval history—and secure his name and cause in a way that no number of Harfleurs could have.

A TANGLE OF ALLEGIANCES

How could a king also be a vassal? This conundrum, unpalatable to the chivalric mindset that shaped late medieval leadership in Western Europe, lay at the root of the Hundred Years' War that pitted England and France against each other from 1337 to 1453.

When William the Conqueror defeated the Anglo-Saxon aristocracy of England in 1066 and the years that followed, he did so as the Duke of Normandy, a vassal of the French crown. Hence the awkward situation his heirs found them-selves in: Though sovereign kings of England, they were impelled by law and

custom to pay fealty to the king of France because he still functioned in the Gallic hierarchy as their liege lord.

The kings of England tended to disagree with this interpretation, but in time it simply became an absurdity. Ruling England from the mid-twelfth century until the fifteenth century, the Angevin Plantagenet dynasty ultimately controlled an empire that included not only England, but Aquitaine, Poitou, Anjou, and other rich territories on the continent. The confusion of Anglo-French inheritances and marriage alliances had produced an untenable situation: The crown of France controlled less real estate within its own country than did its ostensible English vassal.

Unsurprisingly, war ensued. France, eager to expand, clashed with English monarchs determined to maintain what they believed was their legitimate inheritance. Through intermittent warfare, France conquered much of what had been part of Plantagenet territories on the continent.

After 1204, only Aquitaine, in southwestern France, remained Plantagenet territory. Also known as Gascony, the region was still considered a duchy by the French, requiring its owner, the king of England, to pay homage to the Parisian throne as the Duke of Aquitaine—a new spin on the old issue that had set the English and French against each other in the first place, and that inspired several attempts by the French to seize the region by force of arms. For their part, English sovereigns never gave up on the dream of getting back all the territories on the continent that they had lost to France.

Adding fuel to these smoldering fires was a succession crisis. In 1328, Charles IV of France died without a direct heir, taking the senior Capetian line with him to the grave. Among those willing to make a claim for the throne was none other than Edward III, king of England and a grandson of the late Charles IV. The French had their own ideas, and placed a counter-claimant on the throne without consulting Edward. Known as Philippe VI, he marked the commencement of the Valois dynasty.

Edward III might have left it at that had the French not made yet another attempt to conquer Aquitaine in 1337. In response to this, he decided to wage war not merely to defend his Gascon possession, but also to conquer all the territories lost by his forebears and seize the throne of France itself. It was time, it seemed, to settle all accounts once and for all. So began the Hundred Years' War.

CHARLES D'ALBRET, FRENCH KING CHARLES VI'S CONSTABLE, AND HIS FELLOW SOLDIERS SUFFER DEFEAT AT THE HANDS OF THE ENGLISH AT AGINCOURT, 1415. D'ALBRET WAS ONE OF THE HIGHEST RANKING NOBLES ON THE FIELD THAT DAY TO LOSE HIS LIFE.

Private Collection / The Stapleton Collection / The Bridgeman Art Library International

OF TREATIES, USURPATIONS, AND FACTIONS

Edward III proved worthy of his ambitions, dealing the French a series of stunning defeats, capturing the vital port of Calais, and taking his opposite, Jean II, prisoner. The result was the Treaty of Brétigny (1360), in which the English king agreed to renounce his claim to the French throne in exchange for keeping Aquitaine, Poitou, Ponthieu, Guines, and Calais. A huge ransom was also paid for Jean II's freedom, though Edward had to give up his claims to the rich estates in Normandy, Anjou, and Maine.

Peace, however, was not in the cards. Richard II, Edward's successor from 1377, certainly considered it; but he proved an unpopular monarch and fell to a coup by his cousin, Henry IV, in 1399. As a usurper, Henry faced hostility at home and abroad: Rebellious adherents to the old regime required his vigilance in England, while the French refused to recognize his authority altogether. As Henry worked to establish his reign, French opportunists took advantage of his weakness to once again invade Aquitaine. Though initially successful, the effort foundered on divisions within the French nobility that proved explosive.

Charles VI, king of France from 1380 to 1422, had descended into a state of madness that would, over the course of his eventful life, abate only occasionally. Two factions arose to vie for control of the kingdom in his psychological absence: the so-called Armagnacs, led by the Duke of Orleans, and the Burgundians, headed by the Duke of Burgundy, John the Fearless—a dangerous man who lived up to his epithet by having the Duke of Orleans murdered in the streets of Paris in 1407. Charles, the victim's son, rose to manhood nursing a grudge that brooked no quarter.

THE ROUTE OF HENRY V FROM ENGLAND TO AGINCOURT AND THEN CALAIS IS SHOWN IN BLACK ON THE MAP. HENRY INTENDED TO CROSS THE SOMME RIVER AS CLOSE AS POSSIBLE TO THE COAST. THE FRENCH, HOWEVER, FORCED HIM INLAND, ADDING DAYS TO THE JOURNEY AND DRAINING FOOD AND SUPPLIES FROM HIS SICK AND HUNGRY ARMY.

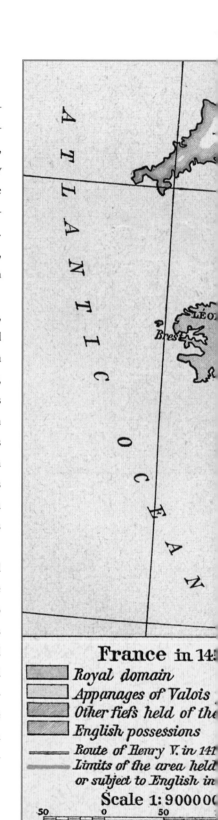

France in 14:
Royal domain
Appanages of Valois
Other fiefs held of the
English possessions
Route of Henry V. in 141
Limits of the area held
or subject to English in
Scale 1 : 9 0 0 0 0 0
50   0   50
Miles

With an unreachable king and an underaged dauphin (heir to the French throne), these two factions were free to decide by intrigue and violence which noble was capable of influencing crown policy. Each hated the other with a vehemence that all but trumped their mutual hatred of England, whose military power was courted by both in the course of their struggle. Though the Armagnac party had grown closer to the throne, the Burgundians remained numerous and powerful outsiders. In this way the stage was set for a decisive return of English power to France. But it would fall to Henry IV's son to make it happen.

Ascending the throne in 1413, Henry V had his hands full. Disquiet remained in England over his father's method of accession. Moreover, the new king had quarreled heatedly with his father during the latter's reign, leaving many in the court wondering what to expect.

Henry gave them an answer soon enough. Casting himself in the role of warrior monarch, he meant to focus his wealthy kingdom's attentions on the venerable enemy. In France lay the hope and future of his reign.

His father, embattled and suffering from illness, may have been unable to enforce the standing claims of English sovereignty across the Channel. But Henry V would make them his life's work—and divert attention away from domestic troubles in the process by giving his subjects a holy mission. Though diplomatic efforts were made to squeeze Charles VI for all he was worth, Henry planned for a war that was all but assured. And no wonder: Henry, sporting his claim to the French throne as an underdog, ambitiously demanded French territory as legal restitutions. If they were turned down, as was virtually certain, he could respond with force and a clear conscience. "By the bowels of Jesus Christ," he wrote to Charles in his final piece of correspondence before taking the leap, "Friend, render what you owe."

Neither Charles, nor the men trusted with acting on his behalf in his illness, rendered anything.

TO ARMS

By the summer of 1415, everything was in place. In and around Southampton on the Channel coast, an army of 12,000 had gathered, along with 1,500 ships to deliver them to the continent. France waited, its principal factions still incapable of working in unison to prepare the kingdom for the storm that was about to break upon it. Indeed, Henry seems to have put feelers out to John the Fearless with the intention of securing the noninterference of the Burgundians in the coming war.

On August 11, Henry's armada made for France, arriving two days later at the mouth of the Seine. By August 17, Henry's army had scouted the countryside and completed the laborious task of disembarkation—all in the curious absence of French interference. The siege of nearby Harfleur began almost immediately.

With around 3,000 armored men-at-arms and three times as many archers, Henry had every reason to be sanguine about taking the port in less than two weeks. But the defenders proved tenacious, and before long, Henry saw his hope of a swift victory vaporize in the summer heat. And then the sickness descended.

Dysentery, or the "Bloody Flux"—the bane of armies since time immemorial—was a virtual guarantee during long sieges in hot weather, where vast numbers of men lived for weeks in conditions of appalling sanitation. Unfortunately for the French, those within the town were also vulnerable to the scourge, weakening Harfleur's bid to play for time. Moreover, Henry managed the crisis with impressive skill and celerity, systematically recording the names of all those who were stricken and sending them home on a form of sick leave that many of them would nevertheless not survive. In this way he came close to purging the army of the contagion and preserving at least a core of his force.

A CONTEMPORARY PORTRAIT OF CHARLES VI RECEIVING THE WORK OF POET PIERRE SALMON. CHARLES, EMOTIONALLY UNSTABLE, LEFT THE FATE OF HIS KINGDOM TO HIS PRINCIPAL SUBORDINATES.

© SuperStock / SuperStock
1443-329-I-P30G

These measures proved enough to maintain the pressure on the port's dwindling reserves of resistance. Harfleur, abandoned by a France that was still scurrying to organize a proper response to the English invasion, formally surrendered on September 22. Henry had won his prize. But at what cost?

MARCH OF THE DOOMED

Dysentery had ravaged Henry V's men, and continued to spread, when the king found himself forced to divide his dwindling army even further. Harfleur needed a garrison strong enough to keep it under English dominion—a force that, after careful consideration, numbered 1,200 men.

This left him with some 6,000 warriors: not quite 1,000 men-at-arms and around 5,000 archers. With these he intended to march farther up the coast to Calais, a large English-controlled port offering plenty of provisions and a return to England. Such a journey in force through the contested territories of Normandy and Ponthieu would serve to galvanize his claims to them and taunt the French.

During the first week of October, then, Henry and his army departed Harfleur by the Montvilliers road, marching north and east—toward the great Somme River, which they needed to cross as close to the coast as possible to make good time to Calais. Though most of the men were no doubt mounted (even many of the archers in the English army had been indentured with horses), the host drew a large train of camp followers in tow along with those archers without a mount, slowing its progress to a pedestrian pace.

The army carried just eight days' worth of provisions, more than enough to get them through a fight with the French and on to Calais. Or so they thought.

On October 13, having reached the great river, Henry turned inland to find the nearest crossing point above the estuary. Reconnaissance soon told him, however, that an enemy force of 6,000 waited to oppose him on the opposite bank. Turning southeastward, the English hugged the river in search of the next ford, all the while shadowed by the French across the watercourse. For six days Henry and his force searched for a way across, only to find themselves farther inland than they had ever intended to go and watched from across the Somme by an enemy that grew stronger with every company brought thither by rumor of the English.

Food ran out. The Bloody Flux raged.

After stealing a forced march on their watchful enemies, Henry's men managed to come across a pair of causeways at Bethencourt and Voyennes that, after some effort at repair, proved adequate

AN ENGLISH ARCHER WITH LONGBOW, C. 1500. THE LONGBOW WAS ORIGINALLY A WELSH WEAPON LATER EMBRACED BY THE ENGLISH. AT AGINCOURT, COMMON MEN LIKE THESE PROVED THE UNDOING OF THE FLOWER OF FRENCH CHIVALRY.

Getty Images

to bear the army's progress to the north bank. All were across by the morning of October 20—at least four days beyond the date Henry had planned to be in Calais. Having marched more than 60 miles (96.5 km) inland, he still had more than 100 miles (161 km) yet to go—with a growing French enemy hot on his heels.

The ensuing days for the English must have been a blur of trudging agony. Autumn had arrived in her gusty glory, dumping rain on Henry's ragged men as they forced their way forward toward Calais, which had become something of a Holy Grail by this point.

Hunger now defined their state, pulling at their strength even as it exhorted them to greater effort. The French were nowhere in sight, despite evidence of their presence—broad stretches of churned-up road reminded the English that somewhere, just over the horizon, a mighty host gathered to destroy them, well-fed and vengeful.

Those Frenchmen may well have smelled the English coming long before they saw them. Even as they were racked by dysentery and deprived of proper food, Henry's men had been ordered to remain in a state of readiness on the march for fear of imminent battle. This meant that men-at-arms accustomed to riding with their kit in tow now rode fully armored in the saddle for days—weeks—at a stretch, trapping their suffering bodies in a kind of prison. Under the rain, corrosion began to appear where normal care had become impossible, allowing rusty water to creep into clothes and over flesh that had grown mephitic from neglect. The stench must have been insufferable.

Ironically, the archers, social inferiors, would have fared better without the enclosing burden of armor. But they had the responsibility of maintaining the battle readiness of their weapons against the weather. And their weapons were special indeed.

The longbow has become a legend in the English-speaking world, and for good reason. Originally a Welsh weapon that the English embraced after learning to dread it, the longbow represented a superlative in European arms. It was certainly long, around six feet (1.8 m) when unstrung, requiring impressive strength to pull, and years of practice to master. Bow-staves were made of yew, their flexibility born of a perfect symmetry of sapwood and heartwood, and their strings fashioned of animal gut, the whole protected by layers of wax. The mightiest bows had a draw-weight of 180 pounds (81 kg), an awesome force. Henry V's archers typically drew around 150 pounds (68 kg).

This meant that they could loose a deadly missile up to around 300 yards (274 m), though their effective limit was closer to 250 yards (228 m). The weapon was useless, however, without extensive training. Since the late fourteenth century, archery practice on a weekly basis was required for all able-bodied Englishmen between the ages of sixteen and sixty. Far from coming like a bolt from the blue, this law meant to hone what was already a fixture of English culture into a war-winning weapon system—one on which Henry would rely heavily in the clash he knew was coming.

Late in the afternoon of October 24, that clash seemed imminent. Henry's scouts reported the presence of an enormous French force straddling the road just ahead, barring the way to Calais.

The English had set out from Harfleur with the intention of striking a blow for their king's rights and possessions. They would now be fighting for their very lives.

ST. CRISPIN'S DAY

The French response to Henry's invasion had been sclerotic. With a confused king on the throne and the realm sundered by factions, it is hardly surprising. Ultimately, however, an army began to gather at Rouen, composed mostly of Armagnacs but also including some from the Burgundian faction who believed the peril of their kingdom trumped their allegiance to John the Fearless.

By the time the English were crossing the Somme, this force was on the move and gathering up smaller contingents as it went, slowly accreting into a great army. Though the king and his young heir were absent to keep them from danger, some of the most important leaders in France had assembled to smite the English. They included Charles d'Albret, the king's constable, and the Marshal of France, Jean le Meingre Boucicaut, one of the most celebrated paladins of the chivalric age. The two leading military officers of the crown, they were accompanied by a profusion of elite French chivalry, including four dukes, a dozen counts, and great throngs of knights and lords. Though some advised a cautious approach based on allowing the English to pass and then working to reclaim Harfleur, the urge to give battle raged too furiously throughout the ranks. A blow simply had to be struck.

And so it went. The French, having massed a truly daunting host of armor-clad killers, watched the paltry English stagger through the countryside like beggars on a pilgrimage, and took heart. D'Albret and his council, satisfied that they had played for time long enough to both swell their own ranks and exploit the enemy's burrowing hunger, sensed the time to strike.

As the two armies came within view of each other on the 24th, the French arrayed themselves for battle while watching their outnumbered English adversaries do the same. Light soon faded as the armies squared off, however, eventually compelling the French, confident in their numbers, to begin breaking off to find quarters for the night in the nearby village of Agincourt. Battle would wait until the following morning.

October 25, St. Crispin's Day, dawned wet and miserable. The English had spent an awful night huddling beneath the rain in strict silence, per Henry's order, though they were helpless to stop the growling in their stomachs. Most of the archers had been surviving on nuts and uncooked vegetables for weeks. Dysentery was rife. Under such appalling conditions, the English must have found sleep difficult at best, their minds racing with images of the morrow's slaughter at the hands of French soldiers who had shadowed them for days like ravens smelling a feast. Priests labored through the night hearing confessions.

Both armies had formed up for battle before the sun had broken free of the horizon. The field on which they were about to make history lay roughly near the center of a triangle formed by the villages of Tramecourt, Maisoncelles, and Agincourt. Recently sown with winter wheat, it had become a mud plain, deep and viscous. Toward the north, the French straddled the Calais road along a front some 1,200 yards (1 km) wide, their line bracketed to east and west by a pair of forests. A thousand yards (0.9 km) to the south, the gap between the trees narrowed to around 900 yards (0.8 km). It was here that Henry, having camped his men near Maisoncelles the night before, ordered them into line.

The forests were clearly significant. While the French looked on them as a nuisance, limiting their deployment and forcing them to stack their greater numbers in depth, the English saw these arboreal barriers as a valuable asset. Henry could rely on them to guard his flanks and prevent the French from making the sort of broad sweeping movements that their huge numbers of mounted knights would normally allow.

Just 900 English men-at-arms now stood ready, or mostly ready, for battle. Esquires, knights, great earls, and dukes, these were the fighting landlords and their retinues of men whose ability to stand firm in a melee made them a necessity on any battlefield.

Since the commencement of the Hundred Years' War, the manner in which they practiced their deadly craft had undergone a revolution of sorts. Advancements in metallurgy, recruitment, weaponry, and other spheres had begun to undermine the unchallenged supremacy that mounted knights had enjoyed since the eleventh century. Close formations of heavily armored infantry now posed a problem that charging cavalry could not always solve, requiring attackers to respond in kind. Though the mobility of mounted chivalry still had a major role to play, battles between Western Europe's finest warriors increasingly took place on

foot—great clashes of men encased in plate armor and advancing on each other in closed ranks to bludgeon with weapons designed to puncture an enemy's metallic carapace, including battle axes, spike-headed war hammers, and lances carefully shortened for close-in work.

With only 900 of these professionals, Henry faced a horde of heavily armored enemies. His much-more-numerous archers were going to be decisive, and he deployed them accordingly. At the center of his line, the king placed the men-at-arms in three divisions, or "battles." In between these, he placed two wedges of archers. The rest of his longbowmen he placed on the wings in two large groups.

In addition to their missile weapons, Henry's archers carried crude wooden stakes that had been sharpened at both ends. On his orders, they hammered these into the ground in front of their positions, their points facing toward the French to thwart charging enemies. Then they stood ready and waited.

And waited. As the sun climbed over a soggy landscape, the two enemy forces stood immobile, each daring the other to make the first move. For the French, staying put had its advantages. Henry's men were hungry, exhausted, and sick. Many of them soiled themselves throughout the morning, seized by the indignity of dysentery and powerless to leave their positions. With every hour they grew weaker.

Henry knew this as well as the French, and decided to break the stalemate. He ordered his line forward to within 300 yards (274 m) of the enemy—close enough to make the sting of his archers felt, but still within the narrower part of the ploughed land with woods on either flank. After allowing the archers to pound their stakes home, he waited for the reaction that his new proximity might inspire.

He didn't have long to wait.

GALLOPING FURY AND WHISTLING DEATH

We shall never know precisely how many French fought at Agincourt. What is certain is that they outnumbered the English, quite conceivably by as much as six to one. Recent scholarship based on a reappraisal of documents from the period supports, controversially, a ratio closer to two to one in favor of the French. At least four to one is a ratio espoused by a majority of historians working from the available evidence, which, on both sides, makes a point of remarking on the stark, almost ridiculous disparity in numbers that chilly October morning.

But with so many powerful nobles on the field, the French were at once awash in leadership and devoid of direction. The plan agreed on by Constable d'Albret and his fellow leaders, such as it was, provided for the deployment of a vanguard in front, backed by a main battle. These two divisions, the most important in the French formation, were composed of dismounted men-at-arms. D'Albret and virtually all the other leading nobles of the army placed themselves in the van, creating a concentration of leadership that was based more on mutual enmity than on sound military judgment. On the wings stood two squadrons of mounted men-at-arms composed of men hand-picked for their superior equestrian skills. To these was given the job of riding down the English archers—a prelude to the main fighting upon which the French plan depended for success.

Archers using a smaller bow than their English counterparts and crossbowmen, whose skills were held in less regard in the French camp than in the English, were relegated to positions behind the front line on the wings—precisely the place they should be if their purpose was to make virtually no contribution to the battle. Along with them went the crude artillery and their skilled gunners, of whom the French seem to have had a modest number that day, though their purpose and performance remain extremely vague. In the rear of the French army waited a mounted reserve, composed of all those men-at-arms who weren't important or influential enough to be put in the other, more vital units.

Not long after seeing the English line advance to its new position, the mounted wings swung into action. They waited a bit longer than they should have, perhaps owing to the fact that many had wandered off during the interminable prelude to activity, thereby allowing Henry to settle his men into a proper defensive position. The English decision to move forward, in other words, may have surprised the French, whose overconfident throngs had begun to lose their edge during the long morning—and whose numbers and confused command structure prohibited the timely dissemination of orders. By the time they readied themselves for a reaction, Henry had completed his redeployment.

Presently the two French wings of cavalry rolled forward, their heavy mounts throwing clods of mud in the effort to create momentum. At the other end of the field, Henry's archers grew taut with coiled energy, exhorted and disciplined by their captains. Then Sir Thomas Erpingham, the king's commander of archers standing near the center of the line with Henry, gave the signal with a mighty shout: "Now strike!"

Nearly as one, 5,000 English bowmen pointed their knocked arrows skyward and released them, loosing a great whistling cloud over the field. A moment later, it came clattering down on the oncoming Frenchmen. Tipped with the long bodkin, a heavy iron head shaped and sharpened specifically to puncture armor plate, the arrows raked their Gallic targets, wounding riders and sending screaming horses rolling into the dirt. Those knights who survived the fusillade came up short on the porcupines of wooden stakes, many of them impaling their mounts or being shot from the saddle at oblique range in the chaos of reeling horses.

A palpable thrill must now have rippled through the English archers, whose steady calm and prowess had blunted the first attempt on their lines by the mighty French. But this was merely the beginning; and Henry's archers had no idea just how much would be demanded of them before this bloody day was done.

A MORTAL PRESS

The French vanguard had already begun its long march toward the English when their mounted comrades, shocked and stricken by English marksmanship, came galloping back in disorder. Somewhere in the middle of the field, these two bodies of men—retreating cavalry and advancing infantry—collided, further hampering the French assault. By the time they had freed themselves from this unintentional melee, the men-at-arms resumed their exhausting walk toward Henry's center, only to be welcomed by barrages of arrows on a flat trajectory. With the range gradually closing, the vaunted sheets of steel plate that made men-at-arms so formidable were proving less and less effective. The French van had become a massed, slow-moving target for adrenaline-fueled bowmen whose greatest problem at the moment was getting more missiles to loose—an issue that must have been solved by youths and other noncombatants making constant runs between the baggage train and the front line.

Henry's archers could fire ten shots per minute, making the French situation truly perilous. But two other factors were proving just as lethal. First, the mud— by all accounts, it was a quagmire at Agincourt, sapping the strength of the French men-at-arms as they strode like crude automatons through the muck. With the front line moving so slowly, the main battle chose not to wait, following on the vanguard's heels as soon as it was able—and running into a morass that had been perfectly churned first by panicked horsemen and then by a great host of strutting, metal-clad warriors. The French advance soon slowed to a crawl.

The other factor that hampered France's fighting men that day was more cerebral. Warfare in the early fifteenth century was as much a means of personal advancement as a contest between opposing factions. The force that had gathered to oppose England represented the flower of French chivalry. There were some lowborn in their midst, such as crossbowmen, but the vast majority of glittering, armored fighters were of, or associated with, the nobility. The cost of armor and weapons, as well as the amount of training needed to use them effectively, limited the profession of men-at-arms on both sides to those born into privilege, as well as their retainers and retinues. To these men, the only achievement in life greater than the defeat of other professional warriors was the capture of one to be ransomed by his family. The higher the captive on the feudal ladder, the bigger the ransom. An economy of hostages thrived during periods of war.

Consequently, the advancing French men-at-arms ignored the archers on the enemy flanks to concentrate on the three battles of the English center. There, where King Henry V's banner flew alongside those of the principal nobility of England, lay the jackpot: all the great men of Britannia who had survived the ordeal of Harfleur and the march that followed, whose ransom was worth fighting for. As far as the French were concerned, the archers were already supposed to be banished from the field; the fact that they weren't was not alarming enough to distract the French nobility's attention away from what they considered their only worthy opponent: the small coterie of English "equals" at the center.

The effect of all these considerations was dramatic. Drawn to the 900 men-at-arms at Henry's center, the French funneled downward into an increasingly narrower approach, all the while encouraged to do so by the English longbowmen whose volleys savaged their flanks. With each labored step through the deeply churned mud, the ranks of French warriors came closer to the source of their torment, forcing them to wade into the flights of arrows, heads down, as if they were walking into a gale. By the time their front line reached the English, they must have been desperate to vent their wrath.

It was at this point that Henry and his fellow men-at-arms came into their own, reeling at first before the weight of the French assault but soon gathering their strength for a retaliation that allowed them to stand their ground and meet the oncoming fury.

ENGLAND'S WARRIORS WERE PRESSED TO THE LIMIT, BUT FRANCE'S WERE DOOMED BY A TRAP THEY NEVER SAW COMING.

Henry, using the battlefield itself as a tool, had turned the drastically greater French numbers to his own favor. In the melee that followed, England's warriors were pressed to the limit, but France's were doomed by a trap they never saw coming. With the main French division coming on behind them and completely unaware of the situation at the front, the men of the vanguard became crushed between their own confused countrymen and the deadly English, whose furiously hacking knights began piling victims before them like cordwood.

Meanwhile, those French on the flanks who tried to break the curse of the archers were met with irresistible volleys at oblique range. Bodkin-tipped missiles at such close quarters must have reaped a frightful harvest, punching clean through the finest armor. When the arrows ran out, the bowmen took up their heavy mallets, daggers, and swords to overwhelm weakened French men-at-arms in swarms and either kill them or claim them as prizes.

The French men-at-arms at Agincourt must have felt like victims of a panicked mob, caught in a press of fellow warriors that neither allowed them to wield their weapons effectively nor spared them from butchery by predatory English who, all too aware of the disparity in numbers, were willing to err on the side of mercilessness as the issue became confused. The front line at Agincourt was as violent and unsparing a grudge match as any in the long, ugly history of the Middle Ages.

JUDGMENT AT AGINCOURT

Though prisoners were taken during the battle, most of the French men-at-arms were murdered where they fell. The archers, pressing in from the flanks as the French stumbled and staggered over their own dead, set upon the wounded and dispatched them with a dagger thrust or a crushing blow with a mallet. Corpses began to litter the muddy field in ghastly heaps, especially along the front ranks.

Through several hours of this hell, the English managed to receive wave after wave of French assailants until too many had fallen to continue. Many of the French had been simply trampled to death in the mud after losing their footing in the congestion. The lucky ones were discovered by the English, who, after the battle had subsided, ranged across the field in search of wounded prisoners.

Tragically, many of these were rescued only to be butchered. Late in the battle, the French rearguard, largely leaderless and having done nothing all day, rallied behind the late-arriving Duke of Brabant to make a last-ditch effort to save the honor of France. As if this weren't enough, an attack was also made late in the battle on the English baggage train by plunderers, allegedly local peasants spurred by opportunistic nobles. Though the Duke's attack evaporated under a hail of arrows, Henry saw these two developments as evidence that he may have been losing control of the situation against unknown odds. He acted rashly, ordering all but the most prestigious prisoners—scores of men—put to death.

A brutally practical measure intended to free his men from the burden of guarding captives in the face of a renewed enemy assault, this decision has echoed down the centuries as an atrocity. But against the day's appalling death toll, it seems almost like a footnote. Despite the era's obsession with the rules of chivalry, medieval warfare was a bloody, savage business.

In the end, the English were incredulous at their achievement. No reliable tally of French dead exists from contemporary sources, though it cannot be doubted that the kingdom's chivalric class had been gutted. Among the slain were three dukes and eight counts. Constable d'Albret, one of the highest-ranking nobles on the field, also lost his life—along with six other close relatives of King Charles VI. France's ruling caste had been decimated, punching huge gaps in the social fabric of the kingdom. For this, Henry had lost a fraction of his army.

How? Few battles offer a clearer example of how the confluence of otherwise innocuous circumstances can, in the aggregate, produce a "miracle." Bracketed by the forests, the choice of battlefield—one implicitly agreed upon by both sides in the initial jockeying for advantage that occurred the day before St. Crispin's Day— offered every advantage to the English while downplaying the French strength in numbers. Then there was the mud, which clearly impeded the French advance, further exhausting heavily armored men already hard-pressed by English archery.

Additionally, the French labored under an ad hoc council of sanguinary lords, each bringing a host of jealousies and prideful expectations to a hackneyed command structure that could not hope to replicate the efficiency of Henry's taut, charismatic leadership. Without disciplined control, the French numbers meant next to nothing—indeed, they seem to have contributed to the disaster.

Lastly, there was the longbow and the men who wielded it so efficiently. That this weapon had been embraced by the English generations earlier, rather than dismissed as a Welsh compensation for cowardice, laid the groundwork for the slaughter at Agincourt. In and of itself, the longbow could hardly be interpreted as decisive. But when embraced by an entire culture and appreciated, cultivated as a means of harnessing the common freeman's desire to fight for his king, it proved devastating.

Ultimately, Henry V's vision proved elusive. He was one of England's greatest warrior kings, an asset he used to drive the French to the ropes in this greatest of late medieval contests. But ultimate victory in the Hundred Years' War would go to the French, who, with the help of an extraordinary peasant girl named Joan of Arc, succeeded in purging the English presence from nearly all of France.

CHAPTER 8

NARVA

1700

A KING'S COMING OF AGE MEETS SWEDEN'S FINEST HOUR

10,000 SWEDES VERSUS 40,000 RUSSIANS

AN ENDURING IMAGE EXISTS OF TSAR PETER THE GREAT as a protean genius. Not only was he unusually tall and massive, striding during conversation with his ministers at a pace that required them to break into a trot, he was also quintessentially curious—a natural student who reveled in learning how to build a fortress, make a shoe, sail a vessel, and design a city. This most famous of Russian rulers threw himself into the business of life and death that he may better master the business of statecraft.

In 1700, however, his true "greatness"—and that of his state—still lay in the future. The year was significant: Charles XII, Sweden's newest king, had been on the throne for only three years, and seemed unequal to the task of running a powerful kingdom. One of the mightiest empires in Europe, Sweden dominated northern Christendom with an immaculately drilled army. Her navy sailed virtually unchallenged on the Baltic, which had truly become a "Swedish lake." The tsar, eager to win back lands that Swedish arms had taken from Russia in generations past, contrived to isolate Charles with an anti-Swedish alliance, and then pounce. Whatever its merits as a reason for risking war, Peter's intent at least had the virtue of logic, however ruthless.

His official casus belli, by contrast, proved asinine. According to correspondence from the tsar meant to justify his aggression, in 1697 he had stopped in the Swedish-controlled city of Riga, on his way to a European tour. There, so the story went, he suffered treatment beneath his station—an indignity that now drove him to seek vengeance. That the courts of Europe were expected to accept this as genuine and legitimate was patently ridiculous, but the truth of the matter made the claim even worse. In fact, Peter had indeed stopped in Riga, where, in accordance with his custom of maintaining a low profile to help him gather the sort of practical skills he prized so highly, he had insisted on acting like the servant of his own footmen. Having gone along quietly with the tsar's charade, the good burghers of Riga now served as the excuse for his expansionist agenda.

This was the ego of Peter the Great in action. Excitable, choleric, mercurial, he saw immense things in his future and was in a hurry to get there, however reckless his chosen path. He may well have been a genius, but he could also have been his beloved empire's worst enemy.

Worse, Peter picked a fight with a monarch of considerable, albeit deceptive, ability. Charles XII would prove to be one of the greatest soldier kings in European history—more than a match for his outsized Russian nemesis. In fact, this war—known as the Great Northern War (1700–1721)—would become an epic duel between two eccentric rivals, consuming the Baltic and Eastern European worlds in an ugly grudge match for twenty-one ruinous years. And it was to begin at a town called Narva.

Though only one of these larger-than-life rulers fought in the actual battle, the presence of both was palpable on that November day in 1700 that witnessed an historic triumph of audacity, leadership, and luck over formidable odds.

ROAR OF THE LION CUB

Charles XII has fascinated and befuddled historians ever since his brief and sanguinary reign came to an abrupt end in 1718. Encapsulating the matter neatly, *The Oxford Companion to Military History* calls him "one of the most enigmatic figures in military history, about whom it is impossible to remain equivocal. Either he was a great leader and paragon of military virtue or a belligerent lunatic."

One thing is certain: he was young. Charles XII inherited the throne of Sweden in 1697, not long before his fifteenth birthday. He had been prepared for leadership by his father, better than most young princes of Europe, and impressed his court and regents from the very start. Though terse and opaque, he was possessed of a keen intelligence and eagerness to lead, inspire, and direct.

Such qualities, it was soon discovered, lent themselves more to the military camp than the palace, and Charles threw himself into the exertions of war as if they, and they alone, could dissipate some nagging doubt about court affairs and his contribution to them. Once war had broken out with Russia and its allies in 1700, Charles left Stockholm; he would never return, spending virtually the entirety of his reign as commander of his armies in the field and dying, in 1718, from a wound to the head suffered while laying siege to the Norwegian fortress of Fredriksten.

His royal house, the Vasa, had been at the forefront of military developments since King Gustav Adolf (who reigned from 1611 to 1632) drew on sixteenth-century tactical innovations to produce an army the like of which Europe had never seen. Throughout its gradual emergence from the Middle Ages, early modern Europe had undergone an arms evolution that witnessed, among other things, the return of the pike to battlefield dominance. The weapon that had helped Alexander the Great conquer an empire, the eighteen-foot (5.5 m) pike, enjoyed a resurgence thanks in no small measure to the Renaissance's focus on all things Classical. The quintessential infantry weapon when deployed in massed ranks, the pike dealt the final blow to the mounted knight, whose dominance had been waning for years. Once the arquebus and its heavier offshoot, the musket, began to appear in numbers, infantry formations employing blocks of pikemen flanked by gunpowder weapons became ubiquitous on European battlefields.

The artful interplay between pikemen and musketeers in the heat of combat occupied the greatest military minds of the age. While the "push of pike" dominated for years, relegating musketeers to a supporting role, the advent of

HIGH-STRUNG AND A HEAVY DRINKER, TSAR PETER I THE GREAT DID NOT STICK AROUND FOR THE BATTLE OF NARVA. HIS LEAVING ON THE EVE OF BATTLE HAS BECOME THE SUBJECT OF MUCH HISTORICAL DEBATE.

Jean-Marc Nattier

regimented training sparked ideas that were to change the face of warfare forever. Why not train musket-wielding infantry to fire more rapidly and in disciplined, concentrated salvos? And why not draw them out into broad lines rather than concentrating them in squares along with the pikemen? Such tactics, if executed by soldiers strictly disciplined to behave en masse, might prove devastating.

The Thirty Years' War (1618–1648) and the wars of Louis XIV (who reigned from 1638 to 1715) bore these developments out. Sweden, for its part, maintained its position as a military innovator and, perhaps because of its infamous paucity of manpower, kept ahead of the curve as much as possible. By the dawn of the eighteenth century, Sweden could boast of an army with exacting regimentation, training, loyalty, and élan. Charles XII inherited a kingdom that embraced the entirety of the Baltic, with possessions in what are now Finland, Russia, the Baltic States, Poland, and Germany.

By the end of the century, Sweden's adversaries could do little but seethe. They had long grown accustomed to fearing the Vasa punch, and longed for the day when some weakness might show itself in Stockholm. The death of Charles XI signaled such a moment, leaving a relative pup in charge of the great northern heavyweight. If Tsar Peter dreamed of a new era in earnest, he was in good company: Frederick IV of Denmark-Norway and Augustus, king of Poland and elector of Saxony in modern-day Germany. (An elector was a leader of his province, semi-autonomous, who held the rare privilege of being able to cast a vote for prospective Holy Roman emperors—less than a king, more than a duke, unique to the Holy Roman Empire.) These were two rulers more than happy to bring an end to Swedish control of the Baltic. Augustus, as elector of Saxony, spearheaded the effort, declaring war on Sweden in January 1700. Frederick IV followed suit several months later.

Tsar Peter, wrapping up hostilities with the Ottoman Turks, wasn't able to join the party until August, by which time Charles XII—in a typical display of Vasa pugnacity—had descended with an army on Denmark to force peace on the Danes, who had invaded the Swedish client of Holstein-Gottorp. Across the Baltic, however, on the border between the Swedish provinces of Ingria and Estonia, Peter began operations in earnest by advancing on Narva with the bulk of his army. Should Narva fall, Charles's position on the eastern Baltic coast would be in serious peril. (See map on pages 142–143.)

On October 1, the king of Sweden sailed for Pernau, in Swedish Livonia, with a small army. By heading for the Gulf of Riga, Charles could place himself conveniently between the Russians, to the north and east, and the Saxons, to the south. Once on shore, he could consult with local authorities to decide the best plan of action for what little time remained of the campaigning season.

His subjects in Pernau greeted him warmly, heartened by the presence of their sovereign in such troubled times. It wasn't long before the greater strategic situation became clear: Augustus, scared of a Swedish landing in his rear similar to Charles' incursion into Denmark, cut short his advance north toward Riga and sent his men into winter quarters. Wellingk, the Swedish general in charge of dealing with the Poles and Saxons, was now free to accompany his young king on what became the next obvious target: the relief of Narva.

Time, however, was running out. Soon the snows would fall. More importantly, the Russian army—estimated at around 80,000 strong—was many times greater than any force Charles could possibly assemble.

And the tsar himself was overseeing the siege.

THE RUSSIANS ARE COMING

Twenty-eight-year-old Peter the Great, all six feet, eight inches (2 m) of him, had been on the throne of the Russias since 1682. To historians, his reign represented the beginning of true Russian imperialism. But in his own time, Peter labored just to bring his vast realm up to the level of military, architectural, and scientific excellence that already existed in Europe—to acquire the very cultural sophistication on which Sweden now depended to wage war with a power many times her size.

Yes, the tsar could draw on reserves of manpower that Sweden could not hope to match. But Peter wasn't satisfied with shoveling his peasantry at the enemy like sand on a fire. It wasn't that he held an especially high opinion of his subjects; to the contrary, Peter would end up killing off a great many of them in epic projects deemed vital to Russia's future (not least the building of his new capital at St. Petersburg in the midst of a vast swamp). But such antiquated military tactics would no longer do if Russia were to join the pantheon of great powers.

The tsar needed Western expertise, on which he staked everything, and Western experts, from whom the intellectual capital could be tapped. In time these assets would mold a new Russia. Until then, Peter shamelessly relied on the presence of mercenary foreigners to compensate for his own countrymen's lack of knowledge. Narva was no exception.

Having decided on war with the encouragement of the kings of Denmark and Poland, Tsar Peter invaded Swedish Ingria and invested the fortress town of Narva with around 40,000 troops—half the number that his Swedish enemies had estimated, but still the largest army in the region by far. His intent was to undermine the whole Swedish position east of the Baltic, putting Charles on the defensive.

Narva, whose modest garrison was under the command of Swedish Major-General Henning Rudolf Horn, served as the principal stronghold of the region. This was "the frontier." It was always known that Russia would strike here when war broke out, and Narva's walls were built to stand a typical siege long enough to hold out until relief came.

Peter planned accordingly. Among his troops were veterans of recent action against the Ottoman Turks whose experience under fire would prove invaluable. These men, however, could do little but form the clay from which an army could be molded by more skillful hands—which for Peter was foreign hands. Among his coterie of experts from abroad was one Ludwig Nicolaus von Hallart, sent by Peter's Saxon allies as an expert in siege engineering, and Charles Eugene du Croy, an envoy from Augustus to Peter's army. In addition to these two, Peter's officer corps relied heavily on foreign mercenaries charged with whipping Russian peasants into passable soldiers—Western professionals who usually earned the undying hatred of the men they were expected to command.

As far as Peter was concerned, these awkward arrangements were necessary if he was to take on a European army. The army besieging Narva was typical of the best that Russia could do at this stage, featuring three types of soldiers: cavalry, irregular troops, and infantry levies. The cavalry were probably the tsar's finest fighters, boasting the highest proportion of professional fighting men and nobility, and capable of swift hit-and-run tactics. The irregulars were short on discipline and poorly orga-

KING CHARLES XII OF SWEDEN (1682–1718) WOULD PROVE TO BE ONE OF THE GREATEST SOLDIER KINGS IN EUROPEAN HISTORY—MORE THAN A MATCH FOR PETER THE GREAT, HIS OUTSIZED RUSSIAN NEMESIS.

Private Collection / © Philip Mould Ltd, London / The Bridgeman Art Library International

nized, and the levies, though armed with the latest infantry weapons, were more like militia than anything else.

Nevertheless, these were brave men, inured to the hardships of fighting in northern climes, well fed and supplied, and confident in their numbers. Moreover, Peter wasn't taking any chances. Hallart, his German engineer, knew his business and quickly set about working on Narva with state-of-the-art trenchworks. He had a large train of guns and mortars at his disposal, with which he soon began taking a serious toll on the town's defenses. And his arrangements for the security of the Russian camp were exemplary.

From north to south, the River Narova bowed toward the east like the front of a great "D." Narva sat within the curve of the river's western bank, a bridge connecting it to its suburb, Ivangorod. Another bridge—the only one available to the Russians in case of retreat—spanned the river more than a mile (1.6 km) north of the city. Forming the back of the "D" and extending for four miles (6.5 km), Hallart's line of contravallation cut off the besieged town from any relief, its flanks anchored on the westward-curving banks of the Narova.

The outward-facing defenses of the Russian camp boasted formidable obstacles, including a ditch backed by a rampart crowned with *chevaux de frise* (moveable wooden frames bristling with sharpened spikes), and bastions at regular intervals, the largest of which—known as the *Corpo di Battaglie*—anchored the line at its center. Moreover, the Russians were capable of mounting 140 cannon in these works. Surely a relief army, even one larger than the Swedes were capable of mustering, would blanch at the prospect of assaulting such fortifications.

INTO THE UNKNOWN

"We are unlikely to have time for anything but the pursuit of the enemy," claimed Charles XII on the eve of the Narva campaign, "so that winter quarters will be unnecessary." The Swedish king either didn't know about Peter's extensive works, or didn't care. Once Charles had settled on the relief of Narva as the focus of his remaining effort in 1700, he exhibited an eagerness to take the plunge that worried his principal subordinates.

Youthful, headstrong, keen on proving himself, Charles XII tended to run roughshod over the subtler calculations of the older men sworn to advise him. His counselors fumed as ambassadors from other courts, including that of Louis XIV of France, offered to broker an arrangement between the hostile powers, only to be ignored by the young king. Though his chancery diplomats thought it irresponsible not to consider every possible avenue for state advantage, Charles XII seemed focused on carrying through with the war, as if everything depended on its vigorous execution.

Now, with an army of 10,000, he was determined to launch a forced march in late autumn across territory denuded of supplies to take on a stronger enemy ensconced in siege works. Even Carl Gustav Rhenskiold, the irascible general under whom the king was acquiring his military on-the-job training, was skeptical: "If the king succeeds," he wrote just before the campaign commenced, "there never was any one who had to triumph over such obstacles."

Wesenberg, west of Narva, was chosen as staging point for the campaign. Wellingk and his cavalry rode ahead of the king with orders to stock the town with food, coats, gloves, ammunition, and anything else he could lay his hands on for the coming operation. His horsemen also managed to blunt an advance on Wesenberg by Boris Petrovich Sheremetyev, the tsar's cavalry expert, whose Cossacks had to settle for laying waste the countryside on their return to Narva.

It was through this ravaged landscape that Charles and his army now had to race to the rescue of Horn and his hard-pressed garrison. Before dawn on November 13, the Swedish army left Wesenberg for Narva. Impatient to begin the campaign before winter, Charles had been forced to depart with the knowledge that more regiments had yet to arrive. He could wait no longer, however, settling on a force of 10,000 to perform his desperate gamble.

The going proved nightmarish. The roads had disappeared into slop, forcing an agonizing pace, and the enemy had robbed the countryside of food and fodder. Laboring through the gelid muck, the Swedes passed farms and villages left smoldering by the Russians, their murdered inhabitants scattered like tree boughs on the ground after a storm. At night, sleeping under black skies, the soldiers struggled against the savage cold.

AN ANCIENT STANDBY OF DEFENDERS: CHEVEAUX DE FRIZE, WHOSE WOOD AND IRON POINTS BRISTLED ATOP THE RUSSIAN WORKS AT NARVA.

Library of Congress

CHEVEAUX DE-FRIZE, large points or beams, stuck full of wooden pins, armed with iron, to stop breaches, or to secure a passage of a camp against the enemy's cavalry.

Map labels: Vasa; Lesje; KINGDOM OF NORWAY; KINGDOM OF S[weden]; Nystad; Bergen; Hamar; Gefle; Falun; Börn[g]sund; Christiania; Kongsberg; Moss; Upsala; Åland Is.; Stavanger; Fredrikshald; L. Mälar; Stockholm; Arendal; Bohus; L. Wener; Norrköping; Nyköping; Christiansand; L. Wetter; Göthar R.; Gothenburg; Wisby; Gothlan[d]; Häl-land; Calmar; Öland; NORTH SEA; Jut-land; Helsingborg; Bleking; Brömsebro; Aarhuus; Skåne; Carlskrona; Me[l]; KINGDOM OF DENMARK; Copenhagen; Lund; Malmö; BALTIC SEA; Roeskilde; Königsber[g]; Bornholm; Oliva; Stesvik; Götdorp; Rügen; Danzig; Oldenburg; Elbe R.; Travendal; Stralsund; East Friesland; Wismar; Lübeck; K

KING CHARLES XII OF SWEDEN (RULED 1697-1718) INHERITED A KINGDOM THAT EMBRACED MUCH OF THE BALTIC REGION, SHOWN HERE ABOUT 1740. SWEDEN'S EMPIRE CAME CRASHING DOWN AFTER CHARLES'S DEATH IN 1718, IN PART BECAUSE OF PETER THE GREAT REBUILT HIS ARMY BASED ON LESSONS HE LEARNED AT NARVA.

Under such circumstances, it must have been a relief to spot enemy troops on the fourth day. It was Sheremetyev again, with 6,000 excellent horsemen blocking the exit of Pyhäjöggi Pass, eighteen miles (29 km) from Narva. Taking personal command of a combat formation for the first time in his life, Charles XII led a battalion of his foot guards forward, supported by a detachment of cavalry whose numbers concealed the approach of a battery of eight cannons. Opening fire at close range, this compact, combined-arms force sent the Russian cavalry wheeling. The way east was open again.

Celebrations were short-lived, however. Though the Russians had left equipment and booty in their flight, the Swedes were now desperately low on provisions. The following night, they found themselves forced to pitch camp in what one officer of the engineers called *das sogenannte Drecklager*—"the so-called muck-camp." The fields had flooded, depriving the army of any dry ground and requiring many of them to spend the night standing. Illness now began to race through the ranks. Charles was too far from any sanctuary, too low on food and fodder to continue much longer, and too close to the Russians to turn back. It was now do or die.

On November 19 they reached a plundered manor called Lagena, just seven miles (11 km) from Narva. Charles ordered guns fired to signal their imminent arrival to Horn and his men, who reportedly cheered in response. Then, glad to be back on dry land, however frigid, the Swedes settled down to a fitful sleep. The following day would bring either glory or ruin.

A GIANT'S VIEW OF THINGS

Sheremetyev had made the countryside howl. He had torched the farms, scattered the peasants, pilfered the granaries, and captured a few Swedish officers for good measure. Charles's advance would be a dreadful affair thanks to him.

The clash at Pyhäjöggi Pass had been a shock, but nothing to regret. After all, he had been under orders to detain the Swedes without risking a general engagement, and that he had done. On the 18th he returned to the tsar's camp outside Narva with news of his escapades and the approaching enemy. He was not received warmly.

To begin with, the abandonment of Pyhäjöggi Pass seemed like a setback to the men on the ramparts, if only because an opportunity to use ideal ground against a gifted enemy had been thrown away. Sheremetyev may have been following orders, but his reappearance in camp—trotting past the bastions with his ramshackle noblemen and Cossacks in tow—sent a chill through the men who observed their return. The message was subtle but troubling: The Swedes had been located and engaged, and they had checked the swift Russian riders of the steppe on whose martial abilities so much depended.

Then there were Sheremetyev's prisoners, who soon gave the Russians much more to fret about. One of them boldly informed his interrogators that 30,000 soldiers were coming to relieve Narva, a threefold inflation of facts.

Such matters fed Peter's fertile imagination, sending the tsar slowly but inexorably into a slough of despond. Until now, the war had been a splendid affair. Hitching his wagon onto two of the most formidable powers of the Baltic world, he had picked on a beardless minor in charge of an overstretched empire. What could go wrong? He had raised a large army, settled things with the Ottomans, and made the perfect opening move by investing Narva with an army too big to dislodge without a huge effort—an army raised, for the first time, with Western methods and organized along Western lines.

But Peter was high-strung. He drank often and copiously—indeed, he may well have spent the 18th in an increasingly drunken state of brooding desperation, the doubts falling like mortar shot on his once-infallible plan. The Swedes were coming for him, and something about that stuck in him and refused to wiggle free.

What happened next has been the subject of much historical debate. The tsar, racing about his headquarters in a frantic state, declared his decision to head back to Moscow. His reasons were sound enough. Military convention stipulated that the Swedes would settle down into a sort of countersiege to weaken the Russian defenses with artillery before risking an assault. This would give the tsar time to raise a relief force that, in concert with the army besieging Narva, could ensure the destruction of the enemy from two directions. Additionally, he needed to get in touch with Augustus about renewing the effort against Riga and to treat further with the Turkish ambassador.

Undoubtedly, Peter's role as autocrat of a massive state in the midst of a war posed unique challenges for him. As the very personification of imperial power, he had to be many things—and many places—virtually at once. But one can't help wondering *where* in the world he thought he was likelier to have a greater impact on the course of his nation's history than with his army on the verge of fighting its most important battle against its greatest foe?

Two generals, Weyde and Golovine, stood next in line of command beneath the tsar. Nevertheless, in one of his most infamous acts, a deeply intoxicated Peter gave command to du Croy—a Belgian prince who was unfamiliar with the command structure, knew none of the officers of the line, and spoke almost no Russian. The poor fellow protested, but to no avail. According to Hallart, Peter— "confused and half-mad, wailing and draining glass after glass of brandy"—penned his standing orders to du Croy, left the fate of the siege in his hands, and galloped off to Moscow like a man in a hurry.

Peter the Great's apologists have bent over backward through the years in their attempts to make this whole affair look like anything but an act of abject cowardice, but the question remains: How was this good for the Russian cause?

Debate over that question still occupied the tsar's soldiers when, on the morning of the 20th, they spied lines of blue-clad soldiers emerging out of the forest to the west.

Charles XII had arrived.

NOW WHAT?

The previous night, King Charles had sent a party of his engineers ahead to reconnoiter the Russian works in the moonlight. Their findings proved significant.

To begin with, the Russian breastworks were formidable, presenting an uninterrupted line of wood and earthen defenses that, in tandem with the river, effectively imprisoned Narva and its environs. But as impressive as they appeared, they had two weaknesses. First, they were four miles (6.5 km) long—no besieging army could possibly be present in strength all along its front. Second, the large, central bastion stood opposite a spit of high ground called Hermannsberg on which Swedish guns could be placed to dominate the surrounding terrain.

Working from this information, Rhenskiold developed a plan of attack that pleased his sovereign greatly—for it was daring in the extreme. By ten a.m. on the 20th, Charles's ragtag army had emerged from the woods that had concealed its camp. His men must have made quite a sight as they formed up, an army of wan, drenched fighters whose only consolation in the morning chill was that their ordeal was about to end. Rhenskiold would have preferred an attack at this moment by the Russians, but none came. He had no choice but to take on the breastworks.

Across the field, du Croy, conspicuous in his red uniform, had been inspecting the troops when scouts signaled the Swedish arrival. With little direction needed from him, the Russians deployed into the lines according to unit and began the waiting game they knew was coming. Du Croy and Hallart, experts in the science of war, assumed the Swedes were about to commence approaching the Russian works through trenches and bombardment, a process of exacting methodology that should take days at the least. There was no hurry.

The Swedes complied with convention by moving their artillery up onto Hermannsberg. As Charles's infantry and cavalry began mustering in columns on either end of the high ground, the guns opened fire, sending shot flying into the Russian entrenchments and especially into the large, central Corpo di Battaglie.

As thunderous as this display was, however, it could have but little effect on the enemy works. That suited Rhenskiold fine, for the artillery was the least important element of his plan. What he had in store for the Russians was so preposterously risky as to escape their imaginations entirely.

Not that they didn't speculate. To du Croy and his officers, the assembling of Swedish troops north and south of Hermannsberg was a curiosity: Why were they not busy throwing up entrenchments of their own for a fortified camp?

Noon came and went, and soon all was near readiness. Rhenskiold had instructed the infantry to create what the Swedes call *askiner*—bundles of bound twigs and brush, known commonly as *fascines*, with which assaulting troops can fill a ditch to more easily cross it. Once these were ready and deployed, the troops prepared for the attack.

It was almost two p.m.—and the Swedes, drastically outnumbered, intended to take the enemy position that very afternoon.

STEALING VICTORY IN THE BLOWING SNOW

Having spent most of the morning on the heights directing the bombardment, King Charles galloped north to join the left wing. Here Rhenskiold was in overall command, while the king's *Drabants*—elite mounted guards, gentlemen all—were entrusted to Count Arvid Horn, a favorite of the king. To the south, on the other side of Hermannsberg with its guns pounding away, was the other wing, commanded by Wellingk. Both wings included infantry and cavalry.

Incredibly, outnumbered four to one, the Swedes had further divided their army—a classic no-no in military circles. But Rhenskiold's plan intended to use the two wings in tandem. Moving forward like two tines of a carving fork, the columns would stab the center of the Russian line on either side of the Corpo di Battaglie. Once through, the infantry would turn north and south, respectively, attacking up and down the lines and sweeping the Russians before them. Much of the cavalry would remain behind to prevent escape by the enemy and to reinforce any trouble spots that might arise.

It was a plan of the purest audacity. And things were about to get even stranger. Not long after two p.m., the sky that had been darkening gradually all day turned violent, sending a wind howling from over the woods behind the Swedes. A snow squall followed, and Charles knew it was time. Shouting "with God's help," the wild-eyed youth led the right column forward, giving Wellingk his signal to follow suit.

With a speed seen only in far northern climes, the squall intensified dramatically, filling the battlefield with a swirling white torrent that at times grew opaque. The wind had joined the Swedish ranks, blowing right into the faces of the Russians as they strained to make out the ghostly images in blue coming to kill them. Musketry began to chatter up and down the line from Russians firing desultory volleys into the tempest, and soon they were joined by occasional blasts of artillery. But the shots proved wild and poorly timed.

Then, some thirty paces from the parapet, the Swedes came up short, shouldered their arms, and loosed a roaring fusillade into the hapless Russians, felling them in droves. Into the ditch went the tumbling fascines, which now bore Swedish soldiers into the very teeth of the enemy. A clash of bayonets, swords, and pikes filled the air, the desperate combatants throwing great gouts of breath in their murderous exertion. But despite their fury, the Russians were hard pressed to overcome the confused, wintry hell that had descended on them as if from nowhere. Rhenskiold had made his two breakthroughs.

INCREDIBLY, OUTNUMBERED FOUR TO ONE, THE SWEDES HAD FURTHER DIVIDED THEIR ARMY— A CLASSIC NO-NO IN MILITARY CIRCLES.

The Corpo di Battaglie now remained under guard (and under fire from the Hermannsberg cannon) while the wings broke away from each other to fight up and down the Russian line. Though resistance proved stiff in some quarters, the Russian command structure had all but crumbled. Du Croy, whatever his true abilities, was now merely a foreign spectator trying not to get killed—and probably cursing the tsar of the Russias under his breath. Du Croy would survive the day's carnage; others were not so fortunate. Many of the Russian levies, desperate in the frigid struggle, would murder their foreign officers and make a break for freedom.

Progress was quickest for the Swedish right wing, fighting its way south. While many Russians broke west into the open ground, Charles XII and his cavalry hunted them down or drove them back into the fray. Soon the Russians on the southern half were all but broken—and none too soon, for help was needed on the other end of the line.

To the north, Rhenskiold's wing found itself clashing with a series of strongly fortified positions. Through desperate combat, the Swedes managed to slowly push the Russians onto the swampy ground before the Kamperholm Bridge—the sole route to salvation for retreating Russians. While two of the tsar's finest regiments, the Preobrazhenski and Semenovski Guards, poured fire on their attackers from blockhouses, a horde of refugees from the Russian camp crowded over the bridge. In time it collapsed, sending a stream of camp followers and teamsters splashing into the frigid water.

Afternoon was fading to evening now, and the northern end of the Russian line became a scene of intense violence. The surviving Russian guardsmen, now joined by stragglers and refugees trapped by the collapsed bridge, formed a makeshift laager out of carts and wagons, and maintained their terrific resistance under Russian officers who refused to give quarter. At one point, as reinforcements were brought up from the south, Swedish units began firing on each other in the whirling confusion.

This was the battle's denouement—a drawn-out slugfest that finally brought King Charles himself, who personally led his Drabants against the enemy position while Swedish guns, hauled down from the heights and through the parapet, were trained on the enemy at close range. Soon the artillery began blasting great gaps in the laager, making the Russians' position untenable. By eight o'clock in the evening, they had all surrendered.

Charles XII had his miracle.

THE CUP RUNNETH OVER

Around 2,000 Swedish dead lay on the field by nightfall, their still forms gradually disappearing beneath an accreting blanket of snow. For their loss, Charles XII had claimed nearly 12,000 Russian dead and a mighty throng of captives—far too many for the victorious Swedes to handle in their depleted state.

The only alternative was to set them free. In the days that followed, columns of refugees filed out of Narva bound for Russian territory, their arms surrendered and stacked in great heaps. Only the Russian officers were retained and sent as prisoners to Sweden for future ransom.

So complete was the Swedish victory, and against such formidable odds, that many in the young king's entourage could scarcely believe their good fortune. Charles XII—just eighteen years old—had, in one blustery afternoon, become a legend. Though Rhenskiold had formed the battle plan and ensured its exacting execution, his youthful sovereign had played a crucial role throughout the action, galloping from place to place as he was needed and showing his hungry soldiers how eager he was to share the danger with them. In such times, acts like these made a lasting impression indeed.

Russian incompetence was definitely a factor in the battle's outcome. From the empire's backward training system to the tsar's mercurial, drunken behavior on the eve of the fight, Russia's most dire weaknesses were fully exposed.

By contrast, the Swedish effort was historic, representing the perfect execution of a brash young monarch's gamble. Fortunately for Charles XII, the army he inherited was up to the incredible task he had set before it. Drilled as thoroughly as any army in Europe, the king's professionals fought with a sense of purpose and camaraderie, even when their stomachs were empty, their clothing was soaked and freezing, and their enemy was numerically superior and protected behind retrenchments—an astounding challenge, to say the least. They fought with the bayonet, a relatively new weapon that allowed their muskets to act like ersatz pikes once discharged. At Narva and the battles yet to come, the Swedes would win a reputation for lethality with cold steal in the charge, a tactic that more poorly prepared troops like du Croy's Russians were incapable of withstanding.

And what of the snowstorm? Appearing with providential timing, its severity and direction—confirmed by accounts from both sides—clearly represented the straw that broke the camel's back. If the Russians ever had a real chance that day (and they did, given their enormous numerical superiority), the weather seems to have dashed it. As it had before and would again on countless occasions, the weather played a critical role in the course of the battle.

It wasn't long before all Europe was singing the Swedish king's praises, hailing the arrival of a northern Alexander the Great to bedazzle the age. By contrast the tsar, having abandoned the front, seemed like a cur or, worse, a coward. In the coming years he would prove himself neither, yanking through sheer force of will his countrymen into a new era. Narva represented the nadir of his career.

Convinced that Russia had been thoroughly chastened, Charles turned to other theaters in the war, especially Poland, where he won a series of extraordinary victories. But he had underestimated Peter, who used the long respite to build a new Russian army based on lessons learned at Narva. The result proved

catastrophic for Sweden, which lost its Baltic empire in struggles with Peter and his reinvented military machine. By 1721, Sweden had lost its Alexander (who died in 1718) and its empire, in part because of the late king's obstinate refusal to treat with the enemies of his kingdom. Sweden's glory days passed into memory.

A FRENCH ENGRAVING SHOWS THE RUSSIAN ARMY BESIEGING NARVA. THE SWEDES ENDED UP WITH SO MANY RUSSIAN PRISONERS, THEY HAD TO SET MOST OF THEM FREE; THE REST THEY SENT BACK TO SWEDEN TO HOLD FOR RANSOM.

CHAPTER 9

LEUTHEN
1757

FREDERICK THE GREAT STEALS VICTORY
FROM THE JAWS OF DEFEAT

38,000 PRUSSIANS AGAINST 65,000 AUSTRIANS

EARLY IN THE MORNING OF NOVEMBER 5, 1730, AN EIGHTEEN-year-old prince named Frederick Hohenzollern was forced to witness a nightmare. On the ground floor of the fortress of Custrin, in Brandenburg, Germany, the boy was marched like a prisoner (which in fact he was) to a window looking out on the courtyard. There, a grim spectacle was about to take place. Frederick's father, the uncompromising king of Prussia, had ordered him to witness the punishment of Frederick's close friend, a young army lieutenant named Hans Hermann von Katte. His only crime had been playing a role in Frederick's abortive attempt to escape the tyrannical clutches of his father, the king. For this, the dashing Katte would pay dearly—while Frederick himself looked on.

As the executioners prepared themselves and their victim for the solemn act, the prince, no doubt fighting back tears, shouted a plea for forgiveness to his doomed friend in the courtyard. "Don't give it a thought," replied Katte in perfect French, a devoted companion and cavalier to the end.

Katte was forced to a prone position. Held firmly by a pair of grenadiers at the window, Frederick watched helplessly as the blade fell on the neck of his friend in a heartbeat, sending gouts of crimson splashing on the stones.

Frederick lived with that moment for the rest of his days. But if the guilt over Katte's death was shattering to the heir of Prussia's throne, the crime in which Frederick had enlisted the lieutenant's help had been committed with the purest of intentions: to flee an abusive parent.

King Frederick William I, Frederick's father, was a man of iron purpose. He had envisioned a great future for Prussia, despite the kingdom's lack of resources, population, and territory. To compensate for these weaknesses, the king enforced a new order on his realm that emphasized austerity, discipline, frugality, and piety. He meant to fashion a modern-day Sparta in Central Europe, complete with a state apparatus geared toward sustaining a military establishment of the first order.

There was no room for debate in this atmosphere of severity and absolutism. Frederick, the king's eldest son, was everything his father could not tolerate in an heir: an aesthete, an aspiring philosophe, and an irreligious seeker of knowledge. Frederick composed music, wrote works of history, preferred French to his native German (which he never learned to speak eloquently), and warmed to the secularism of the Enlightenment.

So the king reacted in the only way he thought he could. He beat his son, belittled him, and vented his explosive wrath on him. And when Frederick didn't think he could take it anymore, he conspired to run away into exile. The king, having discovered the plot, thrashed his son about the head with a cane until the blood flowed from his face. He would have had Frederick executed for a traitor had prominent members of the kingdom's elite not appealed to him on the boy's behalf. So the best Frederick William could do was to imprison his wayward son and force him to watch the wanton slaughter of his coconspirator.

Though neither father nor son could know it at the time, there was a colossal irony to it all. Frederick William savaged his child mostly because he believed him unequal to the task of ruling a military power. And yet, this young flutist and litterateur would become the greatest general of his century, transforming the art and science of war in ways that would have made his barbaric father's head spin—and all without any of the Spartan brutality that Frederick William embraced.

The Battle of Leuthen, fought in 1757, would be his signature triumph—a culmination of preparation and bravado that ensured Frederick II "the Great" a place in the pantheon of brilliant commanders.

AN IMPERILED REALM

Since its inception as a kingdom in 1701, Prussia viewed itself as an underdog. Its roots lay in the dynastic consolidation of lands that lacked a contiguous border, resulting in a spattering of territories across northern Europe with its nominal heart in Brandenburg in northeastern Germany.

To the ruling house of Hohenzollern, this fractured geographic situation invited disaster. Unlike Habsburg Austria, another geographically dispersed power with an interest in shaping European affairs, Prussia—with fewer than 2 million subjects—lacked abundant resources to compensate for her diffuse inheritance.

Frederick William's answer to this was to create as centralized an administration as possible while exploiting the military theories of the day to build an army whose potency was out of all proportion to the mediocre state it was intended to defend. The king, who reigned from 1713 to 1740, obsessed over his army, becoming notorious throughout Europe as a penny-pinching tyrant with delusions of grandeur. Nevertheless, the king bequeathed to his hated son a military machine of surprising size and exquisite efficiency.

SAVAGED BY HIS FATHER, WHO THOUGHT HIM UNFIT TO RULE, FREDERICK II THE GREAT (1712-1786) NONETHELESS TURNED OUT TO BE THE GREATEST GENERAL OF THE CENTURY.

Getty Images

Upon assuming the throne at twenty-eight years of age, Frederick II (who reigned from 1740 to 1786) inherited his kingdom's vulnerability. Though he feared and loathed his churlish father, Frederick understood his policy decisions, and had an undying reverence for military preparedness and the utility of force. Almost immediately upon taking the reins of his kingdom, Frederick went to war with Austria over Silesia (in modern-day Poland), the rich region southeast of Brandenburg whose annexation would greatly improve Prussia's geopolitical situation. In his late twenties, the king was still untried, and showed it—Silesia was a mix of triumph and failure. But it laid the groundwork for future improvements, which Frederick codified in a series of manuals over the coming years that represented his passion for intellectual expression.

In a second scrape over Silesia, the Prussians got the better of their Austrian rivals, forcing them to cede Silesia and inspiring Frederick to pen, in 1748, *General Principles of War*. The abused prodigal son had become a warrior philosophe, his manuals in time achieving classic status.

WHILE THE BRITISH FOUGHT FOR AN OVERSEAS EMPIRE, FREDERICK THE GREAT STRUGGLED IN EUROPE AGAINST MIGHTY FOES FOR HIS VERY SURVIVAL.

THE NIGHTMARE MADE REAL

In his reckless seizure of Silesia, Frederick had done his cause little good by alienating existing and potential allies. What gradually ensued in the years that followed has been dubbed a "diplomatic revolution" by historians for its complete shift in traditional alliances. Before long, Frederick's worst nightmare became a reality: An anti-Prussian league was beginning to emerge, headed by France, Austria, and Russia. Fearing extinction, the king preempted his enemies by attacking Saxony in 1756, helping to precipitate what would emerge as history's first true global conflict—the Seven Years' War, which raged from the Caribbean to Canada, and from India to the Mediterranean. It was a slugfest worthy of Enlightenment Europe's labyrinthine diplomacy and its penchant for producing surprises, pitting Great Britain and Prussia against France, Austria, Sweden, Spain, and Russia. While the British fought for an overseas empire, Frederick the Great struggled in Europe against mighty foes for his very survival. To succeed (and the prospects of doing so were dismal indeed), he would need to exploit the idea of interior lines to the utmost, rushing from front to front via the central position of his own kingdom to overwhelm each opponent in turn before they could join forces against him.

Frederick campaigned vigorously with mixed results. In 1756 he achieved little beyond capturing the army of Saxony, but the following year proved much more dramatic. Invading Bohemia, in what is today the Czech Republic, the Prussians dealt their Austrian foes a series of defeats, pushed them back into Prague, and laid siege to the city. Empress Maria Theresa narrowly avoided disaster when a hastily assembled relief army won a surprise victory over Frederick at Kolin, sending him packing back to Prussia.

The king licked his wounds and prepared for a rematch. By autumn an allied army of French troops and contingents representing the Holy Roman Empire marched on him from the west, while an Austrian army prepared to retake Silesia from the south. Though his army still smarted from Kolin, he turned west to meet the French Imperial threat and routed it utterly on November 5 at the Battle of Rossbach in Saxony. Given the disparity in numbers (Frederick was outnumbered by more than two to one), this historic victory would have been enough to ensure the Prussian king's place in the history books.

Indeed, the allied army that had faced him at Rossbach, though laboring under a joint command, was formidable. For days before the battle, as the Prussians approached, the allies did what every eighteenth-century army was expected to do: march and maneuver for position, performing a kind of sparring dance to achieve a decisive geographic orientation toward the enemy that would compel him to withdraw to secure his line of supply. This was standard operating procedure in the age of "limited warfare." Why? For one thing, standing armies were expensive investments. But just as important, the weapons and linear tactics of the time offered little to opposing forces beyond the ability to maul each other severely.

Frederick embraced a different approach. Though he appreciated the need for maneuver warfare, his usual goal was to close with the enemy quickly—to rapidly force a fight that would allow him to deal a decisive blow and spare his relatively impoverished kingdom from a long and costly conflict. "Our wars must be short and lively," he

THE MAP SHOWS CENTRAL EUROPE ABOUT 1786, THE YEAR OF FREDERICK THE GREAT'S DEATH. IMMEDIATELY UPON TAKING THE THRONE IN 1740, FREDERICK WENT TO WAR WITH AUSTRIA OVER SILESIA—THE TERRITORY IN BLUE THAT BORDERS POLAND ON THE LEFT. ULTIMATELY VICTORIOUS, HE USED THE LESSONS LEARNED TO TRIUMPH AT LEUTHEN.

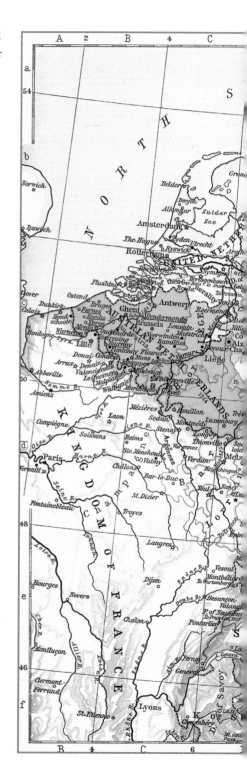

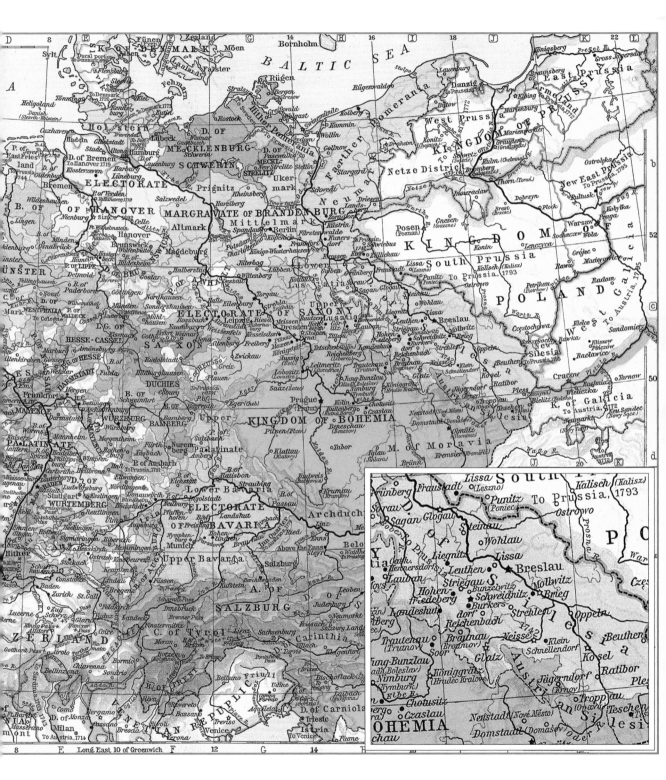

wrote. "It is not in our interests to engage in protracted campaigning." Rossbach was a classic example. Once he was able to pin down the French-Imperials, he dealt them a shattering defeat: At the expense of 500 dead and wounded, Frederick inflicted ten times that many casualties and captured another 5,000 prisoners. It was one of the most humiliating disasters in French history.

Few other commanders of the age could expect to achieve so lopsided a victory. What's more, even as the weather grew ominously cold, Frederick prepared for another fight. As he later wrote, the Rossbach triumph "only gave me the freedom to seek out new dangers." He now meant to march almost 200 miles (320 km) back east to lock horns with the Austrians before the year was out.

BLUE WALLS ON THE MARCH

What kind of military machine enabled the king of Prussia to pull off a success like Rossbach and assume that he could still expect even more from it in winter against daunting odds?

What set Frederick II apart from his contemporaries was an emphasis on aggression. He had at his disposal the very same tools as his numerous enemies; he merely used them in a revolutionary manner. The rigid conventions of Enlightenment-era strategy and tactics usually led to predictable, linear fights between commanders typically wary of committing the regiments their states had spent so much time and effort creating. Caution dominated events.

Frederick's "short and lively" vision of warfare, by contrast, needed an army equal to the task. By the time of the Seven Years' War, drawing on his experiences fighting the Austrians in Silesia, the king had further honed the excellent military establishment he had inherited from his father based on his own preference for decisive violence over maneuver. Practice in peacetime bred efficiency in wartime, and the king held regular maneuvers in which elements of the army were tested in real-life situations. As a result, the king himself could test the effectiveness of various tactics and prepare his men for eventualities. Frequent drill on the parade ground did the rest, turning individual recruits into inexorable walls of blue-clad soldiery.

Observers from all over Europe marveled at the speed and efficiency of Frederick's army, whether it was marching on parade, breaking camp before dawn and forming into columns, or executing complicated turning maneuvers under fire. This was an army sharpened to a knife's edge. Though adhering to the same fundamental principles as other great powers, Frederick could expect more resilience and exertion from his troops in a long march than any commander in Europe.

And that's what he was counting on in the autumn of 1757. The French and Imperials had been wrecked at Rossbach. Now it was time to deal with the Austrians.

WINTER OF DISCONTENT

Silesia, which Frederick had fought so hard the previous decade to conquer, was under attack. While the Prussians had been winning glory at Rossbach, the Austrians had advanced into Prussian territory. In November the Austrians took Schweidnitz and pushed the Duke of Bevern, Frederick's hapless man-on-the-spot, back into Breslau, the capital of Silesia. The city fell on November 25.

Prince Charles of Lorraine, commanding, now faced something of a dilemma. With the exception of Rossbach, this had been a fair campaigning season for Austria and her allies. In addition to retaking much of Silesia by humiliating Prussian arms, the Austrians had also managed to kill one of Frederick's most esteemed generals (Hans Karl von Winterfeldt, in the September Battle of Moys) and even raided Berlin (in October). Now, with December right around the corner, the notion of winter quarters consumed his thoughts.

Few armies in this part of the world campaigned into November, much less December. So why did he keep getting messages that Frederick was racing east with a small army? Did the king honestly intend to reverse his Silesian disasters this late in the season?

Charles, encamped with his huge army outside Breslau, needed to do three things: prepare his men for winter quarters (a massive task all by itself), garrison as much of Silesia as possible, and put himself in some sort of readiness to react to whatever Frederick intended to do.

PRINCE CHARLES OF LORRAINE (1712-1780) WAS THE BROTHER-IN-LAW OF AUSTRIAN EMPRESS MARIA THERESA AND COMMANDER OF THE AUSTRIAN FORCES AT LEUTHEN. AFTER BEING CRUSHED BY FREDERICK THE GREAT, CHARLES WAS RELIEVED OF HIS DUTIES BY MARIA THERESA AND RETURNED TO THE NETHERLANDS, WHICH HE GOVERNED UNTIL HIS DEATH.

Erich Lessing / Art Resource, NY

He maintained a large camp near Breslau while dispersing some of his army in smaller contingents to guard the outlying towns and patrol for signs of enemy activity. Though winter quarters would have to wait until he knew precisely what the king was up to, Charles seems to have believed that he was wrapping up the 1757 season with the usual protocol. And if Frederick should advance on Breslau, as increasingly seemed likely, then the Austrians could receive his attack behind the formidable defensive works outside the town.

Then, on December 2, the prince made an abrupt change of plans. Intelligence had reached the Austrians that Frederick had arrived with plenty of men and guns in Parchwitz, a town near the confluence of the Katzbach and Oder rivers, some thirty miles (48 km) west of Breslau. After much debate with his staff, Charles ordered the main Breslau army out of its trenches, leading it west toward the Prussians. Far from seeking battle, Charles meant to ensure the safety of his winter quarters and his supply lines to the southwest by pushing his zone of control as close as possible to the Katzbach itself, hemming the Prussians in for the winter. It was a practical decision, unanimously agreed upon by the prince's council, and perfectly in line with military convention.

Unfortunately for the Austrians, they were dealing with an enemy that had no use for convention.

"IF WE GO UNDER, ALL IS LOST"

Averaging thirteen miles (21 km) a day, Frederick had driven his army east from Saxony to rescue the situation in Silesia. Winter beckoned, but fair weather reigned, easing the Prussian columns' swift passage. Having left a significant portion of the victorious "Rossbach" army behind, he led just 13,000 men, hoping to link up with remnants of Bevern's shattered command (the duke himself had fallen into enemy hands around Breslau) to deal with the Austrian presence in Silesia.

He maintained a remarkable pace. On November 26 his columns reached Ludwigsdorf while still unaware of Bevern's fate. Two days later they kicked an Austrian garrison out of Parchwitz, which Frederick soon turned into a forward camp on the Katzbach. In just over two weeks, the Prussians had marched more than 190 miles (305 km) to put themselves within four days of Breslau. The situation in Silesia was now anyone's guess.

This was a tremendous feat, putting the merits of Frederick's rigorous training regimen in bold relief. In the ensuing days, the survivors of the defeated Breslau army joined the king, bringing his combined army to around 38,000.

Despite the Prussians' speed and coordination, they still faced incredible odds to meet Frederick's requirement for a decision before year's end. A numerically superior force of Austrians awaited them to the east (though Frederick had no idea just how superior) with snow clouds on the horizon. Somehow, out of all of this, King Frederick meant to scare up a miracle. His options were few, as far as he was concerned. "I must attempt and achieve the impossible, for the salvation of the state is in the balance."

He had certain obvious assets. Among the reinforcements that arrived at Parchwitz were seventy-eight heavy guns, including ten massive fortress pieces known as *Brummers* from the garrison of Glogau.

Still ignorant of Prince Charles's decampment, Frederick intended to assault the Austrians in their entrenchments outside Breslau—a massive undertaking that would have involved the army in an assault on prepared positions against a numerically superior foe. Nevertheless, early on the morning of December 4, Frederick led his army out in the direction of Breslau, a hyperconfident tactician secure in his belief that some sort of incredible victory was still in the offing. "I am marching to attack this position," he told his men. "I fully recognize the dangers attached to this enterprise, but in my present situation I must conquer or die. If we go under, all is lost."

Ahead of the advancing Prussians sat the town of Neumarkt, where an Austrian field bakery churned out bread for Prince Charles's troops. Frederick, accompanied by an advance party of light cavalry, chased the garrison out of town, then prepared for the deployment of the rest of the army to the north and south of the settlement. By evening, messages were arriving confirming that Prince Charles had brought his army up. Contact with the Austrians would doubtless occur the following morning—and it would be a pitched fight on open ground rather than a protracted fight against entrenchments.

Buoyed by this good turn of fortune, Frederick took heart. His sleep that night would doubtless have been a fitful one, however, had he known the truth about enemy numbers. Charles didn't have 39,000 men with him, as Frederick roughly calculated. He had 65,000.

TAMING THE AUSTRIAN BEAST

Several miles to the east, Charles struggled to prepare his unwieldy army for battle. He had seen the wounded streaming back from the Neumarkt collision, and sent orders to hasten the remaining elements of his army forward. Now, deployed somewhat haphazardly along miles of front around the town of Leuthen, his lines hunkered down in the cold night.

In the dawn hours of December 5, Prince Charles and his second in command, Field Marshall Count von Daun (the very general who had defeated Frederick at Kolin), organized their army and maneuvered it into position for the fight they didn't think had been coming when they left the trenches around Breslau. The night had left a dusting of snow on the hard ground, and the day broke cold.

What emerged from their earnest efforts was more than adequate under the circumstances. Arranged in two parallel echelons, as was typical of the age, the Austrian army stretched more than four miles (6 km) along an axis made slightly concave as it faced west, as if anticipating a blow from that direction and hoping to close in around it. Leuthen stood at the left center of the line. In the north, a detachment of grenadiers anchored the far right wing on the village of Nippern. Charles, having left most of his heavy guns at Breslau (he hadn't anticipated needing them), was short on artillery, which he dispersed in five batteries at regular intervals along the line. Infantry stood at the center, with cavalry on the wings—and he had plenty of both.

At the far southern end of the line, the two parallel echelons broke ninety degrees to the southeast, forming a hook at the bottom end of the Austrian formation. These were the forces of Count Leopold Nádasdy-Fogaras, an exceptional Hungarian general known as "Papa Moustache" to his troops. Nádasdy-Fogaras's units, comprising a semi-independent corps of infantry and cavalry, were formed into an angle jutting southwestward. The majority of his command was troops drawn from two German states bound by treaty to provide units to Austria: Bavaria, whose soldiers were reputedly unreliable; and Württemberg, whose Protestant inclinations made it a suspicious ally in the Catholic Habsburg orbit.

The sun hadn't climbed far when the forward Austrian position at Borne, the first town east of Parchwitz, came under fierce and determined attack. The Prussians were coming. As the Austrian survivors came retreating back into the lines, Charles and his staff waited on events, expecting a large Prussian army to materialize momentarily. A defensive posture was necessary, mostly because neither Prince Charles nor any of his principal subordinates were familiar with the ground on which they were about to commit their forces. Looking across the landscape, the Austrians saw a series of low hills and outlying villages that inspired little beyond frantic calculations about the enemy's whereabouts. This was foreign territory, which could prove hazardous for a large army deployed across a long front.

With the fall of Borne, the Austrians could expect a Prussian advance before too long. But toward what part of the line, and in what force would they come?

THE SUN HADN'T CLIMBED FAR WHEN THE FORWARD AUSTRIAN POSITION AT BORNE CAME UNDER DETERMINED ATTACK. THE PRUSSIANS WERE COMING.

As they gazed out toward Borne from high ground at the right center of the Austrian line, Prince Charles and Marshall Daun watched with rapt attention as Prussian cavalry massed along the main road heading east out of Borne, more than two and a half miles (4 km) distant. It was late morning, perhaps by eleven, and the sun shone brilliantly on the snowy plain. The Austrian commanders had taken in the expanse of territory before them, from the thick forests around Nippern in the north, through the flat plain running south before them, to the gentle undulations that almost qualified as hills ("bergs" in German) running south by southeast toward the village of Sagschütz, where "Papa Moustache" glowered with suspicion at his Württemburgers on the left flank. Now, emerging from Borne, Frederick's horsemen massed and made their way forward along the highway that parted the plain, a column of infantry trailing closely behind them.

Charles, with Daun at his side, recalled the Prussian king's penchant for attacking the flanks of his enemies. Was Frederick committing his army to a fight? This was still open to debate, as eighteenth-century armies routinely squared off without coming to blows, their commanders veering off after careful consideration. But if Frederick *were* to offer battle, he would have to get his men into line soon—it was still early in the day, but the December sunlight would not last long.

Would he strike up the middle? No. That would be suicide; besides, Frederick always massed for an all-out assault on one of the wings. This was a critical question for the Austrians: Their line was nearly five miles (6 km) long. Moving reinforcements from one end to the other would take well over an hour. Once battle had been joined, radical redeployments along the line would be impossible.

The prince, on his horse, brooded and, after a long pause, decided. The Prussian mixed force coming out of Borne was too far north to make a stab at the Austrian south wing, a move which would expose it to the entire length of the Austrian line and doom it to destruction. Clearly it was massing for an assault through the woods before Nippern to crash into the Austrian right. Charles's *Corps de Reserve,* held in the rear, was sent to bolster the right wing.

Daun rode off to oversee events on the right himself. Not long afterward, as the Prussians continued to maneuver in confusing ways before Borne, the prince authorized the redeployment of more cavalry from the left wing to further rein-force the right, sending a handful of horse regiments on a long ride behind Leuthen and north to Nippern that would take up much of the next hour.

Just before noon, Charles, still observing the Prussian activity with his staff, saw the enemy begin to break south in closely packed columns. Perhaps an attack was not developing after all. Or maybe Frederick had hoped to lure his enemies into an attack and thought better of it. In any event, many of the units that had just moments ago appeared to be massing for an attack to the north were now making off in the opposite direction. Then the blue lines slowly disappeared as they trailed off to the south, leaving the field altogether.

Charles relaxed in the saddle. "The good fellows are leaving," he said easily. "Let's let them go."

THE HARD SCIENCE OF MAGIC

Sometime around ten in the morning, the king of Prussia had formulated his plan. And though he was not a religious man, he could not help seeing the hand of provi-dence in his enemy's selection of terrain.

For years, Frederick had shaped his battlefield tactics with two closely related concepts in mind. The first involved getting his army in such a position as to be able to attack one of the enemy's wings. Though there was nothing novel about attacking an enemy on his wings or flanks, what Frederick espoused was an order of magnitude more difficult: getting the whole Prussian army, or as much of it as humanly possible, into place on one end of the battlefield to deliver the crushing blow—and doing it with a rapidity that prevented the enemy from realigning itself to receive the new threat head-on.

The other concept dictated what should happen once the army had managed to march itself onto the enemy wing. Ideally, the army would deliver an assault in

THIS BATTLE PLAN OF LEUTHEN, CREATED IN 1915, SHOWS FREDERICK'S FORCES IN BLUE. HE HAD THE CAVALRY MAKE A FEINT AT BORNE AND THEN FACE THE RIGHT FLANK OF THE AUSTRIAN ARMY, IN RED. THE PRUSSIANS, HIDDEN BY THE CAVALRY AND THEN A SERIES OF LOW-LYING HILLS, WERE ABLE TO MARCH SOUTH UNDETECTED AND ATTACK THE RIGHT FLANK OF THE AUSTRIAN FORCES.

akg-images

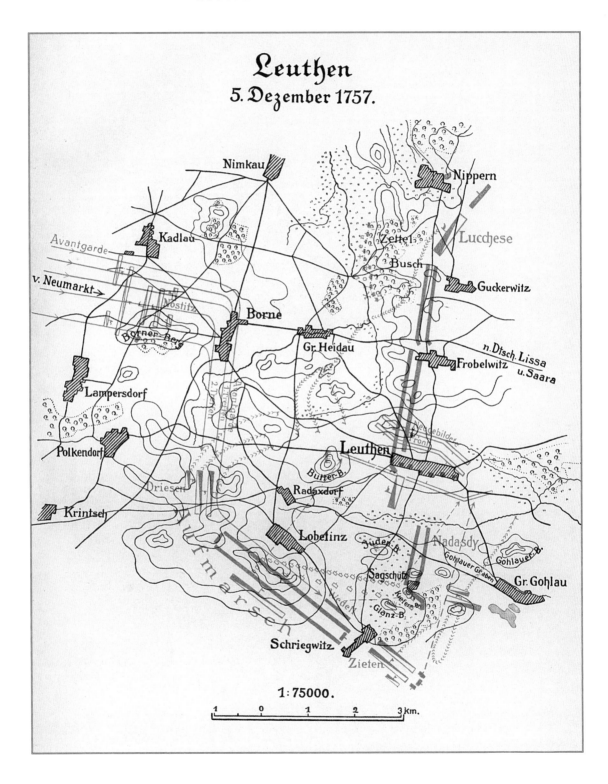

Leuthen
5. Dezember 1757.

Nimkau

Nippern

Kadlau

Zettel

Lucchese

Avantgarde

Busch

v. Neumarkt

Guckerwitz

Nostitz

Borne

n. Dtsch. Lissa
u. Saara

Borner-Berg

Gr. Heidau

Frobelwitz

Lampersdorf

Neugebildete
Front

Polkendorf

Leuthen

Butter-B.

Driesen

Radaxdorf

Krintsch

Aufmarsch

Lobetinz

Juden-B.

Nadasdy

Gohlauer-B.

Gohlauer Graben

Sagschütz

Gr. Gohlau

Kiefern

Glanz-B.

Schriegwitz

Zieten

1:75000.

1   0   1   2   3 km.

"oblique order," with one wing attacking with overwhelming force while the other was "refused," or held back to occupy the attention of the enemy and prepare to exploit developments.

In fact, Frederick had botched his cherished oblique order on several occasions, one of which was at Kolin, not least because his troops had become embroiled in combat with the enemy while in the process of marching to their extreme position. But the king was confident that that wouldn't happen here on the rolling frosted countryside around Leuthen.

Why? Because he had personally conducted maneuvers during peacetime in this very countryside. Unlike Prince Charles of Lorraine, Frederick knew this ground intimately—a stroke of good fortune that electrified him as he saw the enemy's destruction virtually plan itself before his scanning eyes.

The king sat his horse on the Schön-Berg, about a mile (1.6 km) west of Borne, and scanned the long Austrian deployment. Looking south, he saw a cluster of low hills scattered across the landscape, proceeding away from him along an axis roughly parallel with the Austrian line. He had memorized their names during the army's numerous maneuvers here: Schleier-Berg, Sophien-Berg, Wach-Berg. Though hardly more than hillocks, they were enough to screen much of his army as it made its way south, keeping two miles (3 km) between it and the enemy. He would take this approach to bring his forces down and around the Austrian left wing.

Frederick ordered a demonstration of cavalry and infantry be made in front of Borne, intended to make it appear as if he was preparing to continue the attack toward the north of the long Austrian line. But even these forces, in time, would be brought south with the rest of the army.

The plan, though sound and relatively simple in concept, involved profoundly difficult challenges in timing, organization, and deployment. What followed over the next several hours was exquisite proof of the worth of parade-ground drilling—the relentless, consuming repetition of numerous different types of marches in lines, columns, and wings that made battalions of soldiers into instantly responsive, malleable tools of force. The Prussian army was about to give an example of preparation made manifest.

Behind Borne, Frederick and his officers needed to turn four wings—two each of infantry and cavalry—into two lines of combined arms arranged in such a way that they could march in close order quickly enough along the route behind the bergs to deploy at precisely the right place and in precisely the order needed to offer fire on the Austrian flank, all without getting confused or falling behind.

Separating, marching, and morphing in a colossal choreography of blue lines, this enormous realignment was performed with machinelike precision. By eleven thirty, the newly formed pair of parallel lines was making its way south in perfect order. Within another forty-five minutes or so, they were behind the Wach-Berg, where Frederick had them turn half-left to the southeast, putting them on the path from which they would take up their final positions facing northeast. Not long after one o'clock, all the units were in place for an attack, creating a front of infantry with cavalry on the wings.

Looking out from the heights before Sagschütz, Nádasdy-Fogaras's corps saw the battalions deploying and prepared for the worst. Word was sent to the prince that an attack was about to break on the left. But it was too late.

METHODICAL FEROCITY

Having personally overseen the exacting deployments, Frederick was keen to see the spearhead of the advance guard off to its vital task of opening the assault on the right end of the Prussian infantry.

"Lads, take a good look at those whitecoats over there," he shouted to the lead regiment while pointing to the edge of a wood where Croatian infantry waited behind prepared positions. "You've got to drive them from their defenses. You must advance briskly and turn them out with the bayonet." The Prussians were already advancing steadily, their colors flying and drummers sounding the march.

The time was shortly after two o'clock. "It's do or die!" cried Frederick.

Moving on the Croats with measured determination, the lead Prussians bore down with bayonets leveled, sending the "whitecoats" flooding through the woods beyond. Though drawn onward by their success, the advance troops were reminded to proceed at a reasonable pace so as to maintain contact with the units to their left. Frederick had deployed the infantry regiments in such a way that they fell away to the west *en echelon*, creating a staggered front line that, when moving forward, allowed each regiment to open its attack roughly fifteen minutes later than the one to its right. This was the attack in oblique order. The result would be a gradual accretion of violence from one end of the line to the other, at once keeping the enemy off balance and ensuring the cohesion of the Prussian advance.

Beyond the woods lay a stretch of open ground backed by a prominence called the Kiefen-Berg, on which Nádasdy-Fogaras's Württemburgers had dug in. The Prussian attack was full on now, with cavalry joining in and a battery of formidable Brummers moving up the Glanz-Berg in support. As the dark blue lines came on, the Württemburgers opened up with their regimental artillery, only to invite a response from the Brummers a quarter-mile (0.4 km) distant that smashed the guns to pieces and tore ugly gaps in the line. Firing desultory volleys into the advancing Prussians, the defenders on the Kiefen-Berg were beginning to sense the inevitability of their fate when the Prussian line halted, shouldered arms, and erupted in fire and smoke, lashing the hill with a storm of lead.

The soldiers of Württemburg broke and fled, sending a palpable wave of disorder through the ranks of their Bavarian fellows farther up the line to the right. They too took to their heels, completing the crumbling of Nádasdy-Fogaras's southernmost defenses. And still the walls of Prussian infantry marched on, the supporting fire from the Brummers shattering the air like thunder and wreathing the lonely Glanz-Berg in gray smoke.

Prussian arms now closed on Nádasdy-Fogaras's beleaguered corps from the south—Lieutenant General Hans Joachim Zieten's cavalry on the Prussian right, the infantry of the advance guard, and a battery of heavy guns pounding away behind them. The Brummers, having chased their initial targets off the

Kiefen-Berg, now began arching their fire into the soldiers beyond—battle-hard-ened Austrian regulars who were horrified to see their comrades smashed by the twelve-pound (5.4 kg) shot screaming into their ranks. Capable of taking a greater charge of gunpowder due to their stouter construction, the Brummers wreaked long-range butchery on their targets.

The advance guard of the Prussian onslaught pressed on, backed by ranks of supporting infantry whose attacks gradually came into line as the afternoon pro-gressed. Sagschütz fell, and the Prussians mounted a tremendous effort to get a huge battery onto the crest of Juden-Berg, captured ground to the northwest of the town that offered an excellent field of fire. Before long more than forty pieces of ordnance had been wrestled into place on its crest, sending shot crashing into the Austrian lines just south of Leuthen.

Soon the last lines of Austrian defense fell back. Nádasdy-Fogaras's corps had evaporated in retreat, exposing everything south of Leuthen to the Prussians. Merging into a single, well-ordered force of grenadiers and musketeers, the Prussian infantry rolled across the countryside and prepared itself for an attack on the houses that beckoned in the distance: Leuthen itself, where the retreating Austrian defenders were no doubt preparing a line of defense, would have to be taken.

INTO THE CHURCHYARD

As three o'clock approached, the Austrian command, spurred by a frantic Daun (who had raced south from the other end of the line), labored to fix its reeling regiments into the defense line naturally afforded by Leuthen's east–west layout. Gathering within the town and to either side of it, the retreating Austrian army, shaken by its ordeal, sorted itself into a broad barrier to Prussian progress with Leuthen at its heart, and the guns of a battery dominating the heights beyond.

The Prussians regrouped and sorted their battalions into two lines for assault. Then, around three thirty, they rolled forward toward the confines of the town, drums beating a grim and steady pace. Taking fire from the houses as they marched, the bluecoats fell in small and staggered numbers, maintaining their machinelike progress amid the snap of incoming musket balls. Then, as they approached the streets, they rushed the town, sweeping through like a flash flood.

The combat grew frenzied and chaotic. This was no place to wage linear war-fare—the lockstep of the parade ground was useless in the angles and gardens of Leuthen. As the hand-to-hand combat erupted in the streets, the focus of both armies immediately settled on Leuthen's Catholic church, where a stout stonewall with roundels on each corner protected the structure and its yard—and offered Austrian soldiers excellent protection.

The sacred ground had become a death-dealing fortress. As Prussian field guns blasted away at the southern wall, a battalion of infantry stormed a barricaded gate in the east wall. Both effected a breach, and soon the enemies were gutting each other amid the gravestones in a bedlam of bayonets, littering the hallowed yard with blood and corpses.

The Austrians, overwhelmed and outflanked, broke off and vaulted over the north wall in a rout. The church—and, soon enough, the town itself—were in Prussian hands.

Driven steadily northward by Frederick's relentless combined-arms assault, the Austrians were now on their third line of defense of the day. From the Kiefen-Berg around Sagschütz, they had been driven to Leuthen. Now they massed on the heights behind Leuthen. Prince Charles and Marshall Daun scrambled to exert control over their confused situation and to establish a firm, well-defined line facing south to blunt the enemy's inexorable progress.

By the time the Prussians had righted their lines and prepared to advance beyond Leuthen, the sun had long since begun to set. Nevertheless, the advance prepared to continue, with batteries of guns being muscled forward, ammunition trains trundling into town, and cavalry mounts snatching a moment's rest before resuming the action.

When they at last began the march north through the outskirts of Leuthen, the Prussians beheld a chilling panorama. Immediately before them yawned a ditch running the breadth of town. Beyond, cresting the gentle slope rising in front of them, stood a wall of close-ranked infantry, their yards of white coats dominated majestically by a pair of enormous windmills whose blades rounded lazily in the breeze. For the first time during this long, ghastly day, the Austrians had managed to mass a proper battery of heavy artillery, the muzzles of which now began coughing smoke and fire on the western edge of the Austrian line.

In an instant, round shot thudded into flesh all along the left of the Prussian line, scattering the oncoming soldiers. The drums beat on, however, willing the Prussians forward. Though supported by their own guns on a prominence to the left called the Butter-Berg, the blue lines faltered in the trench under the incoming ordnance from the Austrian artillery. Still they staggered on in the desperate hope of engaging the Austrian infantry and silencing its battery, eventually massing in front of the Austrians and unleashing volleys of fire up the slope.

The two armies slammed away at each other north of Leuthen, two great human barriers separated by a roiling bank of smoke. The hour had slipped past four and the light was dimming. And then, off on the far west of the Austrian line, came the low rumble of thousands of hooves. The cavalry was coming.

MOVE AND COUNTERMOVE

To the north, the cavalry that had originally been part of the far northern wing of the Austrian army that morning was making its way south toward the sound of the guns. When Frederick's army had opened its attack in oblique order around Sagschütz, these horsemen were south of Nippern, more than four miles (6.4 km) distant. Now, over two hours later, they were descending on the northwest shoulder of Leuthen in hopes of saving the Austrian army's floundering situation.

Their commander, General Count Joseph Lucchesi d'Averna, a courageous and aggressive cavalryman, now saw the Prussian guns flicking tongues of flame from the distant Butter-Berg in the south, while to the east the long, deep Prussian mass of infantry threatened to push the Austrian defenders off Windmill Hill as it crawled forward through the battle haze.

Riding along the front line of his cuirassiers and dragoons, he exhorted them into formation for a decisive move to the south. He now meant to lead them in a charge against the west flank of the Prussians, sweeping the exposed batteries off the Butter-Berg and savaging the infantry as it fought its way up the slopes of Windmill Hill.

They set off with a flourish at around four thirty, making their way at a slow trot in a counter-clockwise motion to put them in an ideal position to launch a charge into the Prussian flank. Lucchesi had his eye on the prize, carefully managing the mile (1.6 km)-wide front of his formation to ensure its order when it began picking up momentum for the coup de grace.

And then they came—Prussian horsemen, hundreds of them, riding hard from the west. They barreled into Lucchesi's right flank even as he was leading his men into the charge. These were the troopers of Lieutenant General Georg Wilhelm von Driesen, an aged, overweight campaigner who had been ordered to watch the far left wing of the oblique order attack. On this violent and auspicious day, they had sat their horses as spectators of the action until Driesen spotted

Lucchesi's squadrons coming down from the north. Now, fully rested, they took to the hunt with barbaric ferocity, pouncing on the stalking Austrians in a whirlwind of hacking, thrusting swordplay.

Lucchesi's head vanished from an errant cannon shot, sending his body tumbling lifelessly and his men into further disarray. By now the two cavalry formations had embraced in a whirling melee, the blades flashing in the fading sun to cleave and open ugly wounds. The stricken fell and the animals screamed as the fight edged closer to the Austrian infantry on Windmill Hill.

There the prince's last line of defense stood firm before the Prussians attacking out of Leuthen. The Austrian infantry, galvanized by the guttural thumping of their supporting artillery, were rediscovering their true ability by sending a succession of withering volleys into their blue-clad assailants.

Those on the west wing of the Austrian line, however, were having second thoughts as they watched the swift cavalry fight come their way like an approaching hurricane. Lucchesi's cavalry, leaderless and confused, began seeking the protection of Windmill Hill as the Prussians killed their way into them. The routing horsemen smashed into the line, infecting everyone on the ridge with panic. The Prussian infantry drove home the attack, striding up the slope and firing as they went. Now pressed from west and south, the Austrian position wavered and descended into chaos. Those who did not or could not run were ridden down by the Prussian horsemen, slaughtered with the bayonet, or taken captive. The Austrian army had collapsed.

FREDERICK'S GLORY

Darkness descended on the retreating Austrians. That evening, as snow flurries whirled in the torchlight, King Frederick attempted to organize a last effort to cut the enemy off from safety. But it came to nothing in the darkness, and the Austrians made good their escape.

The Battle of Leuthen was over. Of the nearly 65,000 men who fought that day in the name of Maria Theresa, more than 19,000 were dead, wounded, missing, or captured—some 12,000 of the empress's soldiers had become captives of her hated rival. The Prussians had lost around 6,500 dead and wounded, most of them suffered in the desperate fighting for Leuthen itself.

No engagement ever fought by Frederick the Great so perfectly manifested the attack in oblique order as the Battle of Leuthen. He had a handful of crucial assets, all based on his insistence on drill and preparation: confidence in his army's ability to maneuver quickly and efficiently, and, perhaps most importantly, the familiarity he and his officers had with the battlefield itself.

Prince Charles and his cosmopolitan army had shown up with several strikes against them, including weakness in heavy artillery and a lack of preparation, both owing to a conviction on their part that the campaigning season had come to a close and that Frederick would never risk so bold a stroke so late in the year.

They had been sorely mistaken, of course. But they had also compounded their error by deploying along a front too long for the sort of reaction to circumstances that they knew would be required in the event of a battle with the Prussians. Though initially adopted to make their position too long to outflank, the four-mile (6.4 km)-plus Austrian lines in fact had the opposite effect, inviting the infamously predatory Frederick to pounce on one wing confident in the knowledge that the rest of the Austrian army would be slow to come to the rescue.

The Prussians had another advantage: the fact that the man giving commands on the battlefield happened to be their sovereign. Like Charles XII of Sweden, Frederick II viewed it as his obligation to personally lead the army. Though this exposed him to danger, it also electrified his troops with the knowledge that their orders carried not only an undisputed gravitas but also the weight of a monarch's larger view—their orders weren't just battlefield commands, but state policy.

Unfortunately for Prussia, Frederick's approach to grand strategy wasn't nearly as supple or effective as his operational leadership. The Seven Years' War would nearly shatter the proud military machine Frederick had built—hardly surprising given the fact that he was taking on France, Austria, and Russia with only sporadic support from his British ally. His legacy as one of Europe's most successful enlightened despots is assured; nevertheless, his role as warlord whose costly campaigns served mostly to depopulate his little kingdom has endured tenaciously, tainting his achievements.

CHAPTER 10

AUERSTADT
1806

FRANCE'S IRON MARSHAL AVENGES
THE DISASTER OF ROSSBACH

27,000 FRENCH VERSUS 50,000 PRUSSIANS

UNDER MARSHAL DAVOUT'S GUIDANCE, THE INFANTRY regiments formed themselves into squares with artillery at the corners. Then they braced themselves for the onslaught. The morning fog had lifted on October 14, 1806, affording the Marshal and his fellow Frenchmen an excellent view of the Prussian cavalry galloping toward them with murderous intent. Brandishing their broadswords, the tall white plumes of their hats jouncing to the rhythm of the horses, the oncoming Prussians made the earth tremble. Then they broke upon the French squares in a slashing melee, many of the horses veering off to avoid the forest of bayonets leveled to greet them.

Rolling back to regroup, the Prussian cavalry paused briefly then came on again in thundering splendor. Once again they smashed into Davout's infantry squares, many of the riders plunging into the ground as their steeds died beneath them from volleys of shot. The momentum of their charge was terrifying—a force on pounding hooves that promised a dreadful reckoning to all who failed to stand firm before it.

It took grit to defy such horsemen, but these were the infantrymen of Napoleon Bonaparte's Third Corps. They were led by Louis-Nicolas Davout, one of Napoleon's toughest, most reliable marshals. And this—the Battle of Auerstadt—was to be his finest hour.

THE EMPEROR AND HIS MARSHAL

A native-Corsican-turned-French patriot, Napoleon Bonaparte was certainly brilliant. Yet, his vision also unleashed violence that ended up bleeding Europe white. He may have been a forward-thinking product of the Enlightenment, an ingenious political and social innovator who altered civilization; but of all the reasons why the man's name still holds such resonance two centuries later, the majority of them are of military significance.

One of these is the fact that the emperor typically excelled at getting more than enough troops to the point of collision with enemy armies to deliver a decisive defeat. Quick maneuver, superior organization, and outstanding generalship usually ensured that he could bring to the field everything he needed to achieve victory before the shooting even began.

One of the most famous victories of his Grande Armée, however, occurred *without* these circumstances, on a battlefield on which the French found themselves drastically and surprisingly outnumbered. What's more, the emperor wasn't even there, his miscalculation having delegated to one of his chief lieutenants the onerous task of surviving.

The man in question was Louis-Nicolas Davout, and he did a lot more than survive. At Auerstadt, Davout—familiar to his men as "the Iron Marshal"—trounced a much larger Prussian army, achieving one of the most astounding feats of the Napoleonic era.

A EUROPE IN TURMOIL

After becoming sole de facto ruler of the French Republic in 1799, Napoleon spearheaded a series of stunning campaigns against the nation's enemies that resulted in peace by 1802. Having failed to destroy France and the contagion of revolution it had spawned, the great powers and their monarchies now had to accept the reality of a powerful French state with puppet governments in the Netherlands, Switzerland, and northern Italy.

Accept it they did, but not for long. Britain in particular watched with growing concern as "First Consul" Napoleon crowned himself emperor in 1804.

A resumption of hostilities proved inevitable, and just a year after concluding the Peace of Amiens with Napoleon, the British declared war on him. Britain's strengths lay in her industrial vigor, matchless navy, and commercial empire. Her army, however, though well trained, was too small and dispersed across the Crown's overseas possessions to pose any real threat to the nemesis across the Channel. Reality forced an indirect approach: London was happy to open its coffers to anyone willing to attack France on the continent while the Royal Navy bottled up French shipping in the ports.

This was the strategy behind the so-called Third Coalition (the first two having been formed in opposition to Revolutionary France during the 1790s), an alliance of Britain, Austria, Russia, Sweden, and certain German states. Britain's effort to cobble together an effective alliance was aided greatly by Napoleon himself in 1805 when he crowned himself king of Italy. Properly scandalized, Austria and Russia drew their swords and prepared to crush the Corsican upstart.

They failed spectacularly. Striking swiftly, the emperor defeated his enemies in a series of bold military lunges deep into Europe that climaxed in 1805 at Austerlitz, where a combined Austrian and Russian army met catastrophic defeat in what is now the Czech Republic.

But Napoleon exploited his success with characteristic ambition, verily redrawing the map of Europe in the wake of Austria's humiliation and Russia's withdrawal. Looking east at the wheezing Holy Roman Empire, he saw need of consolidation. He therefore replaced its labyrinthine patchwork of polities with sixteen states (ultimately joined by nineteen more) and called it the Confederation of the Rhine. He even elevated his principal allies, Bavaria and Württemberg, to the status of kingdoms for good measure.

This was too much for Prussia, a great power in her own right who considered German affairs her bailiwick. As a rival of Austria's, Prussia was happy to remain neutral during the War of the Third Coalition. Now, however, Berlin bristled at France's temerity. Napoleon, still at war with Britain, urged the Prussians to join him against her. He also demanded that Berlin give up many of its possessions in southern and western Germany in exchange for Hanover—a state still claimed by the British.

THE QUIET HERO: DAVOUT, UNQUESTIONABLY ONE OF NAPOLEON'S FINEST MARSHALS, EARNED THE EMPEROR'S JEALOUSY AFTER HIS BRILLIANT PERFORMANCE AT AUERSTADT.

Getty Images

London cast a suspicious eye toward Berlin even as the other great powers retreated from Austerlitz to lick their wounds. The Prussians stalled for time, sensing that the moment had arrived to mobilize. Only the Kingdom of Saxony seemed ready to join the fray. Other states remained in the anti-French Coalition, but none—except Britain—in a state of actual war. Prussia was virtually alone.

It did not matter. Though having been bested in the scrum of Napoleonic diplomacy, the Prussians were not keen to back down. Since the glory days of Frederick the Great, whose victory at Rossbach in 1757 left a wound on French pride that had yet to heal, Prussia had cultivated an image as the premier military power of Europe. Pride now dictated that she prove it—and teach the "Little Corporal" a lesson he would never forget.

WIELDING A REVOLUTION

Prussian King Frederick William III's choice of war took nerve, for he was taking on the continent's premier military. To defeat the combined forces arrayed against it in the previous decade, Revolutionary France had ruthlessly introduced a *levée en masse*—an expression, in effect, of the state's right to mass conscription in exchange for the privileges of citizenship. These drastic policies paved the way for Napoleon's reforms, which further redefined France's ability to transform potential assets into real military power.

Moreover, the army itself had changed. Borrowing on earlier ideas, Napoleon organized the men into Army Corps, each of which incorporated infantry, artillery, and cavalry into miniature armies. The effect of this innovation on the very nature of campaigning was profound.

Because armies moved only as fast as their infantry, finding and fixing the enemy for battle was always difficult. Your enemy could move as quickly as you could, leading you on a wild goose chase. You could send out cavalry reconnaissance to locate the enemy; but by the time your scouts returned to the main body, the information they carried was already old. All of these factors helped to make war in the eighteenth century of a limited nature, forcing even the best commanders into a game of maneuver.

Napoleon's corps offered a simple and ingenious solution. As they moved through the countryside, these self-contained, combined-arms units represented the dispersion of the Grande Armée for the purpose of engaging the enemy rapidly.

Though scattered to cover as much territory as possible, they also remained just close enough for mutual support. Should any one of them make contact, it could *fix* the enemy army in place with a general engagement and hold out, even if outnumbered, while the others raced to deliver a decisive blow. The system allowed Napoleon to accelerate the pace of war—to find his quarry quickly and attack with the goal of destroying it and forcing peace in a matter of weeks rather than years.

What's more, the individual corps developed traditional bonds of loyalty and camaraderie, fusing horsemen, musketeers, and gunners into a cohesive unit, typically around 30,000 strong, accustomed to taking orders from a single corps commander. Their responses were consequently much quicker, affording faster reactions and greater maneuverability than a traditional force, whose commander was constrained to issue separate orders to different types of combatants to get them where they needed to be.

Though innovators such as Frederick the Great had thought along similar lines, what made Napoleon's corps-based battle plan work was France's immense population and the enlightened institutions put in place to exploit it fully, such as the schools and universities that favored ability over wealth or station. The emperor had a truly large military machine at his disposal.

By October 8, 1806, the finest elements of this army were concentrated in central Germany. Napoleon's forces had been strewn throughout central Europe since the campaigning around Austerlitz. Now, after canceling his previous order to send them home, he massed them for a lunge toward Saxony, where Prussian forces had been gathering.

Three roughly parallel roads led northeast out of Bavaria toward the northeast, each of which now carried a portion of Napoleon's punitive expedition—two corps on each avenue, almost 130,000 men in all, snaking forward behind a screen of probing cavalry. The fate of Prussia had been set in motion.

AN ARMY LIVING IN THE PAST

Frederick the Great put the finishing touches on a military tradition that, stretching back generations, had made a great state out of mediocre material. And though his win–loss record was somewhat ordinary by the end of his life, he was something of a legend in Prussia and the rest of Europe.

Nobody, it seemed, believed this myth more sincerely than the Prussians themselves, who now meant to defend their nation of 10 million subjects against the 35 million citizens of France. Though less significant in the military calculations of a generation ago, this demographic disparity now spoke volumes—as did Berlin's willingness to risk war rather than face humiliation.

Like all the great nations of Europe, Prussia had attentively watched the developments unfolding under Napoleon's regime and made note of their efficacy. She had even incorporated the new corps into her military hierarchy, developing divisions that were charged, broadly speaking, with the same mission.

But rather than creating a fluid structure for the cooperation of all arms, the jury-rigged Prussian response to Napoleonic ideas effectively placed dribs and drabs of cavalry and artillery under infantry officers who had little appreciation of how to use them correctly. Old habits die hard and, though reassigned and organized along fresh lines, Prussian officers were not trained in the new methods.

The French, after all, had had more than a decade of constant warfare to create their new military, and had staffed it not with members of the old privileged caste but with men who had proven their worth in battle. Prussia had neither the hard experience of recent operations nor the willingness to replace the traditional bonds of aristocracy with a meritocracy—an idea against which, it can be argued, they were now going to war.

Nevertheless, Frederick William III was confident, and not without reason. His army was large and well trained in its way. Constant drilling in the Frederickan tradition had made it disciplined and capable of linear tactics that delivered devastating fire in ideal conditions, even if the men and officers lacked the flexibility and innovative spirit that pervaded the Grande Armée.

The army's commanders, however, were another matter. Duke Charles of Brunswick was senior, an intimate of the court in Berlin whose greatest asset seems to have been the fact that he was a nephew of Frederick the Great. Prince Hohenlohe, an aged veteran, brought long experience and little else to his role as general of infantry. And then there was General Ernst von Rüchel, a capable leader and drill-master. Each of these men would wield independent command in the coming campaign, with Brunswick heading up the main army and traveling with the king and queen and much of their court. To Hohenlohe went a smaller army, while von Rüchel commanded an independent corps.

Unfortunately, the sclerotic system within which they were expected to cooperate on a plan emphasized debate between experts rather than action by leaders. While ultimate command resided with the king, he left the details to his principal professionals, whose responsibility it was to formulate strategy by committee. Of the two highest-ranking officers, the Duke of Brunswick, though senior, lacked the official authority to dictate policy outright, while Hohenlohe made a habit of gainsaying virtually everything that came out of his colleague's mouth. Meetings ended in stalemate, the king failed to intervene decisively, and time slipped away as first one plan, then another, were considered and shot down. By the time a strategy was in place, Napoleon—who labored under no such command paralysis—had forced them into a defensive posture.

On October 9, forward elements of both armies had a scuffle near Schleiz, in Saxony, just a day's march from Auerstadt. The following day, at the Battle of Saalfeld, the French V Corps defeated a smaller Prussian and Saxon force and killed Prince Louis Ferdinand, a nephew of Frederick the Great, a composer, and one of the kingdom's most popular young officers. The prince, one of the keenest supporters of war with France, was dearly missed.

It wasn't long before many more of his countrymen were joining him.

CLOSING THE TRAP

There were in fact two battles on October 14, 1806, which is why the conflict—one of the most pivotal of the Napoleonic era—is referred to with a hyphen: Jena-Auerstadt. Having assumed control over events from his dilatory Prussian adversaries, Napoleon moved north with his corps planning, as always, to meet the enemy and destroy as much of his strength as possible in one major clash.

In the days leading up to the battle, the Prussians and Saxons, smarting from their punishment at Saalfeld, attempted to maneuver themselves in such a way as to receive a French attack under favorable conditions while keeping the way north open for a withdrawal. Napoleon, meanwhile, pressed north with his corps while seeking out the enemy. By October 13, Davout, leading the charge, had captured Naumburg, putting his III Corps to the northeast of the whole Prussian army, threatening its escape route. Meanwhile, some twelve miles (19 km) to the southwest, the rest of the Grande Armée began converging on Jena, where the V Corps had made contact with elements of Prince Hohenlohe's army.

That night, messengers raced through both armies, setting in motion the events that would conspire to make the following day's actions both ferocious and peculiar. As King Frederick William III saw it, Davout's capture of the crucial crossroads at Naumburg had precipitated a crisis. Eager to keep his lines of communication open and link up with strategic reserves in Prussia, the king insisted on leading the main army under Brunswick on a race to cross the Unstrutt River to the northeast before Davout could bar the way and complete an encirclement by the French. To ensure the success of this redeployment, Hohenlohe, supported by Rüchel's corps, would need to hold the line at Jena to protect the retreat.

To Napoleon, the situation that was developing at Jena seemed like the opportunity he was waiting for. The V Corps of Marshal Jean Lannes now held a portion of the enemy in a deadly embrace, the two forces camping that night in close proximity after exchanging preliminary blows. Now all he had to do was concentrate the other corps on this spot to deliver the killing thrust: Marshals Michel Ney and Nicolas Soult from the east, Pierre Augereau from the south, and Jean-Baptiste Bernadotte from the north. As for Davout up in Naumburg, he was instructed to march west via Kosen, which would bring him in a position behind the Prussian rear, whence he could strike south—ideally in concert with Bernadotte—to hammer the enemy against the anvil of the rest of the Grande Armée.

FREDERICK WILLIAM III, KING OF PRUSSIA (1787-1861). HIS CONFIDENCE IN HIS ARMY LAY IN ITS LARGE SIZE AND CONSTANT DRILLING IN THE FREDERICKAN TRADITION.

The Wellington Museum, London, UK / The Bridgeman Art Library International

At Jena, Napoleon was able to deploy his army much as he had intended, ultimately precipitating a general engagement that, from early morning until three o'clock that afternoon, raged thunderously on both flanks as well as in the center. Funneling four of his corps into the fight that day, the emperor achieved a significant supremacy of men and firepower, overwhelming the forces of Prince Hohenlohe. Two of his corps, however, failed to arrive. The I Corps dithered uselessly to the north, precipitating a controversy that shadowed its commander Bernadotte. The other, of course, was Davout's III Corps, some 27,000 strong.

So furious had the fighting been that day that Napoleon, even after victory in the mid-afternoon, was convinced that he had faced and routed the whole Prussian army. He had no idea that only Hohenlohe's force had faced him, protecting the withdrawal of the king with the main army to the north. That army—some 50,000 strong, with the kingdom's finest troops—had begun its march toward the Unstrutt, but didn't get far before running smack-dab into the Iron Marshall and the III Corps.

INTO THE DAWN

Louis-Nicolas Davout (or d'Avot, or Davoust) first met Napoleon in 1798. The two officers grew to respect each other's abilities through the political and military maelstrom of the Revolution, forming a relationship cemented by Davout's marriage to a relative of the future emperor in 1801. He said little and did much, becoming the youngest of Napoleon's marshals at just thirty-four years of age—two years before his momentous hour at Auerstadt. Balding and shortsighted, intense and brooding, he had few friends. For his strict drill instruction and battlefield cunning, however, he acquired many admirers. He was a paradigm of the sort of military talent that the French Revolution seemed to produce in profusion.

The marshal received his orders at around three in the morning and had his troops up and moving within an hour. Napoleon's instructions, impelling Davout to engage the Prussian rear, were somewhat vague and the marshal had no clear idea of what lay in front of him. If the emperor had the whole enemy army engaged at Jena, as his orders implied, then what precisely had the Prussians left in their rear, if anything?

He had three divisions at his disposal, one of which, commanded by General Charles-Etienne Gudin, led the way west out of Naumburg. Fog was heavy and Gudin's forward elements passed cautiously through the village of Hassenhausen without encountering anything. Davout, riding with Gudin, received word from one of his aides de camp that the Prussians were approaching ahead from the direction of Auerstadt, and the marshal had his divisional commander start deploying troops on either side of the road.

Suddenly, appearing out of the swirling mist, squadrons of galloping Prussian horsemen descended on the lines north of the road. These were the cavalry of Marshal Prince Gebhard Leberecht von Blücher, whose dragoons drew grapeshot from the French guns even as they drove Gudin's infantry into "squares"—quadrangular formations of bayonet-bristling soldiers intended to defy the approach of cavalry from any quarter.

Blücher's squadrons knew better than to test these human bastions, and veered off in search of reinforcements. The fog persisted, cloistering the anxious soldiers and turning their noise into a reverberating racket. Neither side understood the other's strength and, in the confusion, Blücher lost a battery to a force of French infantry.

By the time Blücher had reinforced his vanguard with cavalry from General von Schmettau's division, which had been forming up for attack outside of Auerstadt to the southwest, the fog had begun to lift, revealing the French positions before him to the west of Hassenhausen. Blücher rode round what appeared to be the French right, then charged, smashing into the blue-coated squares. Davout himself, forced into the center of one of his squares, watched as the gallant Prussians came galloping on, only to recoil and come on again. Blücher, his horse having been shot from under him, retired to the north in some disorder.

Nevertheless, his attack had given Schmettau time to bring his division up, which now deployed around a village called Taugwitz, just down the road from Hassenhausen. Under the personal direction of the Duke of Brunswick, the division—nearly 8,000 strong, with supporting cavalry and artillery batteries—threw skirmishers forward on either side of the road and, around nine o'clock, prepared to move. By nine thirty, they had been joined by the division of Wartensleben on the right, who would approach Hassenhausen on a southerly route. The two divisions now went forward, Schmettau advancing along the road and Wartensleben moving off on the Prussian right, his men concealed by the rolling terrain.

Meanwhile, Gudin's outnumbered division (the general had just 6,500 men engaged before Hassenhausen) was reinforced by another of Davout's divisions, that of General Louis Friant, who deployed his men to the north of Gudin. There, occupying the village of Spielberg, Friant's men extended the French right wing to oppose any attempts by the Prussians to make a dash for the Unstrutt.

The fracas in the fog had now erupted into a general engagement, with each army funneling divisions into the fight in the hopes of finding a weakness somewhere in the other's deployments. While each had managed to get two divisions into line, however, Davout was running out of men.

The Prussians, by contrast, were just getting started.

FATE OF THE DUKE

Southwest of Hassenhausen, the 85 Brigade of Gudin's division stood alone, unaware that their position represented the convergence of the two Prussian divisions that were even then preparing to sweep the village. Sometime after nine thirty they looked west and saw a line of grenadiers bearing down on them,

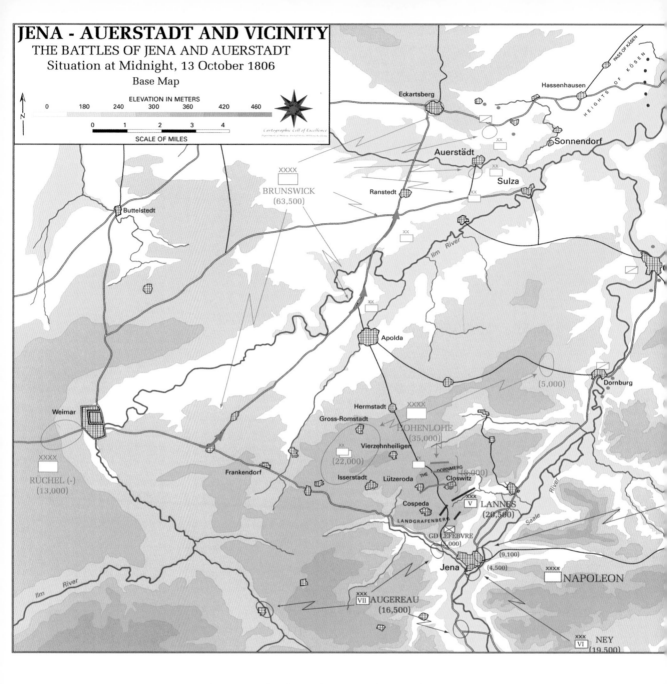

marching in perfect linear formation, their tall bearskin caps making them seem
like giants. Presently this formation, a battalion of heavy infantry belonging to
Schmettau's division, halted, leveled their weapons, and erupted in flashing musketry. This was the close-order firepower that Prussian tactics had emphasized
since Frederick the Great, and the grenadiers poured it on.

The 85th stood firm, returning fire even as many of them toppled in the squalls
of flying lead. Then, at around ten o'clock, it saw a dreadful sight to its left: ranks and

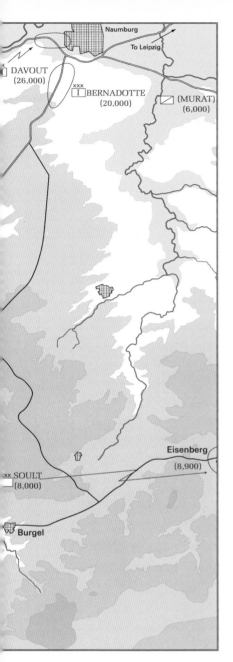

ranks of infantry with accompanying cavalry massing on the plateau stretching off to the south. This was Wartensleben's division, whose arrival came as a complete surprise to the French. Moments later, as the 85th struggled to redeploy while taking fire from the Prussian grenadiers, Wartensleben sent squadrons of dragoons galloping down on them. Seeing their comrades charging from the south, the Prussian grenadiers advanced, pressing home their attack. The 85th broke.

Wartensleben's appearance had come as a shock to Davout, who now saw his soldiers streaming back through Hassenhausen in search of safety. As they reformed themselves behind the village, Davout sent troops from other units into the streets to stop the advancing Prussians, their counterattack supported by 12-pounders. Soon much of Hassenhausen was back in French hands.

The front now settled between the two sides, with Gudin's division anchored in the village and utilizing its cover to counter the two enemy divisions that now riddled its houses and swept its lanes with musketry and grapeshot. To the north, Friant's division skirmished its way south from Spielberg.

Having pushed the French back down the Taugwitz Road, Schmettau's men pressed Hassenhausen from the west while Wartensleben's fought their way north. Soon the Prussians brought up their own 12-pounders and started thundering away. The village began to blow apart beneath a cloud of slivers and masonry.

Though the Prussian king was present in the rear, the Duke of Brunswick was the commander in charge on the royal behest. Looking out on the burning tableau of Hassenhausen, he resolved to take it with a final push of elite infantry, and began issuing orders to the Haustein battalion of grenadiers.

THE REGION OF JENA-AUERSTADT. DAVOUT, ADVANCING FROM THE NORTH, THOUGHT HE WAS CLOSING A TRAP SET BY HIS EMPEROR NEAR JENA. INSTEAD, HE RAN INTO THE BULK OF THE PRUSSIAN ARMY ON HIS OWN.

United States Military Academy

Suddenly a ball struck him full in the face, knocking him from his horse. It was a mortal wound, and he was hurried to the rear. The timing was terrible for the Prussians. To the south, the Duke had been concentrating cavalry, culling them from various units and assigning them to Blücher for a decisive strike, while in the center the Prince of Orange was bringing up his division. Together, these assets represented everything the Prussians needed to crush the hard-pressed corps before them, whose soldiers could be seen clinging to cover in the disintegrating village beneath a hailstorm of incoming ordnance. Now, just as everything was coming together, the Prussians had lost their commander.

At this moment, which was between ten thirty and eleven, the panicked Prussian command staff couldn't know that Davout had his own moment of crisis.

CAN HASSENHAUSEN HOLD?

By late morning, Marshal Davout must have begun to doubt his emperor's conclusion that the bulk of the Prussian army was at Jena. As he looked out to the west and south, all he could see were ranks of Prussians filling the countryside and pouring a deafening rumble of firepower on his men. Though Friant was off on the far right and had yet to engage the enemy fully, Gudin's division was using the broken landscape of Hassenhausen to maximum effect, repulsing a series of assaults from the vantage of crumbled houses and garden walls. Still, these men could not be expected to hang on forever. What Davout needed was his third division, commanded by Charles Antoine Morand, who had been ordered forward early that morning but had yet to arrive.

Then, as if in answer to his thoughts, Morand's brigades appeared on the Naumburg Road, and not a moment too soon. Davout ordered them into the French left, south of the cratered village and opposite Wartensleben's division. With impressive celerity, Morand's men swept in an arc southeast of Hassenhausen, their broad lines making a tide of blue, white, and red.

The Prussians, though reeling from the vacuum in command that came after Brunswick's wounding, were hardly beaten. To the south, Blücher's massed cavalry saw Morand's division coming on and saw their opportunity.

The horsemen charged. First in were Blücher's hussars, resplendent in red uniforms and tall black caps, their curved swords flashing silver in the midday sun. Prince William of Orange, the future William I of the Netherlands, led them personally.

Morand's men, fresh but for the forced march that had brought them to this momentous place and time, formed squares at the double quick, each sporting cannon at their corners like turrets of a redoubt. As the rumbling red wave approached, the French held their fire...and held their fire...until, with the hussars nearly upon them, they heard the hoarse cry to fire and let fly with devastating force, shattering the charge in a hell of smoke and screaming horses.

Down went the Prince of Orange, soon to be picked up and carried to the rear. The countryside crawled with red-jacketed wounded. But the Prussians weren't done, and proceeded to roll their cavalry forward—heavy cuirassiers, proud dragoons, and more swift-riding hussars—only to break on the walls of Morand's squares in assault after assault. South of Hassenhausen, across the rolling landscape stretching away before them, the French soldiers in their squares looked out on a writhing carpet of suffering men and mounts.

Subtly but unequivocally, the initiative had changed hands. Davout, like all good Napoleonic commanders, was gifted in sensing the moment of truth in a battle. He had been on the defensive all morning, holding his own by using the terrain and getting his men into line as efficiently as possible. The job up until then had been obvious: hold on and injure the Prussians as much as possible in the melees that raged up and down the line. Now the enemy was tiring from his exertions, gradually surrendering control over events to the French. It was showing something almost imperceptible—hesitation, indecision, doubt. It was time to strike, and Davout knew it.

NAPOLEON'S EMBARRASSMENT

The Duke of Brunswick was in dying agony and the Prince of Orange had been shot from his horse. Moreover, Schmettau had been badly wounded, as had Wedell, one of Wartensleben's most important brigade commanders. The Prussian command structure had literally been shot full of holes.

More importantly, perhaps, the Prussians had shot their bolt. Blücher's cavalry was blown, the carnage before Hassenhausen—where Prussian infantry in open terrain exchanged blows with French troops in broken cover—had become ghastly, and a lack of direction now defined the army's command structure that only the king could possibly reverse. But before he could do so, the Iron Marshal acted.

Davout gave the order for his divisions to advance. With Friant's men coming down from the north, Gudin advancing out of the ruins of Hassenhausen, and Morand's division scooping up the crumbling enemy resistance to the south, the Prussians could do little but attempt to react defiantly. In a fighting withdrawal, they gave up first Taugwitz, then Poppel, then began falling back on Auerstadt, whence they had begun the day's marching before sunup and whose houses soon burned. Worst of all, the confusion of retreat swamped the already hobbled command structure, preventing the king from effectively drawing on his reserves, which, in comparison to his enemy, were considerable. The Prussian situation devolved into a dispirited, panicked exodus away from the French.

Their losses were catastrophic. In addition to casualties estimated at nearly 15,000, the Prussians lost 150 guns to enemy capture. The French suffered around 7,000 killed and wounded at Auerstadt.

French professionalism had won the day, but not completely. The Prussian tactical system, as dependent on rigid hierarchy as its strategic staff was on diffuse collaboration, began to break down after the Duke of Brunswick's mortal wounding. Moreover, the clumsy deployment of Prussian troops throughout the battle had contributed to defeat. For instance, Brunswick's plan to concentrate cavalry to the south of Hassenhausen had created tremendous logistical challenges in the rear as squadrons from numerous units attempted to make their way over to Blücher, crowding the roads as the Prince of Orange endeavored to bring his badly needed division to the front.

Worst of all, the Prussian lethargy had hampered attempts to get more men into the fight than the French, perhaps the only way that they were going to win this battle. The final analysis is striking: At almost no point in the battle did the Prussians, despite their clear numerical superiority, have more muskets firing on the enemy than the French. Indeed, the whole Prussian "reserve" of two divisions failed even to make it close to the front owing to profound inefficiencies and confusion in the Prussian high command.

These factors proved overwhelming when added to the ability of Davout, whose composed reaction to events personified the sort of cool, efficient performance that earned Napoleon's attention. Davout's men were better trained, more eager to endure the punishments brought by their commander's orders, and less likely to break under adverse circumstances. They proved it at Auerstadt.

For the Prussians, the impact of the double disaster at Jena-Auerstadt was overwhelming. Having completely defeated the enemy army in two simultaneous collisions, Napoleon chased the shattered Prussians right into their own kingdom, commencing a complete collapse of Prussian fortunes that resulted in their capitulation. It also shattered the myth of Prussian invulnerability for the first time since Frederick the Great.

Interestingly, Napoleon refused to admit that his marshal had defeated the bulk of the Prussian army. In response to a report from Davout in the midst of the battle that expounded the immense enemy strength before him, the emperor retorted, "Tell your Marshal he is seeing double." As Davout's eyesight was notoriously bad, this was intended as an extra insult. Even after October 14, when the facts of the day's events were clearer, Napoleon reacted more with suspicion than with admiration. After all, he had in Davout a gifted rival.

Nevertheless, Davout was made Duke of Auerstadt in remembrance of his outstanding achievement that October morning when he had faced the wrath of Prussia and refused to blink.

CHAPTER 11

CHANCELLORSVILLE
1863

HOOKER CAME, HE SAW,
HE GOT CONQUERED

133,500 FEDERALS VERSUS 60,000 CONFEDERATES

IN JANUARY 1863, ABRAHAM LINCOLN WAS PRESIDENT OF a nation that had been at war with itself since the first April of his administration almost two years earlier. Eleven southern states, in open rebellion over the issue of states' rights that had become a casus belli in the nation's ideological divide over slavery, had formed a Confederacy whose armies thwarted the president's attempts at bringing them back into the Union by force. Lincoln had no shortage of matters requiring his urgent attention, from a burgeoning anti-war movement in his own backyard to the overt pro-Confederate sympathies of Europe's great powers. And yet the gravest choice he needed to make involved the selection of a single man.

The war wasn't yet half over and already four men had tried their hand at commanding the eastern armies of the Union, all in varying degrees of failure: Irvin McDowell, George McClellan, John Pope, and Ambrose Burnside. The last—a likeable West Point graduate who had invented an excellent carbine rifle and whose fantastic whisker-appendages gave birth to the word *sideburns*—had just the previous month attacked Robert E. Lee's Army of Northern Virginia at Fredericksburg and suffered a defeat so resounding and gory that he had contemplated personally leading a charge at the enemy ranks as the final act not only of the battle but of his life. Before long he got the sack, too.

The most vocal critic of Burnside was a Massachusetts-born corps commander named Joseph Hooker. Fond of drink and late-night card games, he cultivated an atmosphere at his headquarters that some officers compared to a bar and a brothel. He spoke badly of Burnside, especially after Fredericksburg (and often with whiskey on his breath), making waves that went all the way to the White House. The president took notice not merely because he thought it bad form for a corps commander in the Army of the Potomac to heap derision on his superiors, but also because, in spite of this, Lincoln had pegged him as the next candidate to lead the effort against Robert E. Lee.

A man of considerable drive and resourcefulness, Hooker went on to do much for the Army of the Potomac, including reinvesting it with the confidence and élan that so many defeats had wiped out. Interestingly, he would also lead it to one of its greatest, most ignominious defeats—a battle that would all but finish Joseph Hooker's reputation and elevate those of his Confederate enemies to legendary status.

LEAN AND MEAN

At the beginning of the Civil War, Robert E. Lee was courted by Washington to lead the Union armies. A son of Revolutionary War hero "Light Horse Harry" Lee and a top graduate of West Point, he was widely regarded as one of the finest officers in the U.S. military. He turned down the offer to lead Union troops, citing his allegiance to his beloved Virginia—the very state whose countryside would become the principal battleground over which the fate of the eastern theater would be decided in one bloody clash after another.

Lee went with the Confederacy and, in June 1862, assumed command over the South's principal army in the east, the Army of Northern Virginia. In this crucial role that would win him so many laurels, he established a distinctive modus operandi. Given the colossal disparity in manpower and resources between the North and his own hard-pressed South, Lee developed a preference for closing quickly and aggressively with the enemy and a willingness to overcome his army's long odds by gambling, even if that sometimes meant, ironically, incurring losses the South could ill afford.

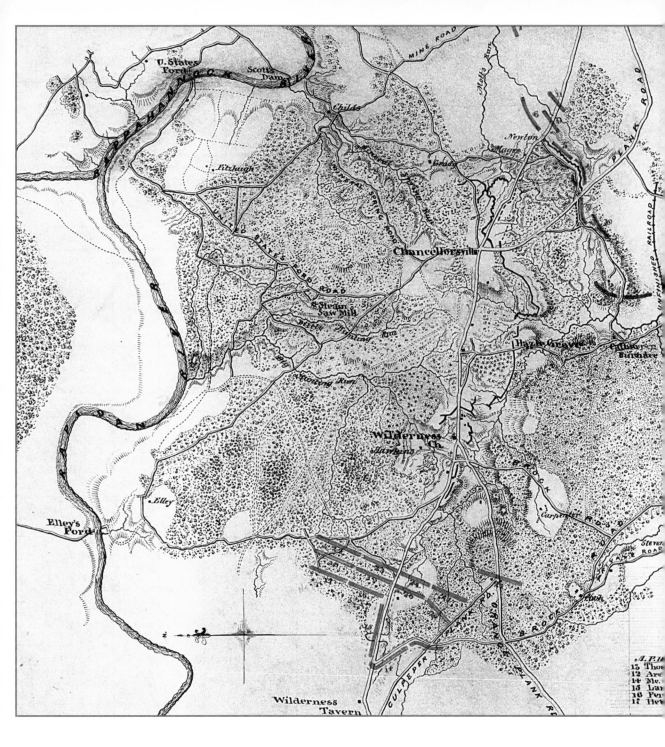

Indeed, warfare had become more destructive. For the first time in history, industrialization was shaping the face and nature of war. Mass production, railroads, and advances in weapons technology and metallurgy all conspired to lend a grinding ferocity to military campaigns. In 1849, a French Army captain named

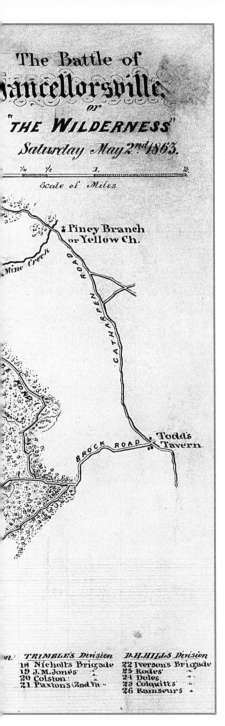

Claude-Etienne Minié patented a new cone-shaped bullet, with grooves running around its base that, when fired, expanded to fit the rifling of a gun barrel. The result was an easier-loading round with greater range and accuracy, which made muskets—most of which were now rifled rather than smoothbore—much deadlier.

Despite these developments, Civil War armies adhered to Napoleonic tactics whose origins lay in the age of smoothbore muskets. Advancing in serried ranks like their predecessors over a generation earlier, they loosed volleys at each other that were at least an order of magnitude more devastating for their long range and precision. Whole regiments fell under such devastating fire, shocking the United States—and the world—with unprecedented casualty rates.

Now, as both armies awaited the spring thaw of 1863, Lee had difficulty envisioning anything ambitious. The calculus of war was brutally simple: 1862 had been a year of violent clashes, and though Lee had won almost all of them, the casualties suffered were felt dearly in the South. Despite his preference for the offensive, he would have to remain on the receiving end of things.

"ONLY THOSE GENERALS WHO GAIN SUCCESSES CAN SET UP DICTATORS"

During McClellan's drive up the peninsula toward Richmond in the spring of 1862, a New York newspaper received a dispatch regarding action in which Joe Hooker's division had participated entitled "Fighting—Joe Hooker." When the dash was accidentally dropped in print, the division commander found himself, by way of pure accident, the owner of a *nom de guerre*.

A MAP OF THE BATTLE OF CHANCELLORSVILLE, SHOWING UNION TROOP DEPLOYMENTS NORTHWEST OF CHANCELLORSVILLE AND THE ARMY OF NORTHERN VIRGINIA SOUTH OF THE WILDERNESS. A PARTIAL LISTING OF CONFEDERATE DIVISIONS SITS AT THE LOWER RIGHT OF THE MAP; THE REMAINING TROOP DIVISION LABELS ARE MISSING.

Library of Congress

"Fighting Joe" stuck. Lee, for one, never liked it, referring to his new opponent as "Mr. F. J. Hooker." But he wasn't the only one. Hooker himself thought the moniker made him sound like some impulsive pugilist. He was a leader, not a scrapper. At least that's what he wanted people to believe—especially the president.

Lincoln wasn't so sure, but he promoted the general anyway, making it official on January 26. He soon found cause to be pleased with his decision. Fighting Joe immediately set out to remake a demoralized army that had become too accustomed to defeat, retraining it from the ground up. Lincoln liked what he saw of Hooker the commander, but could not rid himself of lingering doubts about Hooker the man. Just two days after the general had assumed command over the Army of the Potomac, Lincoln handed him a letter that offered ambivalent observations on the awkward relationship they were about to embark upon. Fighting Joe's past remarks, known to everyone in the country who could read a newspaper, were chief among the president's concerns.

JOSEPH HOOKER'S BUMPTIOUS REMARKS AND STEELY GAZE WERE POOR SUBSTITUTES FOR BOLD COMMAND AT CHANCELLORSVILLE.

"I have heard," Lincoln wrote, "in such way as to believe it, of your recently saying that both the army and the government needed a dictator. Of course it was not for this, but in spite of it, that I have given you the command." Lincoln's sense of humor was in fine form. "Only those generals who gain successes can set up dictators. What I now ask of you is military success, and I will risk the dictatorship."

The campaign Hooker ultimately planned for spring was like no other since the war began. In fact, it smacked of brilliance. Since the Battle of Fredericksburg the previous December, the two armies had been staring at each other over the expanse of the Rappahannock—the Rebels behind and around Fredericksburg, and the Yankees entrenched on Stafford Heights over on the northeast bank, their heavy rifled artillery frowning on the town across the river. Simply put, Hooker intended to leave half of his army in front of Fredericksburg to fix Lee's attention there while he moved the other half in a broad arc to the northwest and south, crossing both the Rappahannock and the Rapidan to appear in Lee's rear. If all went according to plan, by the time the Rebels knew what was happening, they would be sandwiched between two pincers, each of which either matched or out-numbered Lee's whole army.

"My plans are perfect," declared Hooker, "and when I start to carry them out, may God have mercy on Bobby Lee; for I shall have none."

SEVEN CORPS AND A TARGET

By the second year of the war, both sides in the American Civil War, taking their cue from Napoleonic precedent, were dividing their armies into corps—individual mini-armies composed of divisions and capable of bringing infantry and artillery to bear wherever they encountered the enemy. The South favored larger "wings" that performed the same function as corps, but on a grander scale. Lee would main-tain this pattern until the end of the war, dividing his army into two and, eventu-ally, three "corps" whose purpose was to maneuver strategically as self-contained agents of destruction in a grand choreography directed by Lee himself. The army's cavalry, concentrated into a division and later into a whole corps led by self-styled cavalier J. E. B. "Jeb" Stuart, operated independently as the eyes of the army and as a swift and potent raiding force.

The Northern corps, generally smaller than their Confederate counter-parts, were less like wings and more like building blocks to be used in fashioning a greater variety of formations in attack and defense. Consequently they were more numerous—Hooker, in fact, had seven at his disposal in spring 1863, commanded by Generals John Reynolds, Dan Sickles, George Meade, John Sedgwick, Henry Slocum, Darius Couch, and Oliver O. Howard.

He also had a large dedicated cavalry corps. More than 10,000 strong (com-pared to Stuart's 3,500), Major General George Stoneman's troopers were intended to spearhead Hooker's plan, galloping ahead of the infantry to get well into Rebel territory by the time the main forces arrived. Once there they would wreak havoc with Lee's supply lines and harass the expected Confederate retreat toward Richmond. Though ordered to preempt the infantry well in advance, bad weather held up Stoneman's progress. He ended up splashing across the Rappahannock on April 29, by which time all of Hooker's forces were in motion on both fronts.

Fanning out to the west, four of Hooker's corps forded the Rappahannock and Rapidan Rivers at various points. By April 30, they had created a long col-umn of Yankee strength on the far bank of the Rapidan like a snake coiling to

strike directly at the far western end of Lee's position. Meanwhile, elements of the I and VI Corps, under Reynolds and Sedgwick, respectively, had established a bridgehead south of Fredericksburg, hoping to keep Lee's focus in the east. The III Corps under Sickles remained beyond the Rappahannock as a reserve to reinforce whichever wing Hooker chose to deliver the knockout punch once he knew in which direction Lee was reacting.

On May 30, the four corps of Meade, Howard, Slocum, and Couch converged, per Hooker's orders, around the crossroads hamlet of Chancellorsville—an estate centered on a mansion owned by the Chancellor family that stood at the intersection of several local thoroughfares, some ten miles (16 km) due west of Fredericksburg. These forces, having achieved the long hook around Lee's rear that stood as the linchpin of Hooker's plan, were ebullient in their success, and for good reason: in only a few days they had stolen a long march on the enemy.

Unfortunately, these four corps also found themselves in the midst of a vast and forbidding bushland. As they made their way along the roads and tracks toward Chancellorsville, the Federal troops were struck by the verdant tangle that surrounded them in all directions. This was the so-called Wilderness—a countryside defined by old second-growth forests choked with undergrowth, through which only a few narrow tracks offered passage. It was no place to offer battle with superior numbers, and Hooker's generals hoped to press on and meet the enemy in the open farther east.

Not yet, urged Hooker. The commanding general meant to husband his strength before striking—now was not the time to drive home the killing thrust. The following day, May 1, he intended to bring Sickles's corps west, creating a five-corps haymaker to knock Bobby Lee senseless. But in the meantime, consolidation was the key—not attacking prematurely.

May 1 was to be Hooker's decisive day. In the east, Sedgwick and Reynolds were slated to attack out of their bridgehead south of Fredericksburg and watch for opportunities to exploit, while elements of Hooker's right wing around Chancellorsville—now formally charged with delivering the knockout punch—were to advance east in three columns. By two o'clock that afternoon, the heights of Fredericksburg would fall and Lee's army would be trapped or destroyed.

But that's not what happened.

LEE TAKES A CHANCE

If Joe Hooker's plan had a flaw, it involved Stoneman's cavalry. By throwing virtually all of his troopers into a raiding operation through the Virginia countryside, Hooker had denied himself an adequate set of eyes for the advance of his infantry corps. To perform scouting operations for his army in the Wilderness, the Union commander had retained a small force of horsemen who not only had to acquire intelligence on enemy movements but also tangle with Jeb Stuart.

That was a tall order. Since the beginning of the war, the Union had played catch-up in cavalry tactics in both the eastern and western theaters, primarily because so many of the army's great horsemen had gone with the Confederacy. There was also the South's proud equestrian tradition, cultivated by a planter class that cherished horsemanship.

Jeb Stuart personified these assets. Though possessed of an overweening ego and capacity for chivalrous theatrics that even his own men sometimes found irritating, Stuart was a bold, clever, and resourceful leader who knew his business. Moreover, unlike Stoneman, Stuart was still in the vicinity of Fredericksburg, ready to report to Lee on everything his wide-ranging troopers discovered about the enemy. And on April 29 and 30, he had plenty to report.

Outfought and outnumbered, the cavalry escorts of Hooker's great sweeping movement on the right were helpless to drive away Stuart as he prodded, spied upon, and occasionally raided the long blue columns that had come south of the Rapidan several miles from Lee's rear. Clearly this was more than a feint or

ROBERT E. LEE WAS A CONSUMMATE GAMBLER, AND CHANCELLORSVILLE WAS BOTH HIS GREATEST RISK AND GREATEST TRIUMPH.

a reconnaissance in force, as the information he brought back to Lee made clear. Could Hooker be trying a flanking movement?

That was for Lee to decide, and Lee never had trouble deciding. In his headquarters behind Fredericksburg, all he had to do was look to the southeast to see a carpet of blue on this side of the Rappahannock—the formidable bridgehead established by Sedgwick and Reynolds, no doubt ready to strike. How could he deal with both this threat and the one Stuart discovered developing to the west at the same time?

He couldn't. The hard truth was that Lee was already outnumbered before this business began, a fact of life he had long since grown accustomed to. All he could do was attempt to defeat each enemy in detail, one at a time, which meant he had to decide which threat—east or west—was the greater.

Perhaps "Mr. F. J. Hooker" was making a flanking attack after all. At any rate, Stuart had seen an awful lot of so-called blue-bellies on the march around Chancellorsville. So Lee called on his trusted right hand, Lieutenant General Thomas "Stonewall" Jackson, to prepare to move at dawn on May 1 to reinforce the western line, where Major General Dick Anderson's division was already digging in for whatever the Federals were about to throw at him from Chancellorsville.

In characteristic style, Lee was taking a big gamble. To guard the heights behind Fredericksburg against any attack from the Federal lodgment, he left a single division, around 10,000 men. Commanded by Jubal Early, this force would face perhaps four times its strength should the bluecoats explode out of their bridgehead, and Early was ordered to fall back to the south should such a development occur in order to defend the line to Richmond.

The rest of Lee's army—more than four-fifths of it, in fact—was committed to reinforcing Anderson. Lee, having guessed Hooker's game, was convinced that the mass of Northern troops around Chancellorsville posed the greatest threat. It was there, he believed, that this battle would be decided.

Electrified by the prospect of action, Stonewall Jackson got his men moving west that very night. By the time the birds were filling the Wilderness with their discordant music on May Day morning, the vast majority of the Army of Northern Virginia had placed itself to handle the blue juggernaut from the west.

It was these men, skillfully shifted from one front to another, that Hooker's columns ran into as they probed westward along the meager roads leading through the Wilderness out of Chancellorsville on May 1. As reports filtered back to him,

Hooker interpreted the resistance in front of him as more than merely Anderson's back-door guardians. Lee must have taken the measure of his plan and moved accordingly. Hooker, sensing danger and the unknown, called his columns in, ordering them to retreat to the Chancellorsville salient. Many of his generals, however, wondered why they were falling back now that the enemy had been located. Why not press the attack?

JOE HOOKER'S RECKONING

The answer to this question, which has exercised commentators and historians ever since, can best be arrived at by taking a look at the facts that must have crowded Hooker's mind by the afternoon of May 1.

To begin with, the narrowness of the roads leading east out of the Wilderness prevented him from committing anything more than around 30,000 troops to his eastward attack out of Chancellorsville. Second, he had not anticipated so rapid a response by Lee—the hard fighting by the reinforcements brought by Jackson came as a surprise to him. Hooker had hoped to reach Fredericksburg itself by the afternoon of May Day; instead, he had run into the bulk of the Army of Northern Virginia, or at least that's what he thought it was.

Third, Hooker could satisfy himself that he had taken the strategic offensive and succeeded—he had pulled off the feat of getting his huge right hook beyond the Rapidan without incident, positioning the Army of the Potomac for a killer strike. Now that he had put his forces where they needed to be, why not achieve his goal by inviting Lee to attack rather than attacking him?

All of these considerations bore merit. But it has been said by many, from those who were there to academics generations after the fact, that Joe Hooker lost the battle there and then—that, at the first sign of trouble with the legendary Lee, he got cold feet. While such a judgment can be dismissed as hyperbole, one thing is certain: By his actions on May 1, Hooker surrendered the initiative to a foe who thrived on taking it.

A LONGTIME PROTÉGÉ OF ROBERT E. LEE, J.E.B. STUART BROUGHT AN ABUNDANCE OF ÉLAN AND CREATIVITY TO HIS JOB AS CAVALRY CHIEF OF THE ARMY OF NORTHERN VIRGINIA. AT CHANCELLORSVILLE, HE SUCCEEDED TO TEMPORARY COMMAND OF THE II CORPS AFTER THE FALL OF STONEWALL JACKSON.

Library of Congress

DECISION IN THE WILDERNESS

At this point in the war, the Army of Northern Virginia fought with two wings, called *corps*. The I Corps, commanded by James Longstreet, had traditionally acted as the anvil on which the II Corps, commanded by Stonewall Jackson, hammered Union enemies to destruction.

Union threats farther south had compelled Lee to send Longstreet on detached duty with two divisions in southeastern Virginia. Lee took over command of the I Corps directly and consulted closely with Jackson, who remained in command of the hard-charging II Corps. It was this hobbled command structure that found itself coping with the finest plan of attack ever conceived by the Army of the Potomac.

Having blunted and contained the Union breakout from Chancellorsville, the two Confederate commanders huddled together on the first night of May to consider their options. The situation had shifted considerably during the day's fighting. To the northwest, the Union line stretched for miles from a bend in the Rappahannock to a distant point on the Orange Turnpike, its center bowing southward to encompass Chancellorsville. Meade held the eastern end of this long cordon, followed by Couch's men, who formed part of the "turret" around the crossroads, then Slocum, who completed the turret. Howard's corps came next, drawn out on a line to the west along the turnpike. The III Corps of Sickles, having lately arrived from across the river, stood behind Chancellorsville in reserve while, a few miles to the north, Reynolds's corps, summoned west to support Hooker's main effort, was still making its way west on the opposite side of the river with the intention of crossing at U.S. Ford.

Lee and Jackson's combined divisions formed an awkward line to the southeast of the Union line. In all, they had a little more than 40,000 men arrayed against a Union front of more than 70,000.

Very early in the morning of May 2, Lee and Jackson convened a meeting that would go down in history. Sitting in the firelight on a pair of hard tack boxes abandoned by the withdrawing Yankees, they stared at a map of the area around Chancellorsville in the company of two of Jackson's staff: his cartographer, who had provided the map, and his chaplain, who knew the local terrain intimately.

Earlier that day, Stuart had come with information that set Lee's heart racing: The far western end of the Union line, or right flank, was "in the air," meaning it lacked any defensive terrain on which to anchor itself and was vulnerable to attack. Lee and Jackson conferred and concluded that Jackson would hit the Union right, defended by Howard's corps, as long as a path could be found through the green labyrinth of the Wilderness. Now, pointing to the map whose lines shivered in the flickering firelight, the cartographer drew a line with his finger, first west to the nearby ironworks called Catharine Furnace, then south along trails that would deliver the Rebels beyond the observation of Federal posts, then west again until, eventually, a road winding northward gave on to the Orange Plank Road. Once there, having avoided Federal observation in the depth of the thickets, the Confederate attackers would be on the far end of the Union's right wing and sitting astride an avenue to deliver their decisive strike. Simply put, Jackson would lead his entire II Corps on the ten-plus mile (16 km) sojourn outlined by the cartographer, commencing his march as soon as possible in order to place his men in a position to attack before the light of May 2 faded.

Aside from embracing a very ambitious timetable on dubious roads, the plan had one very big caveat: After leaving with his 27,000 or so men on a journey that would take him most of the day, Jackson would leave Lee to face the united Union army with only the divisions of Dick Anderson and Lafayette McLaws, or around 15,000 men. Should the 70,000 or so bluecoats across the way choose to test Lee's line while Stonewall was off path-finding through the Wilderness, the Army of Northern Virginia would be in dire straits indeed.

ODYSSEY OF THE II CORPS

Thomas Jackson was a religious ascetic, hero of the Mexican War, and legendary eccentric. Given to hypochondria and quackery, he sucked on lemons, sometimes during battle, brought his own food to social occasions (stale bread was a staple), exercised by pumping his arms like a chicken, and refused to take pepper in his meals for fear of the pain it allegedly incurred in his left leg.

But if Old Jack was weird, he was also born to fight. When a fellow officer likened his resilience to oncoming Yankees to that of a stone wall during the First Battle of Bull Run in 1861, the epithet stuck. It was ironic, for Jackson's preference was always for movement and attack, a trait that endeared him to Lee, who relied on the former professor to lead the Army of Northern Virginia's most daring flanking movements. Now, on a warm and humid May 2, Lee sent Jackson on the greatest maneuver of his career. The sun was already up by the time his gray and butternut columns wound through the forest, disappearing in the sweltering green gloom.

They did not go unnoticed by the enemy. Dan Sickles's III Corps, having been brought up to fill the front line with its fresh troops, observed columns of rebels moving in the clearings to the south. But by the time Sickles had secured permission from Hooker to attack, the vast majority of Jackson's corps had passed. Union attacks hit the rearguard with some effect, but ended up tangling with Lee's men, who stretched their lines west in order to keep the Yankees busy. What's more, the bluecoats could clearly see that the Southern columns were heading south. Hooker took the movement as evidence of a retreat.

Jackson urged his men on until, around three in the afternoon, Robert Rodes's division reached the turnpike and started deploying into the thicket on either side of the road. His men would form the front line, spread a mile and a half (2.4 km) in the Wilderness and centered on the turnpike, which pointed the way forward toward Howard's unsuspecting bluecoats to the east. The other two divisions of Jackson's corps, those of Raleigh Colston and A. P. Hill, brought up the rear.

Before seeing to the disposition of his men, which took hours in the dense underbrush, Stonewall wrote a message to Lee with the details of his position after a triumphant twelve-mile (19 km) hike in almost complete secrecy. "I hope as soon as practicable to attack. I trust that an ever kind Providence will bless us with great success."

AN ARMY UNDONE

Sometime between five and six o'clock in the evening, men on the far right of Howard's Union corps interrupted their business to watch a crowd of deer and other woodland animals come darting out of the woods to the west as if being flushed by a band of hunters. Well-fed by their own government's beef, the soldiers looked with curiosity more than hunger at the throngs of rabbits leaping through the grass, and wondered aloud at the cause.

They didn't have long to wait for an answer. In the distance, the green Wilderness disgorged a line of Rebels, their gray rags slashed by acres of briars. Close-packed and moving at a pace at once brisk and deliberate, the Southerners came on with a banshee cry that hit the hapless bluecoats like a storm wind—the Rebel yell, a shrill whoop emanating from 20,000 throats that struck deep into Yankee nerves.

The order that sent this malicious wave forward had been brief, even nonchalant. "Are you ready, General Rodes?" asked Jackson with a look at his watch. It had taken the legendary Stonewall some two hours to get his corps into position to unleash his *coup de main*, not least because of the Wilderness itself. "Yes, sir," came the reply.

"You can go forward then."

The surprise was complete. Two cannon and a pair of regiments were all that Howard had consigned to face the westward approach, and these soon collapsed, born eastward on a gale of hollering Rebels. Rodes's men strode along at a ruthless clip, stopping only long enough to shoulder arms and blast away at pockets of resistance. They soon began rolling up the Union right wing like a carpet.

But running down a beaten enemy was hard work, and Jackson's II Corps— short on food and water since setting out early that morning—now quavered in exhaustion. Jackson's overriding order to all his commanders had been to keep up the momentum of attack; at no time were they to slow up or, God forbid, stop. He knew that sheer momentum was their greatest asset. But now, as the sun sank, he was watching an opportunity to destroy the enemy slip from his grasp.

U.S. Ford, a crossing point on the Rappahannock, behind Hooker's lines, offered a clean escape across the river. Once there, Northern forces could travel north to safety and fight another day. Jackson needed to prevent that from happening at all costs, and he now began to obsess over it even as his advancing corps drove its enemies before it. Perhaps the brigades of A. P. Hill's division, having been absent from the attack, could drive home a thrust in that direction.

Night could not be forestalled, however. The Yankees had been shaken, but not crushed. Jackson, the bit between his teeth, now planned that rarest of Civil War actions: a night attack.

Darkness had long since fallen when Old Jack went riding in the direction of the river to see what opportunities presented themselves. By the time he was heading back toward the Confederate lines, he rode in good company: A. P. Hill himself was with him, along with both his and Jackson's staff. And then, as the party approached the Rebel lines, an explosion of musketry greeted them, cutting through the tree limbs and sending the horses into a panic.

A.P. Hill shouted hoarsely in the night. "Cease firing! Cease firing!" he yelled, reigning his horse as the gray smoke wreathed the crime scene. But the assailants, North Carolinians, would not be dissuaded. "Who gave that order?" came a cry from the darkness. "It's a lie! Pour it into them, boys!"

Just twenty paces away, a battalion's worth of shot lit the night in violent flashes, raking the riding party with lead. Among the writhing wounded who soon littered the ground was Jackson, with three bullet wounds. After being laid against a tree by officers who escaped the fusillade, he was heard to mumble, "...my own men. My own men." Tragically, Jackson had proven why night actions were so dangerous: In the confusion of darkness, friendly fire was all too common, especially in a place like the Wilderness.

TO HAZEL GROVE

Despite Jackson's achievement of May 2, dawn broke on a situation little changed from the one that existed before the rout of Howard's corps. Joe Hooker still had an army south of the Rappahannock, and was still hoping to whip Lee in a defensive battle. Lee had done nothing more than ruin a single corps of the Union army, and still had to find a way to crush Hooker's command.

He also needed to reunite the Army of Northern Virginia. Indeed, Lee's situation was quite worrisome. His outnumbered army now lay scattered across miles of real estate in three distinct and separate detachments: Jubal Early and his division protecting Fredericksburg, the divisions of Anderson and McLaws with Lee himself, and the II Corps in the Wilderness to the northwest of Lee's position, regrouped into a frontline facing east. Worst of all, Jackson was out of the fight.

News of Stonewall's unfortunate accident hit Lee hard. Jackson, his left arm amputated high above the elbow, had been replaced by Stuart, whose cavalry had performed such brilliant reconnaissance in the campaign. Now the dashing horseman would be in charge of the whole II Corps—and he had his work cut out for him.

Separated by over a mile (1.6 km) of wilderness, the forces of Lee and Stuart needed to merge. Between them sat the Union corps of Slocum and Sickles, their combined divisions forming a circle around Chancellorsville that bulged south-ward from the rest of Hooker's army, which now formed a pocket anchored on the

A LITHOGRAPH FROM THE LATE NINETEENTH CENTURY SHOWS THE FIGHTING AT CHANCELLORSVILLE. RARELY HAD THE NORTH ENJOYED SO GREAT AN ADVANTAGE IN BATTLE AND SQUANDERED IT SO COMPLETELY.

Library of Congress

river and protecting U.S. Ford. As Lee saw it, Stuart was going to have to fight his way east toward Anderson and McLaws, who would do what they could with their wildly outnumbered force to make it easier on the II Corps. Lee's orders, sent that night via messenger, were clear enough: "Endeavor...to dispossess them of Chancellorsville," a goal that would allow the two wings of the Army of Northern Virginia to meet and face Hooker together.

May 3 broke warm and sunny, promising a pleasant day. And it wasn't long before the Rebels scored their first coup. Hazel Grove, at the extreme southwest of the Yankee position, offered some of the highest ground in the region. From its grassy precipice, one could see in every direction over the green density of the Wilderness. It was a commanding position, and had been occupied by batteries in Dan Sickles's III Corps. Hooker, worried about the position's exposure, ordered Sickles to pull his guns off the hill and retire back toward Chancellorsville. It proved a terrible mistake.

Around six o'clock in the morning, as the Yankee batteries were still hauling their guns north, men of A. P. Hill's division came howling out of the greenery and began pouring fire on the beleaguered gunners. Though supported by infantry, the batteries floundered in the melee, losing six of their pieces. Nevertheless, it was never their intention to defend Hazel Grove, which now belonged to Jeb Stuart.

And he was about to put it to good use indeed.

BURNING UP THE WILDERNESS

Rushing to Hazel Grove, Jeb Stuart ordered Porter Alexander, his artillery chief, to park as many guns on the grassy knoll as he could. Alexander, having prepared for just such an opportunity the night before, soon had seven batteries—twenty-eight guns—banging away. They had quite a shooting gallery spread out before them.

Stretching away to the northeast in a broad ribbon of gray smoke, the two armies clashed in one long, ferocious melee, the rattle of musketry making a din that shook the Wilderness. This was Stuart's gambit—all of A. P. Hill's division, six brigades and a battalion of guns, crashing on the Union front like a wave. Running almost a mile (1.6 km) southwest to northeast, this combat undulated back and forth as Yankee brigades, most of them full of green troops firing from behind fieldworks, opened gaps in the oncoming lines of gray and butternut, only to see them close again. Alexander joined the fray from a distance, sending enfilading fire pounding into the enemy positions from his vantage point on Hazel Grove and torturing blue formations with the whistling violence of incoming ordnance.

As the Rebels advanced astride the Plank Road toward Chancellorsville, their ranks soon shook with the punishment of enemy artillery. On Fairview, a prominence behind the Northern lines, some forty-four Yankee pieces barked away, sending shells and round shot whipping over the heads of their own ducking soldiers to wreak havoc on A. P. Hill's assault. Still the gray ranks came on, howling and firing into the storms of Yankee lead.

Faced with a Rebel lunge toward Chancellorsville that could undo the whole Union position, Hooker elected to send William French, a division commander of the II Corps, to counterattack. Advancing with conspicuous pugnacity, French and his regiments undid the exhausted Rebels north of the plank road, driving them back beyond the Yankee breastworks in a series of firefights.

And so it went, back and forth, Stuart's corps hammering eastward against breastworks that often changed hands several times, their bullet-ridden embankments forming break walls against which dead and wounded gathered in heaps. By nine in the morning Stuart, massing his divisions along the Orange Plank Road, punched through the Union lines, placing the Federal position in peril. At almost the same moment, one of Porter Alexander's rifled artillery pieces scored a crucial hit on Chancellorsville itself. A piece of solid shot struck one of the pillars on the mansion's porch—the very pillar on which Fighting Joe Hooker was leaning his hand while watching the fight. Slammed by large pieces of the shivered column, the general was thrown to the ground, where he lay still. It wasn't long before rumors were racing through the ranks: General Hooker was dead.

MARYE'S HEIGHTS AND BEYOND

By ten thirty, Stuart had linked up with Lee's divisions and taken the whole kitty: Fairview and Chancellorsville itself. Among the dead and dying found by advancing Rebels were throngs of charred corpses, caught wounded when the Wilderness around them went up like a funeral pyre in the furious musketry.

The Confederates' well-coordinated attacks had been conducted with precision and tenacity. But that wasn't the only reason the Army of the Potomac had fallen back that morning.

The truth was that, during the most crucial hour of the battle on May 3, the army had been leaderless. Though not killed by Alexander's near miss, Hooker had been struck senseless and seems to have suffered a concussion. The medical staff could not make a firm diagnosis as nothing seemed outwardly wrong with him; on the other hand, his efforts to sit in his saddle made him dizzy, and he was clearly incapable of lucid, coherent thought at a time when the Confederates were beginning to turn the fight to their favor. By the time a muddled, vomiting Hooker had deferred command to Darius Couch, his senior corps commander, it was ten o'clock and the salient around Chancellorsville was no more.

Hooker's instructions to his surrogate were straightforward enough: pull back. The ring around U.S. Ford was to collapse even further to defend the avenue of extrication across the river. The great "hammer" of the army's right wing, battered, bleeding, and confused, had conceded yet more ground to the numerically inferior foe.

The fighting spirit of the army now wedged in a defensive pocket between Chancellorsville and the Rappahannock may have been hobbled by two days of murderous action, but the bluecoats of Sedgwick's command were just finding their stride. At Fredericksburg, ten miles (16 km) east of Chancellorsville, they received their orders from Hooker to carry the high ground behind Fredericksburg, known as Marye's Heights, and went at it with a vengeance. With Early retiring to the south to protect the road to Richmond, Sedgwick had his road to Chancellorsville and soon headed west with 22,000 men.

Four miles (6.4 km) west of Fredericksburg, he ran into a brigade of Rebels who were soon joined by reinforcements sent by Lee. Lee sensed an easier target in Sedgwick and now began planning the destruction of his corps in a shift to the east away from the main Union force.

Leaving Stuart and the II Corps to deal with Hooker, Lee moved east with the remainder of his forces, which at this point amounted to Anderson's division. With Early coming back north with his division, perhaps Sedgwick could be encircled and pounded into surrender.

THE FINAL ACT

Joe Hooker was feeling much better the morning of May 4. Having rested the previous day while his army took a thrashing around Chancellorsville, he now outlined the final phase of a battle that he, at least, still thought he was controlling.

Today, Fighting Joe believed, Lee was going to hurl his army once again on the Union salient against the river, offering another chance to break the Southerners in a defensive battle. Sedgwick would be given discretionary orders, allowing him to interpret the right time to strike from the east. Should a Rebel attack north not materialize, however, Hooker planned on pulling his army out tomorrow through U.S. Ford, marching east along the Rappahannock, and re-crossing at Bank's Ford closer to Fredericksburg to descend on the Confederates holding Sedgwick up at Salem Church. Either way, he was going to find a way to whip Bobby Lee.

Sedgwick was forbidden to abandon his position south of the river. Should he do so, Hooker's grand maneuver the following day would be useless. Like Lee yesterday, Hooker now meant to reunite his divided army.

As it happened, Lee did indeed mean to spend May 4 on the attack, but not against Joe Hooker. Instead, he had his sights set on John Sedgwick and the VI Corps. Having mustered the strength of three divisions—Early, Anderson, and McLaws—in a line that hugged Sedgwick's horseshoe-shaped position east of Salem Church, he meant to squeeze the enemy's 21,000 troops from all directions with a combined force of 23,000.

At five thirty, three Rebel brigades commenced their march on Sedgwick's left. Here, miles east of the Wilderness, the plain was all but treeless, offering the Yankees a splendid view of the gray lines coming at them—like soldiers on parade, colors flying in the spring breeze. Initially carrying all before them, the Confederates began to lose order in the pace of their advance and, after sending the greenest Union units to flight, ran into stiff resistance. Sedgwick was definitely pressed, but not enough to satisfy Lee. By nightfall the Confederate effort had reaped precious few rewards, leaving Sedgwick in essentially the same position he had occupied before the evening's fireworks.

But Sedgwick saw things differently. Though he had been able to hold on through the evening, the Confederate attacks convinced him, wrongly, that he was wildly outnumbered. A famously conservative commander, Sedgwick allowed himself to believe that, despite Hooker's injunction against doing so, retreating back across the river was the only safe plan to preserve his corps from destruction. So that's what he did.

Hooker, receiving word of this the night of May 4 from Sedgwick's command, despaired. His grand plan, pummeled by so many unforeseen contingencies, had fallen apart. Resigned to the reality of the situation, he authorized the retirement of the forces under his command across U.S. Ford. The week-long Battle of Chancellorsville was over.

AN UNCERTAIN FUTURE

Rarely had the North enjoyed so great an advantage, and squandered it so completely, as at Chancellorsville. James Longstreet, senior of Lee's two leading subordinates, had not even made an appearance, while the other—Jackson—had been mortally wounded. Nevertheless, an army everywhere outnumbered better than two-to-one along the broad Fredericksburg–Chancellorsville front had managed to beat the odds.

How? To begin with, Lee had the advantage of interior lines. But this was hardly enough to counter the vast material and numerical superiority of his foe. Moreover, Lee ditched this advantage altogether with his bold decision on May 2 to send Jackson on a wide flanking maneuver that could have resulted in disaster.

Rather, it seems hard to escape the conclusion that Hooker and his generals were out-generaled on almost every day of the fight. They had failed to retain Stoneman's cavalry to screen the army and reconnoiter Lee's weaknesses. They were unable to provide adequately for the defense of their right flank on May 2, of which Stonewall Jackson made an historic mockery; failed to appreciate the significance of Hazel Grove on May 3, and compounded this mistake by failing to handle their concentrated artillery as well as the Rebels. They had also failed to resume the attack on May 4 when Lee gambled *once again* by attacking Sedgwick and leaving a numerically inferior force near Chancellorsville to deal with the apparently indolent Union forces there. Little wonder the battle has gone down in history as Lee's greatest achievement.

The losses, however, told another story. The Federals had lost just over 17,000 killed, wounded, and missing. For the Confederates, this same figure totaled almost 13,000. This was another striking example of Lee's willingness to incur enormous losses in the quest for battlefield victory against a foe that could replace those losses much more easily. In time he would also lose Stonewall Jackson, who succumbed to pneumonia on May 10, 1863.

As Hooker's Army of the Potomac retired toward Washington in the wake of Chancellorsville, many speculations were made. Lincoln, for one, worried that the nation would erupt upon hearing of yet another setback. The rank and file in the Army of the Potomac began betting on who their next commander would be. And Robert E. Lee floated the idea of a renewed Rebel attack on Northern territory, buoyed by the Chancellorsville victory.

This idea, developed over the coming weeks into an invasion of Pennsylvania, would ultimately result in the Battle of Gettysburg—Lee's greatest defeat and the turning point of the war in the east.

CHAPTER 12

RORKE'S DRIFT
1879

MODERN ARMS AND RAW NERVE
ACHIEVE THE INCREDIBLE

150 BRITISH VERSUS 4,000 ZULUS

IN 1856, QUEEN VICTORIA AUTHORIZED A MEDAL TO BE AWARDED to those British military personnel who had shown outstanding bravery "in the face of the enemy." Inspired by a desire to recognize acts of heroism in the recent Crimean War, it became known as the Victoria Cross—a simple cross pattée, cast from the bronze of captured cannon, featuring a royal crown in the middle surmounted by a lion and the words "For Valour." It was, and is, the highest honor to which any subject of the British Commonwealth could aspire.

In a century and a half just 1,356 have been awarded, and individual medals have been known to fetch hundreds of thousands of pounds at auction. World War I, by far the United Kingdom's costliest conflict, produced just 628 Victoria Cross recipients.

The most ever awarded for a single action was eleven, given to men who fought on January 22–23, 1879, at a remote outpost in what is now South Africa called Rorke's Drift. Occurring on the same day as one of the British Empire's most ignominious defeats, the details of this event—even under the hard scrutiny of historical research—read like adventure fiction.

Though seemingly a case of two peoples—each militaristic in its own way—clashing over matters of empire, profit, and national pride, the nightmarish struggle on those two days between the Zulu and a company of British soldiers occurred over a piece of ground that meant little to anyone. Moreover, the combatants were mere pawns in a campaign whose outcome would be decided on other battlefields. Were it not for those who fought and died heroically on its three acres (12,140 m²) of hell, Rorke's Drift would not have mattered at all.

ISANDLWANA

By the middle of the nineteenth century, southern Africa had become divided into a jumble of independent and semi-independent polities with a range of conflicting interests. The British maintained two colonies along the coast, Natal and the Cape colony, whose intrusive authority had driven the *Boers*—descendants of the region's original Dutch settlers—farther into the interior, where they established two republics, the Orange Free State and the Transvaal.

The push for more land led Boer settlers into conflicts with the indigenous African peoples, inevitably drawing the British in to ensure the security of the region and leading them ultimately toward a policy aimed at uniting the entire Cape area into a single confederation under British control. Fueling this urge was the discovery of diamonds at Kimberley in what is now the Northern Cape, offering the possibility of hitherto unimagined riches.

With a more unified South Africa in mind, the British annexed the Transvaal in 1877, inheriting a border dispute with the formidable Zulu kingdom. Since the 1820s, Zululand had been undergoing a gradual transformation, becoming more centralized by a crown whose reforms had created a loyal governing class and an army of outstanding efficiency. Increasingly ambivalent toward European colonial policy and presenting a geographic obstacle toward British territorial consolidation, the Zulus—by far the strongest African nation in the region—were marked for destruction.

On December 11, 1878, British authorities handed Zulu King Cetshwayo a list of demands he was bound to reject, including the disbanding of the Zulu army, severe indemnities of cattle to be paid in compensation for crimes against British subjects perpetrated by Zulu men, and the return of Christian missionaries to Zululand. The British gave him a month to comply, time the king used to prepare his nation for a war that now seemed inevitable.

THE DEFENSE OF RORKE'S DRIFT PORTRAYS THE ACTION INSIDE THE WALL OF MEALIE BAGS THE BRITISH ERECTED AS A BARRIER TO DEFEND THEMSELVES FROM THE ZULU.

To Lieutenant General Lord Chelmsford, charged with invading Zululand, the coming campaign presented few challenges beyond the immense logistical requirements for a modern army of almost 16,000 soldiers. As far as he was concerned, the Zulu were no different from the Xhosa, another nation in southern Africa against whom the British had fought a series of wars and whose warriors ultimately proved no match for European weaponry and military professionalism. While waiting for a response from the king that he knew would never come, Chelmsford made preparations to penetrate Zululand with three separate columns, the middle of which—personally commanded by Chelmsford himself—was slated to cross the frontier at a place called Rorke's Drift, where preparations had been made to facilitate the spanning of the Mzinyathi River, which formed the border between Natal and the Zulu kingdom.

On January 11, the columns got moving, commencing what came to be known as the Anglo-Zulu War. Chelmsford's column wound its way east after crossing the river. Everything depended on bringing the Zulus to battle as soon as possible without letting them slip behind him to attack British territory, a mission the general hoped to pull off in concert with the other two columns to the north and south.

Rain swamped the tracks, which brought things to a crawl. By January 20, having successfully skirmished with a group of nearby Zulus and burned their settlements, Chelmsford's men had slogged their way to an immense tower of rock known as Isandlwana, in whose long shadow they made camp.

On the night of January 21, the general received reconnaissance reports stating that a substantial Zulu force was nearby. At dawn the following morning, he led around half of his men out of camp in search of the enemy, hoping to find the Zulus before they got round his column and headed for Natal.

At the foot of Isandlwana, around 1,700 soldiers — British regulars and native allies — stayed behind to guard the camp itself. Few of them would live to see dusk.

A QUIET PLACE IN THE REAR

Back at Rorke's Drift, as Chelmsford and his expedition excitedly set out to track down their Zulu prey, the only action was the buzzing of flies under the growing morning heat. Unlikely to witness anything more than an enemy scouting party, the post was under the direction of Major Spalding, deputy acting adjutant and quartermaster-general, whose job title bespoke the rear-area nature of his command. This was a tiny place lost in the striking wilderness of plain, gorge, and cliff that surrounded it.

More than thirty years earlier, an Irish hunter named Jim Rorke purchased land on the Natal side of the Mzinyathi River at the foot of a majestic rise known as Shiyane. There, about half a mile (804 m) from the river, he built a house and a store that the Zulu, with whom he traded, called KwaJim, or "Jim's place." To the rest of the world it became known as Rorke's Drift.

Since then the little post had passed to a Swedish missionary named Otto Witt, who turned the store into a church and then, in 1879, saw it coopted by the British army as a supply base. Once a pair of rafts was provided for crossing the nearby river, the mission station at Rorke's Drift became Chelmsford's *entrepôt* into the Zulu kingdom. Supplies and munitions were stored there and ferried across when needed, and a hospital was established to take in the sick and wounded.

Chelmsford needed all the men he could for the invasion of Zululand, leaving Rorke's Drift with a token defense based around the redcoats of B Company, 2nd Battalion, 24th Regiment of Foot, commanded by Lieutenant Gonville Bromhead. With fewer than a hundred effectives, the 2nd/24th was supported by various elements, the most important of which were the several hundred men of the 2nd

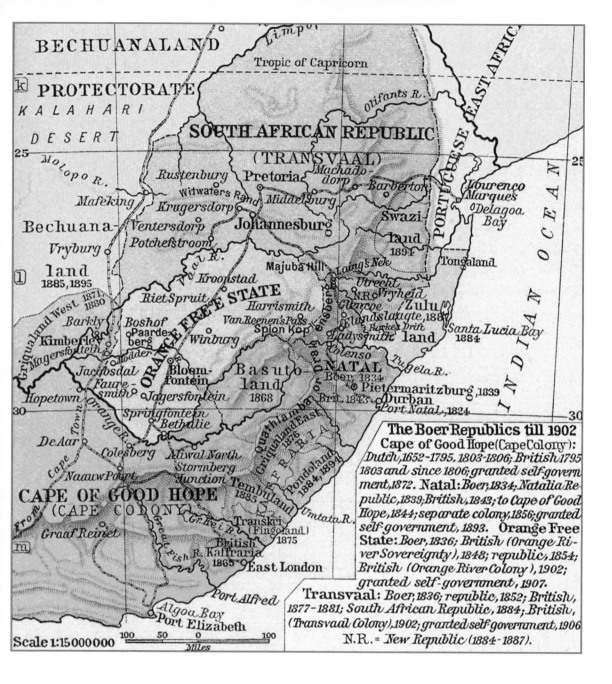

The Boer Republics till 1902

Cape of Good Hope (Cape Colony): Dutch, 1652-1795, 1803-1806; British 1795, 1803 and since 1806; granted self-government, 1872. Natal: Boer, 1834; Natalia Republic, 1839; British, 1843; to Cape of Good Hope, 1844; separate colony, 1856; granted self-government, 1893. Orange Free State: Boer, 1836; British (Orange River Sovereignty), 1848; republic, 1854; British (Orange River Colony), 1902; granted self-government, 1907. Transvaal: Boer, 1836; republic, 1852; British, 1877-1881; South African Republic, 1884; British, (Transvaal Colony), 1902; granted self-government, 1906. N.R. = New Republic (1884-1887).

Scale 1:15 000 000

SOUTHERN AFRICA IN THE LATE NINETEENTH CENTURY: CONFLICTING BRITISH, ZULU, AND BOER INTERESTS ENSURED THE INEVITABILITY OF WAR. RORKE'S DRIFT IS SHOWN TO THE LEFT OF SANTA LUCIA BAY.

Battalion, 3rd Regiment of the Natal Native Contingent (NNC) — native Africans recruited from Natal and led by white officers and non-commissioned officers.

Despite the presence of around 400 armed soldiers, the pace of life at Rorke's Drift since the departure of Chelmsford's column had been virtually somnambulant. Heaps of biscuit boxes and mealie bags filled the yard between the hospital and storehouse, neatly stacked beneath the South African summer sun, while a small team of royal engineers toiled down in the river, half a mile (804 m) away.

These last were led by Lieutenant John Chard, a quiet, thirty-one-year-old officer of engineers who, since January 19, had been present at Rorke's Drift to complete repairs on the two hawser-operated ferries, or *ponts*, that connected the post to the opposite bank. On the morning of January 22, Chard rode to the main column at Isandlwana, some six miles (9.6 km) away, where his superiors merely confirmed that his presence there was not needed. While there, however, he personally observed the flurry of Zulu activity in the area, a fact he dutifully and somewhat worriedly reported upon his return to Major Spalding. Concerned about reinforcements to Rorke's Drift that were supposed to have arrived already from the direction of Helpmekaar (the nearest village in Natal), Spalding prepared to go off in search of them, but not before asking Chard a question.

"Which of you is senior, you or Bromhead?" Chard indicated that he didn't know, sending Spalding back into his tent to check the Army list. There he discovered that the date of Chard's commission to lieutenant preceded that of Bromhead's. "I see you are senior," declared the post commander quite nonchalantly, "so you will be in charge until my return."

As Spalding prepared his horse for the trip, Chard returned to the river to write a letter home and eat some lunch. The sun was high and hot early that afternoon, and a booming could be heard from the east like distant thunder. To the men at the station, they signaled the bark of Chelmsford's artillery guns, whose firing could only mean that a general engagement was at hand.

Down by the river, Chard heard nothing; his position below the ridges that hugged the river shielded him from the distant rumble, allowing him to continue his scribbling while the men worked in the water.

The time passed until, around 3:15 in the afternoon, a pair of riders pulled up on the Zulu side of the river and signaled for permission to cross. Once ferried over, a lieutenant of the Natal Native Contingent named Adendorff, approached Chard with a wild look in his eyes. The man, in as measured a voice as he could muster, gave him a message too incredible to believe: The camp at Isandlwana had been wiped out almost to a man.

FIGHT OR FLIGHT?

Chard let the news sink in for a brief moment and then refused to believe it. Surely Adendorff had bolted too quickly and not seen the outcome? No, assured the NNC officer, he had seen the disaster first-hand. While Chelmsford had been out searching for enemy formations, the main Zulu army had been just over the hill nearby and moved on the camp in his absence like a storm surge over a poorly prepared breakwall.

After issuing orders to the men to secure the crossing and prevent use of the ponts by sinking the cables, Chard galloped back to the mission station, where he found Bromhead's men immersed in frantic activity. While Chard was whiling away the afternoon down by the water, the station itself had been subjected to frenzied warnings by passing fugitives from Isandlwana that the whole Zulu nation was coming to wipe them out. Their manic state betrayed an unwillingness to stick around, and they all kept going for Helpmekaar without reporting to the puzzled onlookers at Rorke's Drift. The countryside suddenly seemed alive with panic.

MAJOR GENERAL LORD CHELMSFORD NEEDED ALL THE MEN HE COULD GET FOR THE INVASION OF ZULULAND, LEAVING RORKE'S DRIFT WITH A TOKEN DEFENSE.

Getty Images

Despite this, Lieutenant Bromhead had things well in hand. Thirty-three-year-old "Gonny" Bromhead was the son of a veteran of Waterloo and a boxer of some renown within the 24th Regiment. Contemporary opinions of him offer a confusion of extremes, from frustration with his apparent hearing loss and abject doubts about his leadership ability, to admiration for his kindhearted devotion to the men under his command. Though he was a veteran of limited action in South Africa, he now found himself answering to an officer of engineers with no combat experience whatsoever and little in the way of infantry training.

Nevertheless, Chard was in command, and he now conferred with Bromhead over their next course of action. By the time Chard had appeared on the scene, his nominal second-in-command had begun preparations for turning Rorke's Drift into a fortress by ordering the mealie bags and biscuit boxes stacked for easy use as barriers. But the question remained: Should they even bother attempting to defend the station against what could turn out to be outrageous odds?

There were several mitigating factors that together made the option of staying nearly plausible. First was the fact that nobody knew for sure whether a Zulu army was even headed for Rorke's Drift. Dreadful reports had come in from those who had been lucky enough to escape the slaughter of Isandlwana, but none of them indicated that Zulus were on their way to Natal. Another consideration was that Chelmsford and some unknown number of British troops were still at large in the Zulu kingdom, having been spared the fate of the camp defenders at Isandlwana. For all anyone knew, they might be dealing with the Zulu army at that very moment.

Then there was the weaponry available to the defenders of Rorke's Drift. The standard issue infantry weapon at the time was the single-shot Martini-Henry rifle, an exemplar of how far technology had come in the Victorian era. Featuring a breech-loading mechanism that allowed the user to easily reload a new round from the rear of the weapon, the Martini-Henry threw a heavy .45 caliber round that, though capable of much longer range, was deadly effective at around 400 yards (365 m) and closer. A trained shooter could get off a round every seven or eight seconds. Just as important, the rifle could hold a bayonet that made it a potently heavy thrusting weapon at close quarters.

Finally, there were the post's human assets. An excellent example of the quality of the mission's defenders was Frank Bourne, color sergeant of B Company and second-in-command to Gonny Bromhead. Just twenty-four years old, the men referred to him as "the kid" behind his back. But Bourne was a natural leader and organizer of men, a fact that everyone in the outfit understood implicitly. The post was also lucky to have Acting Assistant Commissary James Dalton, an old army hand who had seen action in two wars against the Xhosa, one of them as a retired volunteer. Having just volunteered again for the commissariat, which was responsible for supplying the troops with food and equipment, the forty-seven-year-old was, ironically, one of the most experienced military professionals on the spot.

It was Dalton who now approached Chard and Bromhead as they discussed the post's options, and spoke up. The men's only practical option, according to the former sergeant, was to make a stand. Some thirty-five sick and wounded were convalescing in the hospital—men who could neither be left behind nor transported back to Helpmekaar quickly. Should Chard order an evacuation, the little column with its trundling wagons of wounded out in the open would be easy prey for a Zulu force. If enemy warriors indeed were on their way now, the mission station at least offered some protection.

Chard concurred with Dalton—they would defend the mission station.

TO WASH THEIR SPEARS IN THE BLOOD OF THE BRITISH

The Battle of Isandlwana, which claimed over 1,300 British lives, was a classic example of the favored Zulu tactic. Known as "the horns of the bull," it involved an advance in three divisions: the largest, called the chest, advancing forward while two "horns" swung around on the flanks to encircle the enemy. Around 20,000 strong, the Zulus had swamped the beleaguered defenders beneath Isandlwana, the staggered British fire gradually growing silent.

Against the fearsome Martini-Henry rifle, the Zulus relied on a short, heavy stabbing spear called an *Assegai* as well as a lighter one for throwing, and an oval shield made of cowhide. In addition, the illicit arms trade had filled the Zulu kingdom with an eclectic arsenal of antiquated muskets and rifles, allowing more than half of the king's warriors to carry a firearm into battle. Maintenance was spotty at best, however, and good ammunition hard to come by.

Despite their discipline, ferocity, and courage, the Zulus were not full-time fighters like the British they butchered that fateful afternoon. Until they were married, all men of the kingdom pledged themselves fully to the king, who organized his regiments, called *amabutho* (singular: *ibutho*), according to age rather than locale. Each regiment performed several months of public service each year and was called up at times of national emergency. Though married men also belonged to regiments, these stood apart from the younger amabutho, and typically served in a reserve capacity.

Confronted by a three-pronged invasion of his kingdom in 1879, King Cetshwayo called up every regiment at his disposal and, after perceiving Lord Chelmsford's column as the primary threat, set out to intercept it. Not all of the regiments saw action at Isandlwana, however; three amabutho of married men in their 30s and 40s (the uThulwana, uDloko, and inDlondo) and one of younger unmarried men (the inDluyengwe) had formed the reserve, following up the assault behind one of the horns. Between 4,000 and 5,000, the amabutho

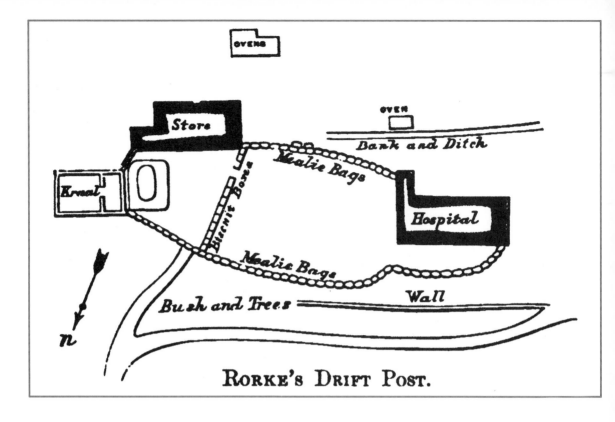

RORKE'S DRIFT POST.

had taken no lives and claimed no prizes, and yearned for something more before returning to their homes.

But the king, who insisted on waging a defensive war within the boundaries of his kingdom, had forbidden any of his warriors from attacking British territory. This was a royal injunction against inciting further reprisals from the British, and one that all of Cetshwayo's generals took seriously. All, that is, except one.

Prince Dabulamanzi kaMpande, half-brother to the king, was known to be impulsive, a bold member of the court who wasn't beyond taking the privileges of his status a bit too far. As commander of the four regiments of the Zulu reserve, he believed it was his duty not only to exploit thoroughly the tremendous success of Isandlwana, but also to offer his men an opportunity at immortality—to "wash the spears of his boys" in the blood of the British, as he admitted in an interview after the war.

Rorke's Drift offered an ideal opportunity to do just that. Crossing the Mzinyathi at two separate points, both of them well downstream from Rorke's Drift, the four Zulu regiments swept west, converging behind the rocky bulk of Shiyane, and approached the mission station from the south.

It was coming on four thirty in the afternoon on January 22, and the day's second momentous battle was just beginning.

THIS DRAWING OF THE RORKE'S DRIFT MISSION STATION SHOWS THE HOSPITAL THAT WOULD ULTIMATELY GO UP IN FLAMES, THE REDOUBT OF MEALIE BAGS ABUTTING THE KRAAL ON THE LEFT, AND THE WALL OF BOXES THAT BIFURCATED THE POST AND TURNED THE YARD NEAREST THE HOSPITAL INTO A NO-MAN'S LAND.

"THE ZULUS ARE COMING"

Conceived as a quiet homestead, converted into a house of God, and appropriated as an army depot, the mission station at Rorke's Drift was about to become the only thing standing between a drastically outnumbered cadre of soldiers and certain death.

For a post whose name would echo down the ages, it wasn't much to look at. By the time Chard and Bromhead had overseen the station's conversion into a bastion with the aid of Dalton, Otto Witt's modest bridgehead of Christianity had been enclosed in a defensible perimeter of 200-lb (91 kg) mealie bags just 100 yards (91.5 m) long from east to west and twenty-five yards (23 m) at its widest. Three structures anchored the circuit: a sturdy stone *kraal*, or rectangular enclosure for livestock, in the east; the hospital, which was a one-story cluster of small rooms, defined the circuit in the west; and, just a few yards to the southwest of the kraal was the Commissariat storehouse. The north wall of mealie bags, stretching eighty yards (73 m) or so from a corner of the kraal to the yard north of the hospital, stood atop a rocky ledge over four feet (1.2 m) high that dropped away abruptly, creating a natural barrier to attack.

The men were still busy completing the barricades when a welcome sight came galloping into view: around 100 Natal Native horsemen led by a white officer, survivors of Isandlwana. Happy to accept their offer of assistance, Chard instructed them to scout around Shiyane, the hill some 350 yards (320 m) to the southeast, for enemy action and to act as a screen to the mission station's continuing efforts at fortification.

Off they went, galloping around the broad base of the massive hill and out of sight. Perhaps fifteen minutes or so passed before they came riding into view again, this time amid the noise of gunshots and with a heightened sense of urgency.

"The Zulus are coming," cried one of the outfit's white riders as they all streamed off toward Helpmekaar, "black as hell and thick as grass!" The enemy army had arrived, and the cavalry was in no mood to come to the rescue.

Chard, nonplussed by the rout, but hardly surprised given what the troopers had already been through that day, had barely begun to register the consequences when the station's other native contingents dropped their weapons nearly as one and began vaulting over the mealie bags to escape. A wholesale defection was underway, with most of the British regulars either too thunderstruck to act or too infuriated to avoid firing their weapons at the fleeing soldiers, some of whom were

white officers of the native contingents. Chard, no line officer, was facing the sort of nervous disintegration that officers with ten times his experience dreaded.

There was nothing to be done. The deserters were gone, the Zulus were just around the spur of Shiyane, and Rorke's Drift had about 150 effective combatants to oppose whatever was about to break upon it.

Chard now had less than half the strength he had started with, and acted quickly. Concerned that he had so long a perimeter to defend with so few troops, he decided to build a stout wall of biscuit boxes through the middle of the enclosure, creating a final barricade behind which the troops could retire to defend a much smaller circumference if need be.

MOST OF THE ZULUS WHO FOUGHT AT RORKE'S DRIFT WERE MARRIED, A FACT DENOTED BY THE CIRCLET WOVEN INTO EACH MAN'S HAIR, KNOWN AS THE *ISICOCO*. THIS PHOTO IS FROM 1880.

This done, the men of B Company, 24th Regiment of Foot, were ordered to their three- and four-foot (0.9 to 1.2 m) walls of mealie bags to await the onslaught. Thanks to Color Sergeant Bourne, each had been issued seventy 45-caliber rounds, as much as they could carry practically. Minus the sick, they numbered ninety-five effectives. Joined by the odd artillerists, hospital corps servicemen, commissary men, and even civilians like ferryman Daniels, they now bore witness to an awesome sight: the onrush of Zulu warriors, swiftly skirting the base of Shiyane on foot beneath a cloud of dust, heading for Rorke's Drift.

SHOOT TO LIVE

It was four thirty in the afternoon, and the men of Rorke's Drift felt the heat both literally and figuratively bearing down on them. The first Zulus to reach the mission station were 500 young men of the inDluyengwe, coming around the western spur of Shiyane, their warriors carrying black shields with white spots. They stooped as they came, pausing to fire weapons, but kept the momentum up, moving through the cover of brush to within 500 yards (0.5 km) of the south wall of the enclosure. Shouting "*Usuthu*," the Zulu war cry, they beat their shields and charged.

Per Chard's orders, the British began firing. Their shots were aimed and staggered, incapable at extreme range of doing little but suppressing movement. But as the Zulus crept closer, the firing picked up, producing a chatter right across the line and forcing the Zulus to ground and into the post's outbuildings, particularly the cookhouse, which stood outside the barricade just twelve or so paces from the rear of the storehouse. From here, the Zulus could offer return fire while covering the advance of their fellows.

The inDluyengwe drew closer and the British poured on the punishment, forcing the Zulus to veer their attack off to the left, around to the front of the mission station. There they crowded into the long grass before rushing over the ledge and across the open ground into the front of the hospital, whose veranda had been heaped with furniture. A series of fierce hand-to-hand struggles ensued on and before the veranda, the British lunging with their bayonets into waves of stabbing Zulus until Color Sergeant Bourne and Lieutenant Bromhead rallied the men and led a charge, driving the enemy back over the ledge.

By now the other three Zulu regiments had shown up in a great mass led by Dabulamanzi himself on a horse. They, too, veered off toward the front of the station to join their fellows in attacking the barricade, massing for assaults that broke against the hospital and eventually all down the line to the left, probing for some weak spot.

The prince now assumed control over events, having begun to understand the nature and extent of the defenses before him. His plan was quite simple: Given the small size of the mission station, he could easily make attacks across the entire front wall to force Chard to defend every foot (30 cm) of barricade. Somewhere, probably near the hospital, a breakthrough was bound to be made. But just as important, Dabulamanzi sent many of his warriors—probably his best marksmen—into the sandstone crags that encircled Shiyane hill like a belt above its base. From there, despite the inaccuracy of their antiquated weapons at such a distance, they could maintain a relatively constant hail of fire on the rear barricade running between the backs of the storehouse and hospital and even beyond it, creating deadly havoc among the British. In time this threat grew weaker, however, as Chard's men began returning accurate fire, their Martini-Henry's zeroing in on the puffs of powder smoke on the heights.

Meanwhile, the assaults along the front barricade continued apace. In the furious hour after five o'clock, constant pressure from the Zulus spawned melees right across the mealie bag wall, with combatants gutting each other at the perimeter in a terrible, sweating intimacy. The British fired when they could, but the enemy assailants were too many and the Zulu clearly feared the bayonet more than the bullet, drawing Chard's men into an exhausting rhythm of upward thrusts to skewer their enemies as they scaled the four-foot (1.2 m) barricade.

Soon the British abandoned the wall in front of the hospital, driven back by throngs of Zulus who swarmed across the veranda and tried to force their way in. Then, at the other end of the station, a column of determined attackers charged up the path that terminated before the storehouse and that offered a way through the rock ledge. There, as they prepared to stab their way onto the barricade, they were met with an explosion of fire from a small party, perhaps six or seven strong, led by Chard. Those who made it to the wall were gored, and the attack broke up.

Nevertheless, as he considered the ease with which the Zulus maintained pressure across the entirety of the front wall even as casualties mounted from the desultory fire coming from the opposite direction off Shiyane and from the outbuildings, Chard couldn't help but worry. Sometime around six o'clock he made the decision to abandon the hospital altogether and pull back behind the barricade of biscuit boxes that bifurcated the yard.

THE LONG AGONY OF RORKE'S DRIFT

By six thirty Chard had completed the withdrawal, creating a new defensible position that now enclosed only the stone rectangle of the kraal, the storehouse, and the yard behind the biscuit boxes. Just over a third the size of the previous perimeter, it presented the British with a much easier task. Moreover, the Zulu snipers on Shiyane had far fewer targets as most of the redcoats were now concealed behind the bulk of the storehouse.

The abandoned hospital, however, now became a battleground all its own. As the Zulus smashed their way through the windows and doors, they found a bizarre warren of tiny rooms defended only by the wounded and a handful of able-bodied soldiers. Soon the thatched roof was ablaze, beneath which a confused struggle raged in claustrophobic surroundings between combatants who barely had enough space to cut or thrust. As the body count rose on both sides, the British made a slow and awkward retreat toward the east end of the building, hacking their way through the thin inner walls with bayonets and a pick. By seven thirty, those who could had fled through a window that gave onto the yard and darted, as fast as they were able, to the safety of the biscuit boxes, all the while harassed by a hail of bullets and spears.

They soon found, however, that they had fled the fire only to land in the frying pan. Inside the barricades, the press of British soldiers crouching behind their makeshift protection offered a steady, deafening fire. Their shoulders sore from the constant recoil of their rifles, most soldiers started firing left-handed. Soon a redoubt was built with the remaining mealie bags, creating a pyramid at the center of the British position. Once hollowed out at the top, it offered an elevated vantage point from which soldiers could fire over the heads of the men at the barricades.

The Zulus were everywhere: firing into the storehouse, clambering atop the mealie bags, crowding over the low walls of the kraal, and taking cover in the dead ground created by the ledge near the hospital to emerge at intervals and take shots at the British line. Scattered about the crowded yard were wounded, many of them leaning on ammunition crates that had been frantically pried open and plundered for more rounds.

Only in the kraal, however, were Dabulamanzi's warriors making headway against the desperate resistance. As sunlight yielded to the glare of the burning hospital, the Zulus vaulted into the teeth of .45 rounds and bayonets, their flashing spears taking a grisly toll. By nine o'clock, the defenders of the kraal had fallen back behind its westernmost wall. Chard was running out of places to retreat from.

The station now lit the night with violence, the flashes of rifle fire stabbing out from the British redoubt to slice through the darkness. Beyond the biscuit box barricade, less than forty yards (36.5 m) away, the inferno of the hospital bathed the yard in bright orange. Those Zulus who attempted to attack across this no-man's land were met with gales of accurate rifle fire, carpeting the ground with dead and wounded.

It was another story on the eastern end of the station. Here darkness concealed the bush, allowing creeping attackers to approach right up to the storehouse or the mealie bag walls. Unfortunately for the Zulus, the captured kraal offered no advantage, as British muzzles now pointed over the far wall to sweep the ground. It was abandoned as an avenue of attack.

Assaults continued for another hour along the only two remaining parts of the wall that offered a chance of success: the short barricade running obliquely from a corner of the storehouse to the inner wall of the kraal, and the long north barricade. Both sides were tiring from the hours of slaughter, but the Zulus had suffered dreadful casualties. Sometime around ten o'clock they launched their final charge, which petered out when the British, their shoulders too bruised to offer aimed shots any longer, simply rested their guns on the barricade and produced a storm of poorly aimed shots.

No longer willing to risk assaulting the British directly, the Zulus maintained a constant fire throughout the night, pinning the defenders behind their gore-spattered protection. Before long, with the men running shorter on water

ZULU KING CETSHWAYO'S
(1832-1884) DEFIANCE OF
BRITISH DEMANDS ON
HIS LAND AND SOVEREIGNTY
LED TO THE TWIN BATTLES
OF ISANDLWANA AND
RORKE'S DRIFT.

Getty Images

than they were on ammunition, Gonny Bromhead lead a small party on a dash into the yard beyond the biscuit boxes to retrieve a water cart, which they hauled up to the barricade and, under fire, ran the wagon's hose over the boxes and into the perimeter.

As the night wore on, the chatter of Zulu fire grew steadily thinner until, in the hours just before dawn, it died out completely.

THE COST OF COURAGE

The British weren't sure that the Zulus had withdrawn until sunup, which brought a frightful scene of carnage. The dead lay everywhere, heaped two or three deep in places. Inside the smoldering, roofless hospital were the charred remains of those who hadn't made it out in time. The British had barely begun to sort through the corpses when, at around seven o'clock, a large group of Zulus rounded the base of Shiyane and took up a position on heights to the southwest. Chard prepared his men for a renewed assault, only to see the Zulus quietly make off the way they'd come, leaving the mission station in peace.

Few commanders indeed can say they had triumphed in the face of twenty-seven-to-one odds, but that is what John Chard had done. At a price of seventeen dead and fourteen wounded, he had successfully endured an attack by more than 4,000 enemy warriors.

The numbers of Zulu dead and wounded, by contrast, remain uncertain. The British buried some 350 in the immediate aftermath of the battle, but in the following weeks, hundreds more bodies were found throughout the surrounding countryside, bringing the total to more than 600. Dabulamanzi had paid dearly for his brash strike.

Though absurdly outnumbered, the British were full-time soldiers who had made a science out of war and combat. The post itself also played a huge role, affording the defenders an excellent opportunity to negate some of the numerical superiority that threatened them. Had Rorke's Drift not been a supply depot with vast quantities of boxes and mealie bags, the outcome would certainly have been very different.

On top of this, the Zulus themselves had been on the march all day. By the time they had descended on the mission station, they had trudged more than fifteen miles (24 km) on little food or water, only to commence a furious, incessant attack for six bloody hours. Overconfidence, and the constant hope that the

British breaking point must be imminent, had drawn them into a slogging match for which they were at best only partly prepared.

In the end, however, technology played the decisive role. Powerful, accurate, versatile, the Martini-Henry rifle had reaped a frightful harvest at Rorke's Drift. Chard's men began the day with 20,000 rounds of ammunition. They greeted the morning of January 23 with just 900.

Though King Cetshwayo lamented his half-brother's costly escapade, the battle at Rorke's Drift made little difference in the struggle that decided the fate of his kingdom. Isandlwana had already assured the return of a British invasion hours before the first shots rang out at Rorke's Drift—revenge, pride, and an imperial agenda demanded the subjugation of Zululand. On July 4, 1879, Chelmsford crowned his second invasion with victory at the Battle of Ulundi, which decisively crushed Cetshwayo's army and led to the partitioning of the kingdom into smaller puppet regimes. It was the end of an era.

CHAPTER 13

TANNENBERG
1914

RUSSIA IS IMPALED ON THE SPIKE
OF THE PICKELHAUBE

200,000 GERMANS VERSUS 400,000 RUSSIANS

O N AUGUST 25, 1914, A CAR SPED ALONG A ROAD IN RURAL East Prussia, in what is today Poland. The uniformed driver needed to catch the automobile ahead, whose trailing dust cloud had only just come into his view.

The driver's name was Lieutenant-Colonel Max Hoffmann, and in his pocket was a scrap of paper on which he had scrawled urgent news. A portly eccentric with a razor-sharp mind and love of food, forty-five-year-old Hoffmann was first general staff officer of the German Eighth Army, which was a thinking man's job for which he was eminently suited. That morning he and his superiors had driven outside of Montowo, roughly forty miles (64 km) southwest of what is today Olsztyn, to consult with one of the army's corps commanders about the timetable for attacking the Russians. Then, on the return journey, the party stopped in town to allow Hoffmann to phone headquarters. He waved the other cars on, explaining that he would catch up with them.

On the phone, Hoffmann was told that a Russian message detailing its dispositions facing the Germans had been broadcast in the clear and intercepted. Hoffmann excitedly scribbled down the details, jumped into his waiting automobile, and raced off in pursuit of his commanding general, Paul von Hindenburg, who now rode in the car ahead.

The space between the speeding vehicles shortened as Hoffmann sounded an alarm by working the horn. Soon the cars were traveling in tandem, and Hoffmann handed the paper to an outstretched hand from the other car.

This was the pace of war a month into World War I: automobiles, telephones, wireless messages…and eggheads performing odd feats of derring-do. Hoffmann, a staff officer responsible for overseeing the operational details that his superior Hindenburg ordered into effect, had airplanes at his disposal to reconnoiter the enemy, railroads to deliver men to the front, and electronic communication with which to transmit vital data in an instant. No state could hope to succeed in war without using these innovations to their maximum potential, choreographing their roles with finesse and precision.

The Tannenberg campaign, which was already unfolding as Hoffmann played action hero on a lonely road in the forests of East Prussia, exposed the gulf that existed between German and Russian approaches to using the technology that was changing warfare's very nature. This would be a fight between two nations that understood the details of modern campaigning differently—and in this case, the devil was very much in the details.

EMPIRES IN FRICTION

When war broke out at the end of July 1914 among the great powers of Europe, two alliances, each forged in the first decade of the new century to prepare for a conflict that many Europeans saw as inevitable, squared off in what promised to be the greatest war that history had ever seen. Germany and Austria-Hungary, the Central Powers, found themselves surrounded by France and the United Kingdom on one side and the Russian Empire on the other. Having foreseen this unfortunate geopolitical situation, the German general staff had developed the so-called "Schlieffen Plan," named for its originator, Alfred Graf von Schlieffen.

Simply put, the plan's intent was to avoid a simultaneous war on two fronts by first knocking out France with a sweeping attack along the English Channel toward Paris. Russia's vast distances and dated infrastructure, it was believed, would prevent the tsar from mobilizing his massive army quickly enough to intervene before Germany had crushed France. Using her excellent rail network, Germany could then redeploy eastward in time to deal with the Russian Bear with the help of Austria.

Though sound enough in theory, the plan had to work in practice, for the danger was acute. By 1871, Germany had been united into a central European state under the firm hand of Prussia, whose monarchs now answered to the title "Kaiser," or Caesar. The German "Reich" (empire) now spanned a huge portion of the continent, from Alsace-Lorraine in the southwest to beyond the banks of the Nemen River in the northeast, which today forms part of the southern border of Lithuania.

Perhaps nowhere was Germany more vulnerable to its enemies than in East Prussia, where the easternmost part of the Reich jutted out toward Russia across what is today northern Poland. The Russian Empire, with control of southern Poland, could attack this salient from both east and south, threatening to encircle German defenders and either push them into the Baltic Sea or destroy them altogether.

Germany's greatest asset in this remote theater was the terrain itself. From the fortified Baltic port of Königsberg (today's Kaliningrad) to the Russian–Polish frontier, a distance of around 100 miles (160 km) north to south, most of East Prussia was forest and marshland. The Masurian Lakes, a formidable wilderness of water and woods some sixty miles (96.5 km) southeast of Königsberg, stood astride any advance into the region from the southeast, forcing invaders to concentrate on two predictable avenues of approach. One would be a lateral advance in the north, straight west toward the eastern defenses of Königsberg; and the other one north by northwest into a stretch of hills around the city of Allenstein, a major rail hub sixty-five miles (105 km) or so due south of Königsberg.

Another asset wasn't nearly as obvious—or picturesque—as the dynamic landscape. It was the railroad system. Based around three major double-track lines connecting the hubs of Insterburg, Königsberg, Marienburg, and Deutsch-Eylau (forming a broad crescent from east to southwest), it was well served and maintained by a professional civilian workforce and offered extraordinary mobility. By contrast, the Russians had only a few single-track lines leading to the East Prussian frontier, all of which changed gauge upon reaching the border, preventing Russian trains from passing any farther.

Despite its exposed position, then, East Prussia was not entirely without defensive advantages. The job of putting them to good use fell to the German Eighth Army, whose role, per strict orders from the general staff, was to hold out against any Russian invasion without getting into too much trouble. Until France was well and truly knocked out of the war, no offensive action was to be undertaken in the east. The Eighth Army, however, soon proved to be full of officers—many of whom would achieve fame in the coming days—of an alarmingly independent nature.

PRITTWITZ, HINDENBURG, AND HOFFMANN

The Russians, playing their assigned role to the hilt, indeed massed two armies, each of which outnumbered the Eighth Army, and sent them rolling toward East Prussia. If the tsar's forces didn't move with quite the lethargy that German planners had predicted, they certainly didn't move with the celerity that defined Western European mobilization efforts. Everything in Russia was vast—its population, its distances, its army, and the hurdles that had to be overcome to create the sort of momentum required to wage modern war.

Time, however, was something Russia didn't have much of. The French, bracing for the German onslaught that was about to break upon their border via Belgium, pressed for action. The onslaught came on August 6, 1914, when Russian combat units began penetrating the East Prussian frontier in the north. These were elements of the Russian First Army, entrusted to General Pavel Karlovich von Rennenkampf, a spectacularly mustachioed cavalry officer of Baltic Prussian birth who was known for his contacts at court and steady performance during the Russo-Japanese War a decade earlier. To him went the northern route, west toward Königsberg, an approach that would bring him into contact with German troops long before General Alexander Samsonov's Second Army had completed its long march into Poland in preparation for the attack from the south.

Hampered by Russia's inadequate rail system, which failed to deliver reinforcements fast enough, Rennenkampf's advance was slow, giving his German adversaries something to think about as they readied themselves for the blow.

They were an interesting bunch. The Eighth Army at this point was still under its prewar commander, General Max von Prittwitz und Gaffron, scion of a venerable Prussian family and now in his sixties. Of the four corps he had at his disposal, the one closest to the frontier belonged to fifty-eight-year-old Lieutenant-General Hermann von François, a descendant of Huguenots who was viewed as unpredictable, a nonconformist—a reputation he now proved was well deserved. Acting on his own authority, François, who had always advocated aggressive tactics in East Prussia during prewar discussions, flatly disobeyed the injunction against an offensive and launched his I Corps, 40,000 strong, at Stallupönen, a rail junction just a few miles inside the German border. There, on August 17, he vindicated his belief in the superiority of German arms and organization by defeating elements of the Russian First Army and taking 3,000 prisoners.

Prittwitz was intrigued, and allowed himself to be talked into a sequel. The Eighth Army was now running its own show in the "Wild East." At Gumbinnen, just west of Stallupönen, Prittwitz threw most of the Eighth Army at the Russians on August 20. What gradually emerged in the heated battle that followed was a stalemate. Then, during the climax of the day's fighting, Prittwitz received reports from the XX Corps in the south, charged with watching the border with Russian Poland on the other side of the Masurian Lakes, that a massive enemy force was crossing the frontier—Samsonov's Second Army was on the move.

The nerve that had allowed Prittwitz to defy general headquarters now crumbled at the notion that he could very well be enveloped and crushed. Defying reports from his corps commanders that the Russians were about to break, he promptly ordered a withdrawal of the Eighth Army all the way to the Vistula River—a move that would surrender the entirety of East Prussia to the Russians.

If Helmuth von Moltke, chief of the general staff, was irritated by the bold insubordination of Prittwitz's attack, he was gravely concerned with his decision to give away a large chunk of the Reich at the slightest setback. Moltke called on Paul von Hindenburg to replace him. Hindenburg, sixty-six years old and a pensioner since 1911, responded to his summons out of retirement with a simple, reassuring "I am ready."

Meanwhile, miles to the east, Prittwitz's order to pull back went into effect, the rows of gray-clad soldiers with their spiked *pickelhaube* helmets gradually entraining for transport westward. One man, however, had ideas that didn't involve flying behind the Vistula. As Prittwitz saw to the withdrawal, still ignorant of his own dismissal, Max Hoffmann toiled away with map and compass, putting the finishing touches on a plan that would offer the Eighth Army a way out of its predicament—and a means of defeating *both* Russian armies.

"A SHEER CATASTROPHE"

The scene along the front line of Rennenkampf's First Army on August 21 could not be more different from the flurry of activity and chuffing trains just twenty miles (32 km) away in the German camp. Determined to rest and regroup after the previous day's fight, Rennenkampf eschewed chasing the enemy and settled into a comfortable inertia.

Though arguably overcautious, especially given his belief that he had routed the enemy at Gumbinnen, Rennenkampf's decision to regroup was reflective of the phlegmatic pace that dominated events on the Russian side in general. Though 1.5 million strong and growing, the Russian army had fewer than 1,200 vehicles at its disposal, which was a staggering deficiency. Contrast this with the observation of a Russian cavalry commander, Lieutenant General Vasili Iosifovich Gurko, who claimed that his troopers "could always see, following the enemy, long columns of motor transport of different types filled with troops." Given the sorry state of the Russian empire's rail network, this meant that much of the supplies, ammunition, and replacements headed for the First and Second Armies would arrive via horse.

There were other problems as well. Once inside East Prussia and beyond the range of its own secure telegraph network, the Russian army was forced to communicate through wireless messages. But the egregious shortage of trained cryptographers and wireless operators left commanders with little option but to broadcast in the clear in the hope that German listeners would not intercept and translate them in time to act.

Though Russian weaponry was excellent, a deficiency in artillery concerned many officers. Russian divisions (there were typically two divisions per corps in both German and Russian armies) were equipped with 25 percent fewer field pieces than their German opposites, and, more worryingly, lacked any counterpart to the excellent German howitzer, whose high angle of trajectory allowed it to pummel enemy positions with indirect fire. Worst of all was the Russian shortage of stockpiled artillery ammunition, a situation described by General A. A. Brussilov, one of the empire's senior commanders, as nothing short of "a sheer catastrophe."

Virtually the only area where Russia excelled was in its cavalry, whose numbers were much greater than Germany's and whose proud tradition and excellent training offset the fact that their very existence on the modern battlefield was soon to become a memory. To these troopers went the task of reconnaissance, a task that, on the German side, now fell primarily to the airplane (every German corps commander had a squadron of six at his beck and call). Though Russia possessed hundreds of serviceable aircraft, their numbers were not distributed effectively throughout the command structure, limiting their usefulness.

Finally, the ethnic realities of the region served to undermine Russia's campaign in East Prussia. Though Germany considered itself an empire, having united under one crown a vast swathe of central and eastern European peoples, East Prussia was part of the monarchy's original heartland. Loyalty would not be an issue here. By contrast, the Russians were not welcome in Poland or the Baltic region, where they were viewed as repressive occupiers, requiring advancing troops to leave garrisons in their wake to secure lines of supply against rebels and guerillas.

Despite these obstacles, Rennenkampf and Samsonov moved forward with a plan of attack that was all but foolproof. Coming at the East Prussian heartland on either side of the Masurian Lakes, they intended to trap the Eighth Army in a vise, the First Army in the north hammering away at the retreating Germans while the Second Army came up from the south to cut off their line of retreat. Should the Russian commanders be able to overcome their logistical challenges, victory would be certain.

That, however, was a tall order. What's more, they hadn't counted on Max Hoffmann and his new pair of superiors.

WAR ON THE RAILS

Hindenburg arrived at Eighth Army headquarters on August 23 with his chief of staff, a tall, brusque, and humorless forty-nine year old named Erich Ludendorff. Having already established a name for himself on the Western Front, Ludendorff had been contacted about his new post by Moltke with the sobering adjunct, "You may yet be able to save the situation in the East."

Greeted by Hoffmann at the Marienburg train station, the two generals—having only just met at the beginning of their journey east—soon found themselves in accord with the Eighth Army's first general staff officer on the next course of action. Though ordered into effect by Hindenburg and Ludendorff, the details of the plan that unfolded over the next few days were mostly the product of Hoffmann's calculations.

The new leadership of the Eighth Army viewed the approach of the two Russian armies as an opportunity rather than a crisis, a shift of perception that underpinned the course of events that followed. Though threatening an envelopment, the two Russian armies were still too far apart to act in tandem, offering the opportunity to destroy them in detail using East Prussia's interior lines. With Rennenkampf moving at a glacial pace from Gumbinnen, an opportunity to shift the Eighth Army to the south presented itself, allowing the Germans to mass their four corps and supporting elements for a decisive strike against Samsonov while Rennenkampf plodded westward. Two of Hindenburg's corps, the XVII and I Reserve, held a central position between the two enemy armies, making it relatively easy to shift them south by foot. The XX Corps already faced the Russian Second Army, and could form the center of a line against it. All that remained was to get the I Corps of François into action.

As it happened, I Corps was already entrained and heading east when Hindenburg's staff ordered it to stop at Deutsch-Eylau and detrain. It was a journey of more than 150 miles (241 km) by rail,

HERMANN VON FRANÇOIS'S STAUNCHLY INDEPENDENT ACTIONS SHAPED EVENTS ON THE RUSSIAN FRONT IN 1914. AN UNPREDICTABLE NONCONFORMIST, HIS CORPS WAS CLOSEST TO THE FRONTIER.

© Classic Image / Alamy

from one end of East Prussia to the other, that happened to put the corps' two divisions on the far left flank of the Russian Second Army and also put Germany's logistical advantage in bold relief.

And what of Rennenkampf? What if he decided to wheel southwest and strike at the rear of the new German formation while it took on Samsonov? This was the great risk of Hoffmann's plan, a contingency he left in the hands of the Eighth Army's only cavalry division. Slowly retreating before the Russian First Army, the cavalry were to screen German movements and delay Rennenkampf's advance— a plan that was bound to fail if Rennenkampf at any time realized how weak the screen in front of him actually was.

If all went according to plan, the Germans would face Samsonov's Second Army with—running southwest to northeast—the I Corps, XX Corps, I Reserve Corps, and XVII Corps, their rear protected by a cavalry screen. Concentrating on the flanks, these four units would trap Samsonov in a pocket and reduce him to nothing.

CHIEF OF THE GENERAL STAFF HELMUTH VON MOLTKE, PICTURED, PULLED PAUL VON HINDENBURG OUT OF RETIREMENT TO REPLACE GENERAL MAX VON PRITTWITZ, WHOSE GIVING AWAY OF LARGE CHUNKS OF THE REICH AT THE SLIGHTEST SETBACK GRAVELY CONCERNED VON MOLTKE.

By August 25, I Corps was in place on the far German right, preparing to attack eastward. It was on this day that Hindenburg, Ludendorff, Hoffmann, and their staffs drove down to Montowo to confer personally with General François at I Corps headquarters. François, irreverent as ever, demurred before his chiefs' demand that he attack the following morning, insisting that I Corps' artillery had yet to arrive by train and that his attack was bound to falter as a result. Ludendorff proved himself equal in truculence to François, loudly insisting that the corps commander comply or else, which brought a conciliatory response.

On the way back to headquarters, Hoffmann received the message he was to hand off to Hindenburg and Ludendorff between speeding cars on the road. It was merely one of several that, over the course of several days, produced an accurate portrait of Russian intentions thanks to the

Russians themselves. Rennenkampf, it seemed, would not intervene in the Eighth Army's attack on Samsonov, his reconnaissance parties having discovered little to nothing of the German redeployment. He would continue to advance west toward Königsberg. In addition, the Russian messages—sent unciphered—detailed the Second Army's deployment in the hill country south of Allenstein. The trap had been set.

GOING FORWARD

The five corps of the Russian Second Army that Hindenburg intended to envelop occupied a sixty-mile (96.5 km) front from Seeben in the southwest to Bischofsburg in the northeast. General Samsonov, commanding, intended to push northward, driving what little German resistance he expected to find before him to be ground against the First Army's advance in the north toward Königsberg.

Once the Germans opened their assault on August 26, officially commencing what became known as the Battle of Tannenberg, the struggle assumed the nature of two sides *attacking into* each other, with only one side—the Germans—fully aware of how the battle was unfolding. Because of the volume of wireless traffic, the scarcity of skilled operators, the haphazard use of aircraft, and the lack of reliable reconnaissance, General Samsonov was entirely unaware for the better part of two days that he was in command of an army that was collapsing on its wings rather than advancing victoriously.

A classic example of this was the battle that raged north of Bischofsburg, twenty miles (32 km) northeast of Allenstein, on August 26 on the far Russian right, where the Russian VI Corps thought that the enemy units spotted in front of it were a screen to mask withdrawing Germans—the Eighth Army, it was believed by the Russians, was still retreating toward the Vistula. The VI Corps commander Blagoveshchenski was disabused of this misconception only after one of his two divisions, the 4th, ran into the German I Reserve Corps while advancing.

A furious fight ensued. As the Russians dug in to receive the attack, the oncoming Germans—some of them, the 6th *Landwehr* Brigade, being older married men originally slated for garrison duty—went to ground as their own artillery began bursting around them. The error was eventually corrected, by which time the Russians had dug themselves in for a fight. As the Germans went forward, the woods erupted with the awful machine rattle of Maxim guns, scything the woods with bullets. Desperate to punch a way through, artillerymen rolled their guns

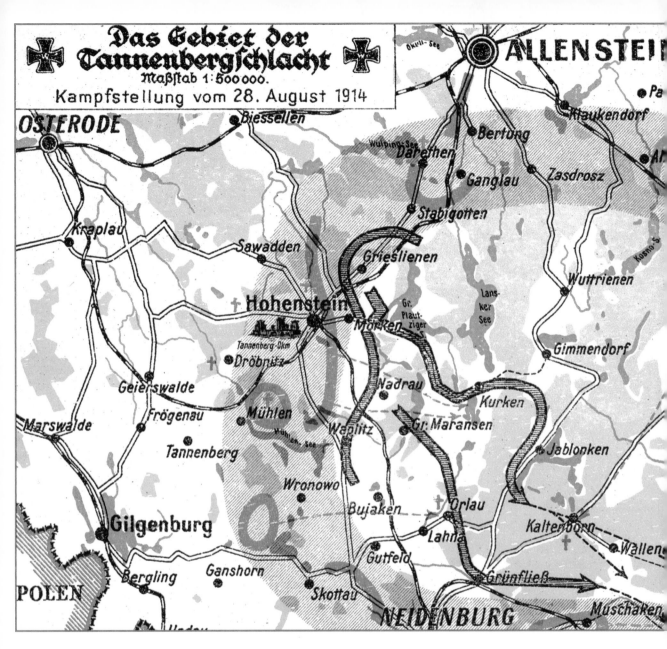

forward and began pulverizing the Russian positions at nearly point-blank range, churning the ground into a wasteland of flesh and debris. Still the Russians held, until, with the sun fading fast, the Germans charged with their last measure of rage even as the 36th Division of the German XVII Corps opened up with its artillery at the other end of the Russian position, pounding everything before it. The Russians broke.

The other division of the Russian VI Corps, the 16th, had attempted to reinforce the embattled 4th Division, marching too quickly to post flank guards who

might have noticed the Germans who, sometime before four o'clock, opened up on them from the woods and sent them retreating south in disarray.

Having begun the day in the hopes of nipping at the heels of a retreating foe, Blagoveshchenski's VI Corps had been shattered. The German attack had hardly been a perfect affair; indeed, deaths from friendly fire, misunderstandings over start times between division commanders, and other errors had marred the day's progress. But the bizarre lack of reliable intelligence on the Russian side had prevented them from ever grasping what they were up against. Indeed, Samsonov, at his headquarters miles to the south in Poland, still believed his right wing was advancing as the sun dipped below the horizon and the men of the VI Corps streamed south on the Ortelsburg road. More than sixty miles (96.5 km) away, on the other end of the Battle of Tannenberg in front of Seeben, thirty-five miles (56 km) southwest of Allenstein, General Francois was up to his old tricks; and even in this, in which blatant insubordination shaped events, the Germans were fortunate.

TIGHTENING THE NOOSE

On August 26, while the XVII and I Reserve Corps were smashing Blagoveshchenski on the German left, François was supposed to be fighting his way east on the right. Instead, he began the day bickering with Ludendorff over the phone.

With the casualties of Gumbinnen still clear in his memory, many of which suffered for lack of artillery support, François still refused to go forward until the I Corps' batteries, still making their way along the crowded rail network, had arrived and deployed. Ahead of his men stretched the Seeben Heights, on which elements of the Russian I Corps stared out over their German foes and dared them to come. François dithered, engaging in a series of shouting matches over the phone

A POSTCARD SHOWS THE BATTLE OF TANNENBERG ON AUGUST 28, 1914. TANNENBERG IS ON THE LEFT, JUST NORTH AND WEST OF GILGENBURG.

Deutsches Historisches Museum, Berlin, Germany / © DHM Angelika Anweiler-Sommer / The Bridgeman Art Library International

with Ludendorff, who finally demanded that the German I Corps go forward at noon. By sometime around one o'clock, the Heights had been taken with the support of just-arrived artillery, but François—who had been expected to take Usdau as well, five miles (8 km) farther east—was content to stay where he was, a final bit of insubordination that ultimately paid dividends.

His reason was sound enough: The 1st Division of his corps, which had spearheaded the assault on Seeben, was too exhausted and depleted of supplies to go farther safely. But François's hesitation had lulled the Russians into underestimating the threat coming from his direction. Operating under this misconception, the center of the Russian advance kept heading north instead of reinforcing the Russian I Corps around Usdau, marching itself further into the trap Hindenburg was attempting to close.

Consequently, when morning broke on August 27, the front had shifted decisively. In the south near Seeben, François, confident with his artillery guns to hand, prepared to smash into the Russian I Corps, while to his left—to the northeast—the German XX Corps occupied the Russian XXIII and XV Corps. Farther to the northeast, the Russian XIII Corps advanced unopposed toward Allenstein, blissfully ignorant of the fact that it was sticking its collective head in a noose; the German XVII and I Reserve Corps could now pounce on the Russian XIII Corps from the northeast now that the Russian VI Corps, unbeknownst to the vast majority of the Russian Second Army, was in full retreat.

This was the situation when, in the foggy predawn hours of August 27, the guns of the German I Corps—sixteen massive 150-mm howitzers accompanied by

GERMAN GENERAL HERMANN VON FRANÇOIS VISITS DESTROYED RUSSIAN COLUMNS, AUGUST 1914. THE RUSSIANS SUFFERED 50,000 KILLED AND WOUNDED, WHILE THE GERMANS SUFFERED 15,000 CASUALTIES.

© INTERFOTO / Alamy

more than twice that many 105-mm howitzers—shattered the sylvan idyll with a
deafening display, sending a shower of shells screaming into the Russian positions
around Usdau. From their vantage point on a hill near Gilgenburg, just a few miles
up the rail line from Usdau, Hindenburg and Ludendorff quietly watched the town
erupt again and again with each shell burst, sensing the pounding rumble even at
this distance.

The infantry of the German I Corps went forward within the hour. François's two divisions—the 1st and 2nd—attacked eastward from the Seeben Heights in two arcs intended to converge on Usdau like a giant thumb and forefinger reaching out to squeeze a bug. Elements of the 2nd Division ran into trouble when, advancing unevenly over broken ground, they emerged onto open terrain clearly visible to artillery of the Russian I Corps. As forward Russian units began pouring machine-gun fire into the hapless Germans, the ominous whine of incoming 122-mm artillery shells gave warning of even worse punishment. Soon the earth quaked with terrific explosions, sending the men into a bedlam of panic and noise and, ultimately, into a rout.

The 1st Division's luck was better that morning. After making contact with the Russian trenches, the German infantry relied on their own artillery to pulverize the enemy in a reversal of what was happening to the 2nd Division. By eleven o'clock, soldiers of the 1st Division had captured Usdau, whose streets had been reduced to a smoking, rubble-strewn abattoir. Amid the appalling stink, it dawned on the Germans that they had turned Samsonov's left flank.

TO BAG AN ARMY

By the night of August 27, Hindenburg and Ludendorff were confident that victory was at hand. Their goal was now to capture the Russian XXIII, XV, and XIII Corps in a giant pocket south of Allenstein. An irony was already apparent: The Russian VI and I Corps, which had been on the wings and whose shattering had made this possible, were also likely to be the only corps to escape the trap. Already on their way to Poland, they were retreating too quickly to be snared by the Germans.

In the north, Rennenkampf's First Army was investing Königsberg, his appreciation of matters to the south still screened by the German cavalry who hampered his advance. And Samsonov was still issuing orders to units that were nowhere near the front.

At Mlawa in Poland, where Samsonov had been keeping his headquarters, events were taking a strange and forbidding turn. Early on the morning of August 28, Samsonov made the unsettling decision to join the XV Corps, where he could personally lend a hand—a clear indication not only that he felt too removed from the front, but also that he had abandoned all hope of shaping the course of the battle and was shirking responsibility in favor of a post that offered him a narrower appreciation of events. It wasn't long afterward that a German zeppelin, appearing over Mlawa like a terrible omen, dropped a few high-explosive bombs on the railway station, blowing a handful of unfortunates to bits, and reminding the Russians who owned the skies.

August 28 was a day of confusion for both sides. As Russian units, still unaware of the scale of their army's predicament, fought with a ferocity born of imminent victory, Hindenburg and Ludendorff pushed their corps commanders harder as the threat of Rennenkampf's descent from the north became more and more acute. Nevertheless, by the end of the day François had advanced deep into the east, creating a cordon of German soldiers to prevent a Russian escape to the south. Frederick von Scholtz's XX Corps continued to deal and receive punishment from elements of the Russian XV and XXIII Corps, while the southwest approach of the XVII and I Reserve Corps served to corral the retreating Russian XIII Corps into the pocket. On August 29, François took Willenburg, cutting off all hope of Russian escape to the south.

> **CONFUSION, LACK OF SUPPLIES (MANY OF THE RUSSIAN UNITS HAD GONE MORE THAN A DAY WITHOUT FOOD), AND A DEARTH OF INFORMATION FROM HIGHER UP IN THE COMMAND STRUCTURE CONSPIRED TO BRING OUT THE WHITE FLAGS.**

This now ensured the destruction of the three Russian corps that found themselves increasingly pressed from all directions. Soon the men of the XXIII, XIII, and XV Corps began surrendering en masse, a process that continued into the next day as Samsonov's great host gradually lost life to the German garrote. Confusion, lack of supplies (many of the Russian units had gone more than a day without food), and a dearth of information from higher up in the command structure conspired to bring out the white flags.

Hindenburg declared victory on August 30. The precise scale of the triumph remains something of a mystery; in the memorable words of historian Dennis Showalter, "Eighth Army headquarters was too busy to tally jots and tittles. On the Russian side nobody was left to keep records." The Germans took some 90,000 prisoners, according to the most reliable records, and dealt their enemies around

50,000 killed and wounded. They also captured an astonishing 500 artillery guns, the hauling of which back to the German heartland further hampered the already distressed East Prussian rail network to its limits. For all this, the Germans suffered somewhere in the neighborhood of 15,000 casualties.

These numbers, like virtually all casualty figures in military history, are open to question. What is not open to question is the state of the Russian Second Army, which had ceased to exist as a coherent fighting force. Samsonov, too horrified by the scale of his failure, wandered off into the woods and shot himself through the head.

TO WHIP ANOTHER ARMY

Despite the scale of their triumph, the men of the German Eighth Army could not rest on their laurels. After all, the Russian First Army still lurked in the north.

The German General Staff had promised to send reinforcements to East Prussia back on August 27, the arrival of which proved invaluable to Hindenburg as he plotted the destruction of Rennenkampf's army. The Russian First Army, having learned of the fate of the Second Army just in time to send help to the south that would not arrive in time, merely invited disaster by spreading itself too thin. Having routed the Second Army in the south, Hindenburg's Eighth Army—reinforced with two corps—now turned on Rennenkampf's scattered units in the Battle of the Masurian Lakes, driving them back during the first two weeks of September. Russian soldiers would not tread on East Prussian soil again until the closing months of World War II.

> **THE RUSSIAN SECOND ARMY HAD CEASED TO EXIST AS A COHERENT FIGHTING FORCE. SAMSONOV, TOO HORRIFIED BY THE SCALE OF HIS FAILURE, WANDERED OFF INTO THE WOODS AND SHOT HIMSELF THROUGH THE HEAD.**

So ended the complete German triumph in the east against Russia in the opening moves of the Great War. It seems impossible to refer to German strengths during this campaign without drawing attention to corresponding Russian failures. In all its facets, the German Eighth Army performed like a reasonably professional army of the industrial age, despite abject failures at certain moments, especially the dropping of artillery shells on friendly troops (which happened on several occasions). But if the Germans seemed to grope their way forward when handling the new tools of destruction at their disposal, the Russians appear to have faltered altogether. Communication and intelligence gathering in particular were far behind German methods, producing a Russian appreciation of events that dwelt in fantasy throughout most of the action of August 26–30. This, despite the tenacious fighting of Russian troops throughout the theater, all but ensured the futility of their efforts.

The victory, conspicuous for its mobility in a war that would be defined by the static attrition of trench warfare, made heroes out of Hindenburg and Ludendorff, who christened it the Battle of Tannenberg. Though the city of Tannenberg lay near the front line, the choice of titles had a deeper significance. In 1410, an army of eastern European allies crushed the Teutonic Knights in the original "Battle of Tannenberg"—a stain on Germanic pride that Hindenburg and Ludendorff meant to expunge with their semantic artifice more than five centuries later. Ironically, their 1914 exploits would vault them to the very top of German affairs, where they would ultimately assume wartime control over the Reich's military destiny—and once again bring ruin upon the Teutonic culture they claimed to represent.

CHAPTER 14

SINGAPORE
1942

A BRILLIANT JAPANESE GAMBIT STEALS
THE GIBRALTAR OF THE EAST

35,000 JAPANESE VERSUS 85,000 COMMONWEALTH TROOPS

ON JANUARY 15, 1942, BRITISH PRIME MINISTER WINSTON Churchill had a lot on his mind. In the midst of a visit to Washington, D.C., to hammer out the shape of the emerging alliance with President Franklin Roosevelt, he had a war with Nazi Germany on his hands in Europe and North Africa, a rocky relationship with the Soviet Union to worry about, and a war in the Far East with Imperial Japan. The conflict that had begun with Adolf Hitler's invasion of Poland in 1939 had truly gone global.

There had been a time when war in Southeast Asia seemed extremely unlikely to Churchill, who believed the Japanese too smart to invite the wrath of the British, Dutch, and Americans, all of whom had deep political and commercial ties to the region. But on December 8, 1941, Japanese forces began landing on the Malay Peninsula right around the time Japanese naval air forces struck the Americans at Pearl Harbor as part of a Pacific-wide offensive. Since those landings, the Japanese had fought their way south through the rubber tree plantations of Malaya (modern-day Malaysia) toward their ultimate goal: Singapore, island fortress of British Southeast Asia—the so-called Gibraltar of the East.

It was with this battle in mind that Churchill took time away from his talks with the Americans to cable General Sir Archibald Wavell, supreme commander of all Allied forces in the Far East, at his headquarters in Java, Indonesia. With the Japanese advancing south, inquired the prime minister, what were Singapore's fortifications like, and were they properly manned to thwart an assault across the narrow Johore Strait that separated Singapore from Malaya?

Only after returning to London did the prime minister receive Wavell's response, dated January 16. In it, the general—a tough old veteran of World War I who had directed successful fighting against the Italians in *this* war before being saddled with the unfolding nightmare in Asia—stated, "Little or nothing was done to construct defenses on north side of island to prevent crossing Johore Strait, though arrangements have been made to blow up causeway."

In his six-volume memoir of the Second World War, rarely does Churchill recall anything with such unbridled alarm. "It was with feelings of painful surprise that I read this message on the morning of the 19th. So there were no permanent fortifications covering the landward side of the naval base and of the city!" Churchill's inquiry had been about a matter so fundamental to military preparedness that, since the advent of war with Japan, he had never given it a thought. "[T]he possibility of Singapore having no landward defenses no more entered into my mind than that of a battleship being launched without a bottom."

His worries were entirely justified. Even as the prime minister fretted over this colossal oversight, British, Indian, and Australian defenders were putting up a last-ditch effort in Johore, southernmost of Malaya's regions and last stop before the Straits themselves. For nearly two months they had endured an Asian blitzkrieg by Japanese veterans of the war in China who sent fireworks arching into the rear of the enemies' positions to make them feel surrounded, avoided frontal attacks to move like wind around the flanks, fixed blown bridges with unnatural speed, and maintained a pace so breathless that much of their momentum, lunging ahead of Japanese supply lines, was maintained by captured largesse.

Only on January 19, as the final line of defense in Malaya stood ready to crumble, was Winston Churchill, half a world away, abruptly disabused of the illusion that these exhausted men had a fortress to retreat to. Though armed to the teeth against a seaward invasion, the island stood naked in the north where it faced the mainland. Singapore had been a disaster waiting to happen for years.

"I warn you," wrote Churchill to General Hastings Ismay, his chief military advisor, "this will be one of the greatest scandals that could possibly be exposed."

PROGRESS AND PREJUDICE

By the advent of the 1930s, Singapore, with a population of nearly a million, had become a central fixture in Britain's Far Eastern strategic considerations. The island was a commercial boom town whose proximity to the shipping lanes also gave it immense military significance. Though derided as a £60 million boondoggle by many in the imperial administration, the colony's impressive naval base—officially opened in 1938—sported a state-of-the-art floating dock of German construction, capable of accommodating the largest warships for repairs.

Such sterling installations belied Singapore's profound vulnerability. Hanging beneath the jungle gloom of Malaya like a ripe fruit ready to be plucked by raiders from the South China Sea, its situation begged for defense against the waters that channeled military efforts in this part of the world. Consequently, authorities installed a series of formidable batteries along the south and east coasts of the island. Dominated by heavy 15-inch (38 cm) guns, these installations ensured a hot welcome for any foe approaching from the sea. Indeed, the naval base itself could only be reached from the east entrance of Johore Strait by first running past a fortified battery of three of these guns that could wreak havoc with attacking vessels.

Anyone looking at a map of Singapore once these batteries had been installed in the 1930s could reach only one conclusion: An enemy invasion of the island was all but doomed. The conspicuous nature of these weapons conspired with a

HAD SINGAPORE, SHOWN HERE, GUARDED A MEDITERRANEAN OR ATLANTIC PATCH OF WATER, ITS FORTIFICATIONS WOULD HAVE RECEIVED FAR GREATER ATTENTION FROM THE BRITISH. THE LACK OF DEFENSES AND UNDERESTIMATION OF THE JAPANESE PROVED TO BE THE UNDOING OF THE BRITISH.

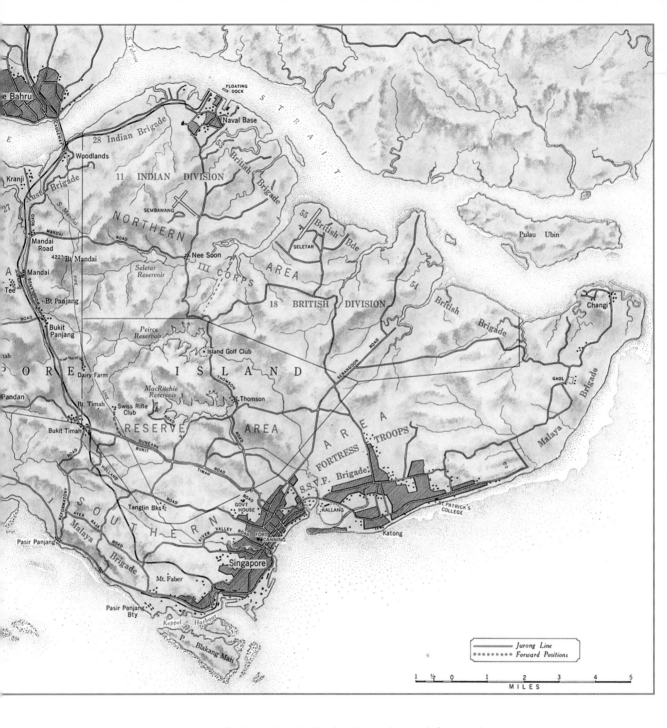

reluctance to commit more funds to the island's already exorbitant defense and the remoteness of the locale to create a sense of complacency. To be sure, strategists interested in theorizing how a battle for Singapore would unfold might insist that the seaward defenses all but ensured an enemy approach from the mainland, and both the Royal Air Force and the Army made substantial commitments to the

defense of Malaya itself for just this contingency. But military orthodoxy, based on
the preeminence of maritime affairs, continued to view the role of the army and air
force as necessary only to hold off whatever came the island's way until the Royal
Navy showed up in force from distant waters to finish off the enemy.

And just who was the enemy in question? Japan, of course—a foe whose image
in the West undermined Allied military preparation. Long before war broke out
in December 1941, Western impressions of Japanese capabilities bordered on the
infantile. The Western perception was that the Japanese were bandy-legged, buck-
toothed, shortsighted incompetents. Their factories produced faulty steel and alu-
minum, and their academies produced unimaginative officer-automatons. Some
bizarre views even held that Japanese bombers flew relatively low for want of the
physical endurance in rarified atmosphere that allowed "white" bomber crews to
achieve high altitude.

As inane as these opinions seem today, they went a long way toward in-
forming hard strategic thinking at the time. Had Singapore guarded a Mediterranean or Atlantic patch of water, its fortifications would have received far
greater attention. As it was, only the Japanese threatened the island's security,
and the Japanese, though clearly capable of massing considerable local strength,
did not warrant sufficient panic in British minds to turn what was really an
exposed commercial possession into a bona fide citadel.

This underestimation of Japanese abilities would prove catastrophic.

AN AMBITIOUS PLAN

Imperial Japan had been at war since 1937, when it commenced a long and costly
attempt to conquer China. This colossal endeavor, mired in stalemate by the time
war broke out in Europe in 1939, continued to function as the focus of Japanese
policy; having committed so much to the "China Incident" and attached the
empire's fate to its outcome, Japanese civilian and military leaders refused to pull
out even in the face of U.S. embargoes, which came in response to Japan's occupation of French Indochina, what is today Vietnam, in the summer of 1940.

Soon cut off from U.S. oil and scrap metal, the urge to expand at the expense
of Western colonial powers immersed in a European war now acquired an air of
necessity—to the south, in remote tropical territories controlled by unpopular
colonial masters fighting for their lives half a world away in Europe, lay a treasure
trove of ore, rubber, oil, and other resources. Why kowtow to U.S. bullying when

you could just steal what you needed from racist interlopers who had no business meddling in Asian affairs in the first place?

Though British, Dutch, and Australian possessions from Burma to New Guinea comprised the principal target for the Japanese, a descent on the Philippines, still in the process of weaning itself off U.S. governance, was also considered necessary. In any event, war with the United States was now seen as inevitable. The result of these calculations was arguably the grandest single offensive in history—an explosion of land, sea, and air operations spanning the Pacific, with near-simultaneous assaults against Pearl Harbor, Wake Island, Guam, the Philippines, Hong Kong, Malaya, and the Dutch East Indies. Even Japan's German allies, who had practically invented lightning war, were a little awed.

Malaya, the world's largest supplier of rubber, was allotted special importance. To carry out the invasion and subsequent drive down the peninsula to Singapore, the army gave General Yamashita Tomoyuki three of its best divisions. One of them, the Imperial Guards, was the emperor's personal troops, selected for their height and physique. The Guards had done no fighting since the Russo-Japanese War of 1904–1905, performing most of their duties at state functions and on the parade ground. Nevertheless, they were eager to put the lie to those who considered them little more than military window dressing.

The other two divisions of Yamashita's 25th Army had acquired a great deal more hands-on experience. Blooded in the savage fighting across China, the 5th and 18th were full of hardened veterans, capable of thinking fast under the hardest pressures, and skilled in unconventional tactics.

To lead these men, the Imperial Japanese Army made an unusual choice in 56-year-old Yamashita, who had seen virtually no action over his long career. But his penetrating mind and strategic acumen had won him posts in the Imperial Headquarters and the Staff College, academic heart of the army's strategic training, as well as

FIELD MARSHAL ARCHIBALD WAVELL, SUPREME COMMANDER OF ALLIED FORCES IN THE FAR EAST DURING THE SINGAPORE DEBACLE, WAS THE ONE WHO INFORMED WINSTON CHURCHILL OF THE LACK OF BRITISH DEFENSES ON SINGAPORE.

The Crown Estate / The Bridgeman Art Library International

attaché in Switzerland, Germany, and Austria during the 1920s and early 1930s. He had also met personally with Adolf Hitler during a diplomatic mission to the Third Reich as recently as 1940.

Confidence in him and his elite 25th Army was high. Despite having just 35,000 men at his disposal (around a third of enemy strength in Malaya and Singapore), Yamashita had 200 tanks and hundreds of first-line aircraft. British numbers in both categories were known to be inadequate (indeed, the Commonwealth had no tanks whatsoever in the region), offering the general—soon to be dubbed the Tiger of Malaya—an opportunity to secure air superiority and to smash resistance along the peninsula's roads.

That, more or less, is what he did.

THE SUN RISES OVER MALAYA

On December 10, 1941, the Japanese put its superior weaponry to good use by sinking HMS *Prince of Wales* and *Repulse*. Winston Churchill himself had sent these two capital ships, a battleship and battle cruiser, respectively, to intimidate the Japanese. Arriving on December 2, with great fanfare, they manifested Britain's conundrum very neatly: Not only were they more than the empire could afford to send to the Far East at the moment, they would also do little to thwart an aggressive foe with near-absolute air superiority.

Caught out in the open while trying to interrupt Japanese landings on the east coast of Malaya, the two ships were sunk by bombers flying out of Japanese Indochina armed with bombs and, of course, torpedoes. No capital ship of such renown had ever fallen to an enemy relying solely on air attack. Sir Thom Phillips, admiral in charge of the little taskforce, went down with his vessels.

Coming just two days after the formal commencement of hostilities, the sinking of the *Prince of Wales* and *Repulse* with 840 lives struck the citizenry and military of Singapore like a cyclone. British pride had, in a real sense, been blown abruptly out of the water.

Those Commonwealth soldiers on the northern end of the Malay Peninsula had long since figured that out. Since the early morning of December 8, they had struggled to hold the invaders back from their landing beaches at Kota Baharu, but not for lack of equipment.

Unlike the Japanese navy's Zero or torpedo designs, the Japanese army was equipped with weapons that were barely up to the standards of their new enemies.

The Arisaka Model 38, for instance, the standard-issue bolt-action rifle issued to the Japanese soldier, was long and somewhat ungainly compared to the British Lee-Enfield, and still managed to fire a smaller round. Submachine guns were virtually unknown at the time in Japanese units, while Commonwealth platoons could rely on the U.S.-made Thompson, or "Tommy" gun, a burdensome but reliable weapon at close range. Perhaps the most ironic difference between the two armies was in armor. Though Japanese tanks were fragile by European standards, they were the only tanks around in Malaya, making them a source of dread for Commonwealth defenders.

Despite these notable insufficiencies, the Japanese embraced a style of warfare that put their confused and desperate enemies to shame in Malaya. Everything the Japanese did emphasized speed, forward momentum, and infiltration. Allied troops, trained to maintain cohesion at all costs, frequently wasted precious moments establishing contact with disparate units and concentrating their strength while Japanese enemies skilled in independent action closed in around them, forcing a surrender or, far less frequently, a fight to the death. And, as if this weren't enough, Japanese control of the seas afforded them the opportunity to make amphibious landings wherever they pleased, which they often did to land troops behind pockets of resistance.

The resulting rout exceeded even Tokyo's expectations. In a little less than two months, the Japanese advanced more than 500 miles (804 km), captured more than 21,000 prisoners, and inflicted another 4,000 casualties. For this, Yamashita had incurred around 5,000 casualties and delivered his men to Johore Strait, beyond which the last Commonwealth defenders retired on January 28 to find what succor they could on the island of Singapore.

Both sides now prepared for a siege, each unaware of the other's weakness. Only one side, however, was willing to gamble all for victory.

GENERAL YAMASHITA TOMOYUKI, THE "TIGER OF MALAYA," WAS COMMANDER OF THE JAPANESE 25TH ARMY, WHICH SWEPT DOWN THE MALAY PENINSULA AND CONQUERED SINGAPORE. JAPANESE CONFIDENCE IN THE GENERAL WAS HIGH DESPITE HIS HAVING SEEN LITTLE ACTION IN HIS LONG CAREER.

Getty Images

TWILIGHT

If the British Empire ever intended Singapore to be a bastion against enemy aggression, its efforts on the island's behalf suggested otherwise. By the time Japanese officers were spying the south shore of the Johore Strait with their binoculars, the British system of civil and military administration had been exposed for the charade it was.

Sir Shenton Thomas, governor of the colony, was a civilian hostile to military intrusion in regional affairs but dependent on the military for defense. Working in tandem with him were three branches of the military—air force, navy, and army—that had long looked on each other with deep suspicion and that now, in a time of war, cooperated awkwardly. With the sinking of the *Prince of Wales* and *Repulse*, as well as the overrunning of the airfields in Malaya, army matters assumed preeminence under the command of Lieutenant-General Arthur Percival, general officer commanding (GOC) of Singapore since April.

Percival's situation was dire as February dawned. In the face of pleas by his best engineering officers to fortify the northern edge of the island as the fight in Malaya deteriorated, Percival had responded with what soon became his mantra: *It would be bad for morale*. Only in late January, as the loss of Malaya seemed assured, did he authorize the discreet construction of defensive works. Unfortunately, much of the civilian labor pool of Chinese and Tamils had left the island, requiring much of the work—such as it was—to be done by soldiers. The result, completed without adequate labor or energetic planning, was predictably underwhelming.

There was a terrible irony in this. Percival had been one of those officers who, in prewar discussions, had always advocated the inevitability of an enemy attack from the mainland. But to him, stopping the enemy in Malaya was the best hope of saving Singapore. With that option gone, he only slowly came to the reasoning behind building up meager works in the north.

This was ludicrous, of course, and quite out of character for a man whose career had been nothing if not distinguished. A skinny fifty-four-year-old with buck teeth and a quiet manner, Percival was a veteran of the fighting in World War I and the Russian Revolution with two Distinguished Service Orders and a Croix de Guerre on his chest. Brave, imaginative, and insightful, he had impressed every officer he ever worked under. Now, for some peculiar reason, his characteristic boldness and sound judgment eluded him.

Other things were slipping from his grasp, including airfields. Though reinforcements of Hawker Hurricane fighter planes had been trickling in since the beginning of the war, they had suffered tremendously in air battles and now had only one airfield, Kallang, left to them on the island; Singapore's other three were within range of Japanese artillery stationed in Johore, and were abandoned at the end of January.

Despite the fact that Japanese planes now all but owned the skies over the island, Percival's situation was far from hopeless. Indeed, he still had more than 80,000 men on the island, their rough treatment during the long retreat down Malaya somewhat ameliorated by the recent arrival of the British 18th Division, which, though green, was at least fresh. He had some 225 guns at his disposal (though he didn't know it, Yamashita had 200), with virtually unlimited ammunition.

Nor were the million or so civilian refugees likely to use up all the food and supplies anytime soon. Hong Kong capitulated on Christmas partly because of a lack of water, something that could never happen on Singapore with its vast reservoirs. Tens of thousands of pigs and dairy cows, along with stores brought in before the war, could feed everyone on the island for six months. Though the docks were crowded with civilians departing the island daily, many continued to go to work, golf, and gather for drinks as if the bombs landing in their midst were an exotic local phenomenon to be endured like the monsoon.

THE A6M2 ZERO-SEN WAS DESIGNED BY MITSUBISHI FOR THE IMPERIAL JAPANESE NAVY. THIS FIGHTER PLANE BOASTED UNPRECEDENTED RANGE AND MANEUVERABILITY, DOMINATING THE SKIES OVER THE JAPANESE EXPANSION IN 1941-42.

For his part, Percival was sure of two things: first, that the Japanese would take more than a week from the destruction of the causeway on January 31, 1942, to plan their assault; and second, that the assault would come on the northeast shore of the Strait. This was because the northwest, on the other side of the breached causeway, with its tangle of brackish creeks and mangrove swamps, made an ideal—and therefore predictable—target for the Japanese. Percival believed they would come on the eastern side of the causeway.

But this was little more than a gut feeling. In the end, Percival had seventy-two miles (115 km) of coastline to defend. After all, the Japanese had used small landings to their great advantage during the Malaya campaign; how could he be sure they wouldn't complement a thrust across the Strait with a sea landing in the south? Consequently, he put his strongest force along the northeast coast: the Indian III Corps, comprised of the Indian 11th Division, British 18th Division, and the 15th Indian Brigade. A thin line of troops guarded the southern beaches, including the city itself, while the Australian 8th Division, reinforced by the 44th Indian Brigade, guarded the northwest part of the island.

Nighttime patrols undertaken by the Australians to the far side of the Straights seemed to confirm Percival's hunch that the assault would come in the east. Though they discovered signs of increased Japanese activity across from the Australian positions, they turned up no sign of boats. Then, on February 8, they saw Japanese troops swarming over Ubin Island, a four-and-a-half-mile (7 km) long piece of rocky ground that parted the eastern Straights. Combined with the thunderous bombardment that now rained on the northern shore since the previous day, the Japanese activity pointed to only one conclusion: the assault was beginning.

DEATH IN THE DARKNESS

For Yamashita, the moment had arrived. He had taken as long as he could under the circumstances to mass his men at their staging areas along the coast of Johore in preparation for the attack. Time was against him: The enemy was busy enhancing its defenses, and the initiative, so carefully maintained since the first landings in December, must be maintained to keep the British off-balance.

He had sent elements of the Imperial Guards off to invade Ubin Island to create a diversion. In fact, as darkness fell on the evening of February 8, Yamashita planned on sending the real attack into the northwestern shore of Singapore, where the span of water was less than half a mile (0.8 km) wide, and where he knew through reliable intelligence that the Australian division waited in poorly prepared positions. The invasion itself would be carried out by the tough veterans of the 5th and 18th Divisions.

The eclectic assortment of boats, so carefully hidden from Australian reconnaissance missions by concealing them in the jungle, now breasted the waters of the Strait carrying around 4,000 troops from both divisions—as many men as the boats could carry in a single wave of assault. It was sometime between eight thirty and nine, and the Japanese stooped low in their craft—assault boats, inflatable boats, and an assortment of other types—as the moon rose and the *whoosh* of their own artillery shells sliced the air above them to flash and rumble into the island ahead.

Suddenly, flare guns hurled a handful of incandescent plumes into the sky, illuminating the little fleet in deadly brilliance. On the boats went, their motors making a buzzing over the water that drowned out all but the largest shell bursts. But nothing happened. The Japanese couldn't know it, but their artillery barrage had broken all the telephone lines connecting the Australian defenders with their headquarters and artillery. Nobody but those at the water's edge was aware of the flotilla's approach.

Then, as the shore grew close, the mangroves burst into jagged flashes, sending streams of tracer bullets coursing into the boats. Rifle fire soon joined the noise, followed by the *crump* of mortars, their bombs plunging into the water in huge white plumes. Boats lurched upward as they were struck with mortar fire, screams carried over the water through the chatter of weapons, and bodies began bobbing in the waves.

Forging ahead through the knifing phosphorescence of the tracers, the Japanese pulled their boats up into the countless inlets that penetrated the coast and, using the swift infiltration tactics that had served them so well since the beginning of the war, got in among and behind the Australians, systematically exterminating them in a series of desperate firefights. The boats that survived went back to carry in more waves of men, pouring troops into the battle. By one in the morning, after some four hours of furious fighting, the Japanese had nearly routed the 22nd Brigade of the Australian 8th Division.

The Japanese now had a toehold on the island, the ultimate nightmare of every British officer who had ever contemplated the defense of Singapore. How? In addition to the lack of artillery support due to severed telephony, the Australian 22nd Brigade had been one of the most thinly dispersed of all Percival's defending units. Also, Brigadier Harold Taylor had issued orders to his men to fall back if they felt themselves being overrun, which amounted to an invitation to head for the rear as soon as the fighting on February 8 got heated. As a result, the situation descended into confusion quickly, adding to the chaos created by Yamashita's deadly waves of attacking infantry. Though the Japanese suffered terrible casualties that night, the 22nd Brigade had been smashed.

As the Australians streamed inland toward the Jurong Line, a natural piece of defensive ground that challenged any lunges into the interior from the west, the Allied response during the early morning hours of February 9 was thwarted not only by a growing sense of defeatism in the ranks, but by Percival himself, who still refused to believe that the attack had been more than a diversion. Paralyzed by this, he hesitated to channel forces from the other coasts to support the gap that had been torn open in the northwest.

That night, Yamashita undermined the Jurong Line by sending the Imperial Guards across the Strait just east of the waters that had witnessed the previous night's assault. Though suffering much heavier casualties than their fellows on the night of the February 8, the Guards came ashore and, by their very presence just east of the Jurong Line, rendered it untenable.

The fight now shifted to the heart of the island.

REALITY AND PERCEPTION

The February 9 assault had been a disaster for the Imperial Guards. Attacking across a much narrower front, they came under scything fire from the Australian 27th Brigade, whose mortars and Vickers machine guns soon littered the water with corpses. Those who escaped the bullets had to brave burning oil slicks floating down from the bombed naval base, which turned much of the Straight into a floating crematorium.

Only Allied incompetence saved the Guards. Receiving a garbled message that seemed to indicate a withdrawal, the 27th Brigade proceeded to pull back even as it was about to destroy the Imperial Guards. It was a fatal mistake. Once onshore, the Guards, in conjunction with the 5th and 18th Divisions farther west, now threatened the Jurong Line with annihilation.

Yamashita's tanks were soon ferried over, spearheading the attack. By February 11, the Commonwealth defenders had been pushed back to a pocket in the south of the island, defending the outskirts of Singapore city, the Japanese having driven their attack forward along the main trunk road that ran from north to south. At this point Yamashita sent word to Percival asking for a British surrender: "My sincere respect is due to your army which, true to the traditional spirit of Great Britain, is bravely defending Singapore which now stands isolated and unaided." Yamashita had more than compliments in mind, however. "I expect that Your Excellency accepting my advice will give up this meaningless and desperate resistance and promptly order the entire front to cease hostilities...."

Though the Japanese general was as keen as any commander to bring a quick resolution to a victorious campaign, Yamashita's message had been sent out of a sense of emergency. In fact, his situation was critical.

Back in December, he had been slated to command a fourth division in his 25th Army. He had turned it down, not least because he believed four divisions were more than Malaya's logistical system could handle. It was a prescient decision, and his calculations about Malaya's supply limitations now proved woefully correct. Having advanced so far, so fast, he now found himself at the tail end of a supply line that snaked its way along the length of Malaya and over the sea at a time when Japanese logistics were barely up to the task. As a result, even as the muzzles of his guns pointed at the suburbs of Singapore city, he was at a loss to find enough shells to make their presence decisive. Indeed, his army—still around a third of his enemy's strength—was nearly out of ammunition.

The Japanese, however, had captured the reservoirs and the center of the island, whose high ground around Bukit Timah offered a commanding position. Unaware of Yamashita's supply situation (indeed, Percival had been laboring under the wild delusion that the Japanese invaders numbered nearly 150,000, mostly on account of the overwhelming speed and ferocity of their attack down Malaya), Percival, after agonizing reflection, decided to negotiate terms with the Japanese on February 15, barely a week after the invasion of Singapore began.

Percival and a small coterie of officers walked through the lines, white flag flying, and were escorted to the Ford factory building near the center of the island. There, meeting face to face, Yamashita and Percival met not as equals but as one commander, Yamashita, determined to bully his opposite into surrendering soon enough to forego the need to call for Japanese reinforcements, which would have been a career-destroyer. Percival, deflated and too intelligent to see any hope in continued resistance, acquiesced.

Churchill called what followed "the worst disaster and largest capitulation in British history," and technically he was right. The number of people who entered captivity that day surpassed 120,000, more than 80,000 of whom were in uniform, unlike anything that had ever occurred in the annals of British military setbacks. Yamashita, who suffered nearly 5,000 casualties in the attack on Singapore alone, was left with around 26,000 effectives, presenting a stunning disparity in numbers.

Air and naval superiority were significant, no doubt. With fewer than 150 obsolete aircraft to defend Malaya and Singapore at the outbreak of war, the Commonwealth was strapped from the beginning. Even when scores of updated machines were sent in, their numbers and deployment were no match for the curtain of airpower that Japan had extended across the region. By February 8, the Royal Air Force had ceased even making an appearance over Singapore. As for the *Prince of Wales* and *Repulse*, their presence was never more than a show of force to begin with; their destruction merely served as a propaganda defeat of the first order.

Then again, how much could the United Kingdom and its allies really be expected to contribute given the severity of the war already underway in Europe against Hitler? Though this must also be taken into consideration, the fact remains that Yamashita attacked with a mere three divisions, and not simply because Japan believed the British to be overstretched. Three divisions, according to Yamashita and his staff, were about the limit that a Malayan campaign could handle under the circumstances. Clearly there was room for the forces already defending Malaya and Singapore to coordinate a defense that would cripple, if not thwart altogether, the Japanese invasion.

The most important factors were always on the ground, where the Japanese, despite smaller numbers in the theater at all times, were able to exploit their greater experience and tactical fluidity. Significantly, this initially came as a terrible shock to the men of Percival's command, who had been inculcated with a deep lack of respect for Japanese arms. This, perhaps more than any other factor, decided the course of events. For though other commands have suffered from a heterogeneous force mix under a hackneyed command structure that cracked in the face of extreme adversity, not all of them were doomed. The leaders in Singapore, however, seem to have reacted with a lethargy whose roots lay in prewar racist mythology. By the time they understood the full scale of the Japanese onslaught and the brilliance behind it, the time had passed for deliberate countermeasures. The result was a catastrophe of historic proportions.

BIBLIOGRAPHY

Barber, Noel. *Sinister Twilight: The Fall of Singapore*. London: Collins, 1968.

Barker, Juliet. *Agincourt: Henry V and the Battle That Made England*. New York: Little, Brown and Company, 2005.

Bengtsson, Frans G. *The Life of Charles XII: King of Sweden, 1697 – 1718*. London: MacMillan and Company, 1960.

Boatner, Mark M., III. *The Civil War Dictionary*. New York: Vintage, 1991.

Boss, Roy. *Justinian's Wars: Belisarius, Narses and the Reconquest of the West*. Stockport, UK: Montvert, 1993.

Browning, Robert. *Justinian and Theodora*. London: Thames and Hudson, 1987.

Connolly, Peter. *Greece and Rome at War*. London: Greenhill Books, 1998.

Davis, Paul K. *100 Decisive Battles from Ancient Times to the Present*. New York: Oxford University Press, 2001.

Duffy, Christopher. *The Military Life of Frederick the Great*. New York: Atheneum, 1986.

Duffy, Christopher. *Prussia's Glory: Rossbach and Leuthen, 1757*. Chicago: The Emperor's Press, 2003.

Foote, Shelby. *The Civil War: A Narrative: Fredericksburg to Meridian*. New York: Vintage, 1986.

Fraser, David. *Frederick the Great*. New York: Fromm International, 2001.

Gibbon, Edward. *The History of the Decline and Fall of the Roman Empire*. New York: The Penguin Press, 1994.

Godloy, Eveline Charlotte. *Charles XII of Sweden: A Study in Kingship*. London: W. Collins, 1928.

Goldsworthy, Adrian. *Cannae*. London: Cassell & Co., 2001.

Goldsworthy, Adrian. *The Complete Roman Army*. London: Thames and Hudson, 2003.

Goldsworthy, Adrian. *The Fall of Carthage: The Punic Wars 265 – 146 BC*. London: Cassell & Co., 2003.

Green, Miranda, ed. *The Celtic World*. London: Routledge, 1995.

Haldon, John. *The Byzantine Wars*. Stroud, UK: Tempus, 2001.

Hammond, N. G. L. *The Genius of Alexander the Great*. Chapel Hill, NC: University of North Carolina Press, 1997.

Hatton, R. M. *Charles XII of Sweden*. London: Weidenfeld and Nicolson, 1968.

Holland, Tom. *Persian Fire: The First World Empire and the Battle for the West*. New York: Doubleday, 2005.

Holmes, Richard, edit. *The Oxford Companion to Military History*. Oxford: Oxford University Press, 2001.

Hourtouille, F.-G. *Jena-Auerstaedt: The Triumph of the Eagle*. Paris: Histoire & Collections, 2005.

Keegan, John. *The Face of Battle*. New York: Viking Press, 1976.

Knight, Ian. *Rorke's Drift, 1879: "Pinned Like Rats in a Hole."* Oxford: Osprey Publishing, 1996.

Lancel, Serge; Nevill, Antonia, trans. *Carthage: A History*. Malden, MA: Blackwell Publishers, 1997.

Lendon, J. E. *Soldiers and Ghosts: A History of Battle in Classical Antiquity*. New Haven, CT: Yale University Press, 2005.

Liddell Hart, B.H. *Strategy*. Second Edition. London: Faber and Faber Ltd., 1954.

Long, E. B. with Long, Barbara. *The Civil War Day By Day: An Almanac 1861 – 1865*. New York: Doubleday, 1971.

Lonsdale, David J. *Alexander the Great, Killer of Men: History's Greatest Conqueror and the Macedonian Art of War*. New York: Carroll & Graf, 2004.

McDevitte, W.A. and Bohn, W.S., transl. *Caesar's Commentaries on the Gallic and Civil Wars*. New York: Harper and Brothers, 1869.

Maude, Col. F. N., C. B. *The Jena Campaign, 1806*. Mechanicsville, Pennsylvania: Stackpole Books, 1998.

Meier, Christian. *Caesar: A Biography*. New York: Basic Books, 1982.

Norwich, John Julius. *A Short History of Byzantium*. New York: Alfred A. Knopf, 1997.

Procopius, translated by Dewing, H.B. *History of the Wars*, Books III – IV. Cambridge, Massachusetts: Harvard University Press, 2000.

Rawlinson, George, trans. *The Histories of Herodotus*. New York: Book-of-the-Month Club, 1997.

Riasanovsky, Nicholas V. *A History of Russia*. Fifth Edition. New York: Oxford University Press, 1993.

Sampson, Gareth C. *The Defeat of Rome in the East: Crassus, the Parthians, and the Disastrous Battle of Carrhae, 53 BC*. Philadelphia: Casemate, 2008.

Sears, Stephen W. *Chancellorsville*. New York: Houghton Mifflin, 1996.

Showalter, Dennis E. *Tannenberg: Clash of Empires, 1914*. Washington, D.C.: Brassey's, 2004.

Smith, Colin. *Singapore Burning: Heroism and Surrender in World War II*. London: Penguin, 2006.

Snook, Mike, Lieutenant Colonel. *Like Wolves on the Fold: The Defense of Rorke's Drift*.

Strauss, Barry. *The Battle of Salamis: The Naval Encounter That Saved Greece—and Western Civilization*. New York: Simon & Schuster, 2004.

Sweetman, John. *Tannenberg 1914*. London: Cassell, 2002.

ABOUT THE AUTHOR

Cormac O'Brien is the author of *The Forgotten History of America*, *Fallen Empires*; *Secret Lives of the U.S. Presidents* (more than 100,000 copies in print); and *Secret Lives of the First Ladies* (more than 30,000 copies in print). He has been a featured speaker at the Jimmy Carter Presidential Library, and has been a guest on many radio programs, including National Public Radio and the BBC. He lives in New Jersey.

ACKNOWLEDGMENTS

I would like to express my gratitude to publisher Will Kiester, who allowed me to turn a beloved idea into this extraordinary book. And to Cara Connors goes my heartfelt thanks for her editing skill, patience, insight, and dedication.

INDEX